For Chris

Settler
Militarism

JULIET
NEBOLON

Settler
Militarism

WORLD WAR II IN HAWAI'I AND THE MAKING OF US EMPIRE

Duke University Press   Durham and London   2024

Project Editor: Lisa Lawley
Designed by Matthew Tauch
Typeset in MeropeBasic by Westchester Publishing Services

Library of Congress Cataloging-in-Publication Data
Names: Nebolon, Juliet, [date] author.
Title: Settler militarism : World War II in Hawai'i and the making of
US empire / Juliet Nebolon.
Other titles: World War II in Hawai'i and the making of US empire
Description: Durham : Duke University Press, 2024. | Includes
bibliographical references and index.
Identifiers: LCCN 2024003242 (print)
LCCN 2024003243 (ebook)
ISBN 9781478031017 (paperback)
ISBN 9781478026778 (hardcover)
ISBN 9781478060031 (ebook)
Subjects: LCSH: Settler colonialism—Hawaii—History. | Martial law—
Hawaii—History—20th century. | World War, 1939–1945—Hawaii. |
Hawaiians—Ethnic identity—History. | United States—Armed
Forces—Hawaii—History. | Hawaii—Colonization—Social aspects. |
BISAC: SOCIAL SCIENCE / Ethnic Studies / American / General | SOCIAL
SCIENCE / Ethnic Studies / American / Native American Studies
Classification: LCC DU627.5 .N436 2024 (print) | LCC DU627.5 (ebook) |
DDC 940.53/969—dc23/eng/20240430
LC record available at https://lccn.loc.gov/2024003242
LC ebook record available at https://lccn.loc.gov/2024003243

Cover art: Lehuauakea, *Huliau Me Ka Māuiki'iki'i (Revolution and the
Solstice)*, 2022. Oil, ink, and metal leaf on wood panel, 18 × 24 in.
Photo courtesy of Mario Gallucci.

Contents

Acknowledgments

I could not have written this book without the help, support, and knowledge of so many people. My academic journey began at Wesleyan University, where advisers Alex Dupuy and J. Kēhaulani Kauanui instilled in me a love for learning, research, and creative thinking. My greatest thanks go to Kēhaulani Kauanui, whose conviction and fortitude continually inspire me and who has offered crucial insight, unflinching critique, and kindness at every stage. I continue to be indebted to her mentorship. As a graduate student at Yale University, I was lucky to work with brilliant advisers. My committee chair, Mary Lui, single-handedly trained me to conduct archival research, listened to and corralled my expansive ambitions, and provided honest, incisive feedback on numerous drafts of my chapters. Thank you to Matthew Frye Jacobson for sharing his encyclopedic knowledge of American cultural history and for his true generosity as a teacher. Inderpal Grewal guided my understandings of transnational feminism and offered vital advice at key moments. I am also grateful for all that I learned in classes and conversation with Jean-Christophe Agnew, Jafari Allen, Laura Barraclough, Ned Blackhawk, Daniel Botsman, Daphne Brooks, Alicia Schmidt Camacho, Hazel Carby, Michael Denning, Kathryn Dudley, Crystal Feimster, Zareena Grewal, Greta LaFleur, Albert Laguna, Kathryn Lofton, Joanne Meyerowitz, Stephen Pitti, Joanna Radin, and Laura Wexler. At Yale, friends and members of my cohort provided kind feedback and camaraderie: Susie An, Melissa Castillo-Garsow, Melanie Chambliss, Karla Cornejo Villavicencio, Marilyn Flores, Arielle Gorin, Holly Miowak Guise, Fadila Habchi, Christopher Kramaric, Najwa Mayer, Kaneesha Parsard, Sebi Pérez, Joey Plaster, Melissa Paa Redwood, Tyler Rogers, Ashanti Shih, Aaron Sweeney, Bo Tao, Randa Tawil, Quan Tran, and Heather Vermeulen. Thank you to LiLi Johnson and Courtney Sato for their friendship, support, and insight during these years and after.

I am grateful to have spent two years as a postdoctoral fellow at the Charles Warren Center for Studies in American History at Harvard University. Thank you to Walter Johnson, Arthur Patton-Hock, and Monnikue McCall for creating a generative space in which to make the transition from graduate student to scholar, and especially to Walter for his generous guidance and support during this period. I'm so grateful for the mentorship and friendship of Genevieve Clutario, who offered encouragement and advice as I navigated writing, teaching, and the job market. Genevieve, Vince Brown, Dean Itsuji Saranillio, Nayan Shah, Penny Von Eschen, and Robin D. G. Kelley offered invaluable criticism and insight on a very early draft of this manuscript that greatly impacted the trajectory of the project. Leanne Day became a close friend while we were living in Boston, and I'm so thankful for her friendship and incisive understanding of my work. During these years at the Warren Center, I was lucky to receive mentorship, friendship, insight, and reinforcement from David Armitage, Melissa Castillo-Garsow, Chris Clements, Eleanor Craig, Christina Davidson, Philip Deloria, Ruodi Duan, Nick Estes, Garrett Felber, Elizabeth Hinton, Lauren Kaminsky, Ju Yon Kim, Tej Nagaraja, Kristin Oberiano, Stuart Schrader, Kristina Shull, and Kirsten Weld.

I have such good fortune to work at Trinity College surrounded by outstanding colleagues and intellectual interlocutors. Davarian Baldwin's mentorship and leadership are inspiring and indispensable. Deepest admiration for Christina Heatherton and Jordan Camp, whom I am so lucky to know and work alongside. Amanda Guzmán has continually been a source of good sense and humor, and I am so grateful for her friendship and our lunches. Without the hard work and expertise of Veronica Zuñiga, our program and collective project could not function. I treasure the research community we have created in our Entangled Histories cluster at the Trinity Social Justice Institute: thank you to Christina, Jordan, Davarian, Amanda, Diana Aldrete, Mary McNeil, Channon Miller, and Leniqueca Welcome for your commitment to making this space what it is. Thank you as well to colleagues who have offered support, insight, or friendship over the years: Zayde Antrim, Jeffrey Bayliss, Benjamin Carbonetti, Sonia Cardenas, Elise Castillo, Dario Euraque, Scott Gac, Cheryl Greenberg, Christopher Hager, Isaac Kamola, Anne Lambright, Seth Markle, Steve Marston, Reo Matsuzaki, Rebecca Pappas, Diana Paulin, Ibrahim Shikaki, Tom Wickman, Stephanie Wong, and Hilary Wyss. Thank you to Jeffrey Liszka and Yolanda Bergstrom-Lynch for their hard work with library materials and digital collections that enriches our classrooms and campus. I am lucky to teach wonderful students, for whom

I have great respect and from whom I have learned so much: thank you in particular to Natalie Tanaka, Felipe De La Cruz, and Momo Djebli.

Many others have impacted this work by contributing critical engagement or constructive critique over the years. And many, whether they may remember or not, offered kind encouragement or advice at pivotal moments in this project's journey. Thank you to Hōkūlani Aikau, Wesley Attewell, Abigail Boggs, Leslie Bow, Jodi Byrd, Keith Camacho, Christopher Capozzola, Clint Carroll, Jason Chang, Cindy I-Fen Cheng, Megumi Chibana, Kandice Chuh, Patrick Chung, Christian Ayne Crouch, Robert Culp, Joseph Darda, Iyko Day, Adrian De Leon, Tabetha Ewing, Keith Feldman, Andrew Friedman, Candace Fujikane, Takashi Fujitani, Evyn Lê Espiritu Gandhi, Rebekah Garrison, Alyosha Goldstein, Vernadette Vicuña Gonzalez, Rebecca Herman, Lauren Hirshberg, Hiʻilei Hobart, Rebecca Hogue, Daniel HoSang, Michael Innis-Jiménez, Khalil Anthony Johnson, Kyle Kajihiro, Eng-Beng Lim, Lori Kido Lopez, Jodi Kim, Lili Kim, Paul Kramer, Jana Lipman, Uahikea Maile, Simeon Man, Nayan Shah, Laurel Mei-Singh, Max Mishler, Mary X. Mitchell, Emily Mitchell-Eaton, Christian Hart Nakarado, Tiara Naʻputi, Logan Narikawa, Richard Nisa, Jean O'Brien, Gary Okihiro, Josephine Ong, A. Naomi Paik, ʻUmi Perkins, Khury Petersen-Smith, Joel Pfister, Laura Pulido, Chandan Reddy, Roberto Saba, Dean Saranillio, Cathy Schlund-Vials, Rebecca Schreiber, Noenoe K. Silva, Seema Sohi, Kim TallBear, Eric Tang, Ty Kawika P. Tengan, Wesley Ueunten, Julie Weise, Joseph Weiss, Tessa Winkelmann, Lisa Yoneyama, and Timothy Yu.

The knowledge and hard work of archivists and librarians have been invaluable to this project, especially Sherman Seki at the Archives and Manuscripts Department in the Hamilton Library at the University of Hawaiʻi at Mānoa; the archival staff at the Hawaiian and Pacific Collection in the Hamilton Library at the University of Hawaiʻi at Mānoa; Marcia Kemble at the Japanese Cultural Center of Hawaiʻi; Eric Vanslander at the National Archives in College Park, MD; William Greene at the National Archives in San Bruno, CA; the Northern Mariana Islands Museum of History and Culture in Saipan, N.M.I.; and Kalani Kaanaana at the Hawaii Medical Library at the Queen's Medical Center in Honolulu. Gwen Sinclair at the Government Documents Collection in the Hamilton Library at the University of Hawaiʻi at Mānoa generously shared her research and collection of newspaper articles that pertained to US military landholdings. I likewise acknowledge the *Honolulu Star-Advertiser* for allowing me to reprint some of the images in this book.

I could not have completed my research for this project without financial support from the American Studies Program, the Yale Club of San Francisco, the John F. Enders Research Fellowship, and the Smith Richardson Foundation at Yale University; the Charles Warren Center at Harvard University; and Trinity College. An American Council of Learned Societies Fellowship offered critical support toward the completion of this project. Opportunities to present or workshop portions of this manuscript yielded invaluable feedback and discussion that strengthened the work. Thank you to Charles Geisler, Raymond Craib, Paul Nadasdy, and the participants of the Summer Institute on Contested Global Landscapes at Cornell University; Cathy Schlund-Vials and the participants of the Bodies Living with Violence Workshop at the University of Connecticut; Joanna Radin and participants of "Cold War Indigeneity in Science and Medicine" at Yale University; Mary Lui and members of the Yale Asian American Studies Working Group; Margot Canaday, Nancy Cott, Robert Self, and participants of "The Intimate State: Gender, Sexuality, and Governance in Modern U.S. History" at Brown University; the History Department and participants of the "New Approaches to Gender and Migration in the U.S. since 1900" at Bates College; Katherine Achacoso, Halena Kapuni-Reynolds, Logan Narikawa, and participants of "(Re)mapping Indigenous and Settler Geographies in the Pacific" at the University of Hawai'i at Mānoa; Paul Kramer and participants of "Social Landscapes of U.S. Military Empire" at Vanderbilt University; Christina Heatherton, Jordan Camp, and members of the Entangled Histories Research Cluster at the Trinity Social Justice Institute; and Roberto Saba, Katie Brewer Ball, and members of the Indigenous Studies Research Network at Wesleyan University.

An early version of chapter 2 appeared as "'Life Given Straight from the Heart': Settler Militarism, Biopolitics, and Public Health in Hawai'i during World War II," *American Quarterly* 69, no. 1 (2017): 23–45. I sincerely thank the two anonymous reviewers and the AQ Editorial Board, particularly Hōkūlani Aikau, for their feedback on this article during the revision process, which was also very influential for my overall project. A previous version of chapter 5 appeared as "Settler-Military Camps: Internment and Prisoner of War Camps across the Pacific Islands during World War II," *Journal of Asian American Studies* 24, no. 2 (2021): 299–335.

Ken Wissoker believed in this project since our first meeting at the Association for Asian American Studies conference, and I have truly valued his vital advice and direction. Thank you to the editorial board and staff at Duke University Press, especially Joshua Gutterman Tranen and Kate Mullen for their support throughout the revision and production process and Lisa Lawley for her hard work as project editor. Thank you to Donald Pharr for his careful copyedits and Andrew Ascherl for his meticulous work creating the index. I deeply appreciate the two external reviewers for their careful engagement with my work and their insightful, capacious, and generous feedback, which greatly transformed the project and improved my writing.

I am eternally grateful for wonderful family and friends. Thank you so much to the Changs in Honolulu for opening their homes to me. I am lucky to have had the company of extended family during my research trips. I am thankful for the love and support of the Nebolon and McCluskey families in California; and the Michael, Lowe, Mark, Dow, and Ng families in Massachusetts. My best friend, Lily Fesler, has been a constant source of support, laughter, and adventure since we met in our dorm room on the first day of college. Thank you to my dad, whose enthusiasm each time I express my passions has fostered my belief in myself. I have a lifetime of gratitude for my mom, whose love, experience, and insight have given me the confidence to pursue my personal and intellectual ambitions, and who has encouraged and thought with me throughout this project. As my mother, companion, confidant, and teacher, she is my guidepost and my inspiration.

Finally, I am so fortunate to share my life with Chris Michael and Joss Nebolon-Michael. Joss, who came into the world just as I finished this book, already brings me immeasurable joy with each gleeful smile, curious babble, and discerning glance. I cannot wait to know the person he becomes. Words cannot fully express my gratitude for Chris, who for sixteen years has continued to teach me what it means to truly be a partner in every imaginable way. He has supported my dreams before his own, but our journey together already exceeds them. This book is dedicated to Chris: almost half of my life has been made with you, and I still love you more each day.

Introduction

Settler Militarism, Racial Liberal Biopolitics,
and Social Reproduction

Two wartime photographs publicized key US imperatives of martial law during World War II in Hawai'i. The first, published in the *Honolulu Star-Bulletin* in April 1942, depicts a high school student in O'ahu, Susan Kang, receiving a vaccination from US Army captain H. R. Meiz, supervised by Colonel Edgar King, a surgeon, and M. F. Haralson, the commissioner for the Territorial Board of Health (figure I.1).[1] The caption reads, "Susan Kang . . . answers the citywide 'call to arms' and is immunized against typhoid," thus linking this vaccination to patriotic military defense under martial law in Hawai'i during World War II. In fact, Kang was one of 363,000 civilians who were subject to mandatory vaccinations by military order in the islands. Kang is standing facing away from the supervising white male officials, who, instead of looking at her face, are focusing intently on the sight of the injection, with the number of personnel far exceeding the need for the proper execution of the procedure. Meiz's firm grip on Kang's arm implies that she is being subjected involuntarily, and he looks down and leans slightly away from her—as though he is holding an animal, not a human being. This dehumanizing portrayal suggests a racial and gendered difference between these individuals that paradoxically otherizes this young girl while also portraying her as a model for wartime patriotism and assimilation.

Another photograph, thought to have been taken by the US Navy, depicts four women defense laborers, Isabel Nascimento, Catherine Ohumukini, Harriet Garcia, and Sally Young, smiling as they move pallets at a storehouse (figure I.2). The happy faces of the four women pictured here belie the reality of the acute labor shortage during this period, in which the US Army unilaterally froze employment and wages, required many laborers to work seventy hours per week, and criminalized absenteeism.[2] As Samuel Kamaka Jr. remembers, when the war started, "We were frozen to our jobs, so we couldn't leave or run away and go away to school, so everything was in confusion. . . . We had twelve-hour shifts. . . . We worked six, six days a week and we had a lot of overtime, of course. . . . I think it was sixty-five cents an hour."[3] The US military government employed workers, in conjunction with an unprecedented acquisition of Hawaiian land, to clear and industrialize landscapes for use as bases, training grounds, ammunitions storage, and other military installations.

Taken together, these two photographs demonstrate how the patriotic necessity of the health of all people in Hawai'i was fundamental to extreme wartime requirements for total labor mobilization in the service of war. That is, after a settler colonial history in which disease itself had been complicit in the deaths of many Kanaka Maoli (the Indigenous people of Hawai'i), the pressures of wartime mobilization led the military government to target the optimal health of all lives—white, Asian, and Hawaiian—even as it perpetuated militarized racial logics that demonized Japanese immigrants and settler colonial structures that naturalized white possession and denied Native sovereignty.[4] Thus, these photographs illuminate select components of the social reproduction of US settler militarism: in these unsettling racialized, gendered, and biopolitical scenes, we can see the imprint of a martial law government working to reconcile its wartime capitalist dependence on nonwhite life and labor with its colonial and military desires to otherize, dispossess, and deplete the vitality of those same lives. Significantly, mandatory vaccination and labor were only a part of this biopolitical, capitalist project that sought to cultivate and purportedly "improve" people and land in Hawai'i, specifically to intensify the racialized and colonial expropriation of life and land as a wartime resource.

Throughout this period the US military unilaterally acquired Hawaiian land at an unprecedented rate, conscripting spaces to fortify militarized biopolitical projects that socially reproduced the uneven racialized, gendered, and colonial relations of this imperial war. Further, just as mandatory immunization cultivated health to boost labor productivity, so too did blood banks collect biological resources from this "healthy" population, reporting donation statistics via a racial hierarchy of patriotic service. Homemaking campaigns targeted immigrant families as a central unit of wartime social reproduction, promoted assimilation to American nutritional standards and

2

FIGURE I.1 · The caption of this photograph in the *Honolulu Star-Bulletin* is "ANSWER 'CALL TO ARMS'": Susan Kang, student at Farrington high school, answers the citywide 'call to arms' and is immunized against typhoid by Capt. H. R. Meiz of the army. Looking on (*left to right*) are Col. Edgar King, Hawaiian department surgeon, and M. F. Haralson, territorial health commissioner and administrator of the emergency medical service of the office of civilian defense." *Honolulu Star-Bulletin*, April 8, 1942. Hawaii War Records Depository HWRD 0738, UHM Library Digital Image Collections.

domestic customs, and masked the persistence of Native Hawaiian food cultures and land-based epistemologies of health. In wartime schools, teachers cultivated "proper" Americanized language, speech, and citizenship in the classroom while training students of all races in gendered wartime vocational skills. Beyond these biopolitical projects that both incorporated and differentiated diverse peoples in Hawai'i, the US military government interned Japanese settlers it deemed "disloyal" or "unassimilable" in military camps across the United States, Hawai'i, and the Pacific Islands.[5]

The World War II period in Hawai'i remains surprisingly understudied, despite its significance as the site of the longest imposition of martial law in US history (1941–44). The declaration of a state of emergency after the bombing of Pearl Harbor validated the defense of the United States by any

FIGURE I.2 · From back of print: "Isabel Nascimento (*back left*), Catherine Ohumukini (*right*), Harriet Garcia (*front left*), and Sally Young working on pallets. (Scene at store-house)." United States Navy ?, undated. Hawaii War Records Depository HWRD 2164, UHM Library Digital Image Collections.

means necessary: a democratic state at war can monopolize instruments of violence, intern populations, place an entire territory under martial law, and subjugate citizens and others with impunity. The extended period of martial law that followed transformed the wartime "state of emergency" into a technique of governance, through which the military state's suspension of constitutional rights permitted and innovated means for the administration of daily life. The mechanisms of martial law transformed not only landscapes and security measures but also standards for health and well-being, access to geographic mobility, language and cultural production, responsibilities of citizenship, and the economics of the home and family—all in the name of military defense and mobilization.

At 3:30 p.m. on December 7, 1941, the afternoon of the Japanese bombing of Pearl Harbor, Territorial Governor Joseph B. Poindexter declared martial law in Hawai'i.[6] This measure, enacted in consultation with President Franklin D. Roosevelt, authorized Walter C. Short as the military governor

4

of Hawaiʻi and suspended the power of the territorial government.[7] General Delos C. Emmons, who replaced Short as military governor on December 17, announced via the *New York Times* that "martial law in Hawaii has been purposely designed to meet war conditions of military and vital necessity which were forced upon these islands by a new type of fast long-range invasion warfare." The military government in Hawaiʻi justified the enactment of martial law to the US government and the American public with its assertion of the "constant threat of repetition" of an aerial attack and because of the supposed threat of local Japanese informants living within Hawaiʻi itself.[8] The US War Department originally planned to evacuate all Japanese, who constituted more than a third of Hawaiʻi's population, but concerns about a labor shortage and its possible effects on wartime productivity led Emmons to eventually abort this plan. Emmons also reasoned that Nisei in Hawaiʻi could possibly serve as useful translators and soldiers during the war.[9] As in other instances of US martial law in colonial contexts, the US military enacted measures in Hawaiʻi to restrict and surveil civilian activity, including the immediate apprehension of "prime suspects," the fingerprinting and photographing of all civilians age six and older, and nightly blackouts and curfews.[10] The military also authorized orders to surveil and censor other domains of civilian life, such as news media, personal correspondence, radio signals, women's occupational statuses, noncitizens' home addresses, educational curriculum, foreign language instruction, and public health and sanitation.[11]

Hawaiʻi took on dual functions as both "home front" and "war front" during World War II: Hawaiʻi's location at the intersection of these spaces is illustrative of how the islands constituted both a US settler colony that was "included" in the US nation-state and a vital military outpost that connected the United States to the rest of the Pacific Theater. For these reasons, the martial law period in Hawaiʻi is an important era in which to analyze the convergence of these two settler and military regimes. I use the term *settler militarism* to refer to the dynamics through which settler colonialism and militarization simultaneously perpetuated, legitimated, and concealed one another during World War II.[12] Settler colonialism is a colonial project that—in contrast to franchise colonialism, which primarily uses Native peoples as a source of labor and capital—is predicated on land acquisition and the replacement, or elimination, of Indigenous peoples. Haunani-Kay Trask's work has been foundational to the study of settler colonialism in Hawaiʻi, as have the other contributors to *Asian Settler Colonialism: From Local Governance to the Habits of Everyday Life in Hawaiʻi*, edited by Candace Fujikane and Jonathan Okamura.[13] Militarization is the process by which military logics, force, occupation, and expansion come to be accepted as a solution or logical inevitability by the government and the general public.[14] Both projects are not merely political but are also cultural, social, economic, racialized, and gendered regimes that continually rearticulate themselves into everyday life in both hyper-visible and ostensibly invisible forms.

Settler militarism is thus a transnational and imperial dynamic through which structures of settler colonialism and militarization share mutual investments in land acquisition and the continued dispossession of Indigenous peoples. In Hawai'i and the Pacific Islands, settler militarism—though always complex, varying, and contested—emerged in the late nineteenth century, intensified during the World War II period, and continues to be elaborated in new, perverse forms today. Significantly, although settler militarism has operated across various locations throughout US history, it was never inevitable, is always unfinished, and is fundamentally reactive in nature: it is always responding to the continuing vitality of Native life and claims to sovereignty.[15] Settler colonialism is by definition incomplete: even as it desires totality via the social reproduction of the racial, gendered, and economic conditions that fortify it, it by necessity can never be total.[16] As Dean Itsuji Saranillio argues, conceiving of white supremacist structures such as settler colonialism in Hawai'i as "emerging from positions of weakness, not strength," more precisely illuminates both the desires and the inherent flaws of these regimes.[17] That is, every history of conquest, dispossession, and exploitation has produced its own contradictions as well as the conditions of its own challenge and demise.

Furthermore, an examination of the history of US settler militarism challenges dominant exceptionalist narratives of the World War II period in Hawai'i, which depict violent carceral projects such as internment, militarized land acquisition, and martial law as necessary aberrations during an otherwise "good war" fought in the name of liberal democracy.[18] That is, the period of martial law in Hawai'i was certainly unprecedented in many ways, but US military governance also built upon long-standing colonial, racial, and gendered dynamics in the islands that would continue to evolve and proliferate even after martial law was lifted in 1944. Scholars in Hawaiian studies such as Haunani-Kay Trask, Noenoe K. Silva, and Saranillio have already traced how the US military has played an integral role in securing settler claims to land in Hawai'i throughout history.[19] Trask and Silva discuss the involvement of the US military both in King Kalākaua's forced signing of the 1887 Bayonet Constitution and in the 1893 overthrow of Queen

6

Lili'uokalani. Trask further observes that the 1876 Reciprocity Treaty, which allowed for the duty-free trade of sugar between the islands and the US continent, also ceded Pu'uloa (now Pearl Harbor) to the United States for use as a military base upon its renewal in 1887.[20] This led to the illegal annexation of Hawai'i through the 1898 Newlands Resolution, which was a domestic US Congress resolution not recognized by international law that included the seizure of 1.8 million acres of Hawaiian Kingdom Crown Lands and Government Lands.[21] Significantly, Silva notes that Congress passed this resolution in order to secure the use of Hawai'i as a coaling station during the Spanish-American War.[22] Kanaka Maoli widely protested against this resolution and US annexation in 1898 through petitions that were signed by more than 38,000 of the population of 40,000.[23] In Hawai'i, the ever-changing structure of settler colonialism has always been intertwined with US military expansion. Yet despite these shared investments, settler and military relations have not always been smooth and sometimes were even extremely tense. For example, as Saranillio notes, there have often been frictions between the federal government and the Big Five sugar corporations, which monopolized the plantation economy, the territorial government, and affiliated legal and cultural institutions.[24] One period when these tensions came to a head was during the 1931 Massie case, which ended in the mistrial of five Hawaiian, Japanese, and Chinese men accused of beating and raping Thalia Massie, the wife of a naval officer. In the aftermath a US admiral incited the lynching of the accused, resulting in the death of Joseph Kahahawai. Unhappy with the supposed inability of the Big Five to govern and "control" the multiracial population in Hawai'i, US congressmen attempted unsuccessfully to place Hawai'i under a military commission.[25]

The specific collaboration of settler and military projects in the islands—while indeed sometimes fraught—laid the groundwork for their escalation during World War II and beyond. For example, on December 7, 1941, Governor Poindexter's power to declare martial law was derived from US settler colonial legislation: Section 67 of the 1900 Hawaiian Organic Act granted the territorial governor the power to "suspend the privilege of the writ of habeas corpus or place the territory or any part thereof under martial law."[26] In the wake of the bombing of Pearl Harbor, discourses of "military necessity" against the Japanese enemy rationalized the US military presence and accelerated its acquisition of land. Over the course of the war, the US military occupied an all-time high of 648,666 acres of land in Hawai'i, which was more than eighteen times the 35,750 acres that it had used in 1940.[27] Vernadette Vicuña Gonzalez observes that the US government constructed the bombing of Pearl Harbor as the *principal* violent event that led to Hawaiʻi's supposed "inclusion" in the United States. That is, militarized, patriotic tropes of collective injury and sacrifice have masked past and present US settler colonialism, including the 1893 overthrow, the 1898 unlawful annexation, and Hawaiʻi statehood in 1959.[28] Furthermore, as Fujikane, Okamura, and Saranillio have illustrated, in Hawaiʻi the patriotic and militarized narrative of the "World War II Nisei soldier" created the conditions for Asian settlers, and particularly Japanese settlers, to benefit from postwar movements for American citizenship, Hawaiian statehood, and civil rights—over and against Native Hawaiian resistance to these movements.[29]

Building on and indebted to this previous work in Hawaiian studies, the concept of settler militarism necessitates that we consider the regimes of settler colonialism and militarization in the Pacific Islands and Asia—as well as the racial triangulation of Indigenous peoples, Asian settlers, and white settlers—as intertwined. At the same time, we must recognize the dangers of combining these histories and structures uncritically via inclusionary rather than relational analyses. Although US wars have informed the experiences of Asian and Pacific Islander communities and their diaspora throughout history, we must acknowledge that the terms *Asia/Pacific* and *transpacific* are necessarily militarized and colonial categories.[30] The use of these terms without attending to these violent histories, as well as to the specificities of Pacific Indigenous peoples, histories, and struggles, simply rehearses settler, military, and colonial logics.[31] In this book I interrogate the settler military epistemologies that have engendered these categorizations, understanding that it is the history of US and Japanese colonialism, settler migration, militarization, and empire—not any inherent similarity between these areas or between Pacific Islander and Asian peoples—that has led Asia and the Pacific Islands to be considered by some to be one region. With this dynamic tension in mind, this book draws from Pacific Indigenous studies and Asian American studies and works to bring these fields into productive and closer conversation. As a mixed-race Asian American settler whose maternal grandparents and their siblings crossed the Pacific in the 1940s fleeing the Japanese bombings of China, my family history's imbrication with settler colonial wartime migration animates my responsibility to research settler military histories and the violent structures they have engendered. This book is written with the intention that understanding the historical entanglements of settler colonialism, capitalism, and military empire—which continue to structure our present—is integral to envisioning and strengthening solidarities across racialized and settler colonial contexts. I offer this book with the hope that this relational research can contribute to further work that moves us closer to a reimagined future.

Accordingly, *Settler Militarism* builds upon recent work in American studies that elaborates settler colonialism as a relational analytic that is "constitutively entangled" with other formations such as white supremacy, racial capitalism, incarceration, immigration control, militarism, and overseas empire.[32] I argue that Hawai'i during World War II exemplifies a specific convergence of settler colonialism and militarization, but history is replete with examples of settler militarism in other arrangements and geographic contexts. For example, nineteenth-century US westward expansion was inextricably tied to and bolstered by the utilization of US military power, and today every US military base and former internment camp in the continental United States sits on Indigenous land.[33] Further, we cannot consider US overseas military basing without interrogating the history of settler colonialism that underlies and supports it. For example, although US military buildup in South Korea does not require the replacement of Korean sovereignty with US sovereignty, US military expansion during and after the Korean War was predicated on the use of military bases located in US settler colonies such as Hawai'i and Guam. The US military presence in South Korea endures today because of the maintenance of this network of settler military bases. Moreover, although the US occupation of Okinawa technically ended in 1972, US militarization in Okinawa has historically bolstered and masked Japanese settler colonialism in the island, and this continues even today: almost 75 percent of the US military installations in Japan are located in Okinawa, and US military installations cover 20 percent of the island, yet Okinawa does not even make up 1 percent of the total land area of Japan.[34] Thus, although it is outside the scope of this study, the dynamic of settler militarism surely permeates contexts beyond the World War II period in Hawai'i.

Racial Liberal Biopolitics

In addition, Hawai'i was a principally *biopolitical* space under martial law: in this book I examine settler militarism in ways that animate and complicate Michel Foucault's theory of biopolitics and its technologies of rule that "'make' live and 'let' die."[35] That is, biopower helps us to analyze the kinds of power that life-cultivating institutions can wield, but there are specificities—such as those that govern colonial, racialized, and capitalist contexts—that Foucault's writings do not fully explain. Because Foucault considers power as amorphous and nonspecific, strictly Foucauldian interpretations of biopower cannot imagine power working differentially or there being differential levels of acquiescence to these projects.[36] For example, Silvia Federici argues that Foucauldian notions of biopower cannot account for how its "make live" imperative to reproduce the population targets men and women's bodies and livelihoods in highly differentiated ways. Likewise, I argue that biopower is not amorphous or undifferentiated: rather, the textures of its techniques seek to produce and order life according to the specific and varying racialized, gendered, and colonial desires of settler militarism, capitalism, and US empire.

During World War II, these asymmetrical dynamics were complex and rapidly changing. Over the course of the war, Hawai'i's population grew from approximately 423,000 to 500,000 as large numbers of soldiers and defense workers arrived from the continent to aid in military mobilization. Additionally, many civilians moved from the neighbor islands to O'ahu, hoping to be employed in defense work.[37] In 1940 women accounted for only 42 percent of the population in the islands, and after the bombing of Pearl Harbor, the influx of servicemen and defense laborers, coupled with the evacuation of many (mostly white) women to the US continent, led men to far outnumber women in the territory. Thus, gender dynamics in Hawai'i were different from those in the continental United States, where women outnumbered men during the World War II period.[38] In 1940 Asian settlers made up at least 56 percent of the population in the islands, whereas white settlers made up 25 percent, and Native Hawaiians made up 15 percent. Japanese alone accounted for 37 percent of the total population, numbering at over 157,000. For comparison, this is more than the total number of Japanese Americans who were interned in the entire US continent during World War II.[39] Eighty percent of the population in Hawai'i were US citizens at this time.[40] All of this created a very specific wartime regime designed particularly for civilians living in Hawai'i that was characterized by a series of martial law policies that used logics of race, gender, and indigeneity as a means to regulate Hawai'i's racially diverse population during wartime. Furthermore, Hawai'i, which has throughout history been depicted as a "multiracial paradise," played a particular role at the intersection of US and Japanese empires, both of which used antiracism as an empire-building discourse. Just as the United States portrayed itself as an antiracist liberal power over and against Japan and other Axis enemies such as Germany, Japan portrayed its Greater East Asia Co-Prosperity Sphere as an antiracist alternative to Western imperialism and white supremacy, including US empire.[41] Thus, although it is significant that martial law projects incorporated individuals of all racial groups during the war in a way that US wartime projects in the continent did not, there were domestic and transnational reasons why inclusionary racial logics were fostered selectively in some spaces but not in others.

Scholars such as Jodi Melamed or Mary Dudziak generally consider the racial liberal transition to have taken place in the United States during the postwar or Cold War period, but in Hawai'i discourses of antiracism, tolerance, and inclusion proliferated during World War II, even alongside militarized racist rhetoric that demonized the "Japanese enemy."[42] In Foucault's theorization of biopolitical governmentality and its "apparatus of security," he states that "instead of a binary division between the permitted and the prohibited, one establishes an average considered as optimal on the one hand, and, on the other, a bandwidth of the acceptable that must not be exceeded."[43] Wendy Brown articulates "tolerance" as a specific element of this biopower: "It is a singular form of such management insofar as it involves the simultaneous incorporation and maintenance of the otherness of the tolerated element."[44] In Hawai'i a biopolitical logic of "tolerance" preserved asymmetrical dynamics of racial otherness within a liberal democratic rhetoric of inclusion—that is, via "racial liberalism." Likewise, martial law projects in Hawai'i did not exclude nonwhite others outright via racist policies; rather, the US military government "tolerated" the racial difference of diverse peoples out of a military necessity for total labor mobilization in the islands and created a "bandwidth of the acceptable" for wartime behavior on the part of these peoples. Furthermore, military documents of the period professed triumphantly that during World War II, Hawai'i "became a *laboratory* for the study of martial law," connoting imagery of the islands as controlled environments in which experiments were conducted upon bodies, populations, and landscapes in order to boost military strength and productivity.[45] Describing Hawai'i as a "laboratory" suggests that this "experiment" concerned the extent to which these protracted conditions of biopolitical control and racial liberalism in Hawai'i could serve as a successful model for other current and future US military occupations in the Pacific Islands, Asia, or, indeed, throughout the world.

As this wartime regime of racial liberalism included all racial groups in the biopolitical administration, it simultaneously continued to intensify the classification of these racially differentiated peoples while denying Hawaiian indigeneity. For example, as I explain in chapter 2, the Honolulu Blood Bank accepted donations from those of any race throughout the war—which was not always the case in the US continent. Yet the military government also published monthly statistics of which racial group was donating the most blood, which "included" Hawaiians as a so-called racial group rather than acknowledging Hawaiian indigeneity and sovereign rights to land. As Jodi Melamed argues, official antiracism does not eliminate racial difference but rather accentuates a hierarchy of differential racialization through veiled racial codes of privilege and stigma, thus fortifying the conditions for legitimate state violence.[46] Racial liberal programs in Hawai'i, from blood donation to English-only education, compelled broad wartime participation without accounting for structural inequalities created by past and present racial and colonial violence. In fact, pressures to demonstrate patriotism via participation and labor were most acute for racialized peoples and noncitizens—particularly those who were suspected of disloyalty—as well as for Kanaka Maoli, who were granted citizenship under the 1900 Hawaiian Organic Act, which designated Hawai'i as a US territory.[47] Overall, racial liberal inclusion contributed to a biopolitical regime of social ordering and reproduction during the war in Hawai'i: I use the term *racial liberal biopolitics* to refer to this dynamic. Yet, in actuality, the US military government's biopolitical regime of racial inclusion was far from "inclusive," and furthermore it was reliant upon spaces of racial exclusion and incarceration: as chapter 5 explores, the US military imprisoned Asian settlers and Indigenous peoples in internment and prisoner-of-war camps across Hawai'i, the Marshall Islands, and the Northern Mariana Islands during this period.

Furthermore, racial liberal biopolitics in wartime Hawai'i was specifically a means through which the military government denied Hawaiian sovereignty and naturalized Hawaiian dispossession for the purposes of settler military buildup and expansion. Aileen Moreton-Robinson's work illustrates how settler colonial logics of white possession operate "through the racialized application of disciplinary knowledges and regulatory mechanisms [i.e., biopower], which function together to preclude recognition of Indigenous sovereignty."[48] In Hawai'i the US military government's racial liberal biopolitical projects worked against Hawaiian sovereignty by seeking to reproduce the conditions of settler militarism: that is, by intensifying racial differentiation, masking indigeneity, and rationalizing militarized land acquisition. Racial liberalism thus not only incorporated to differentiate, but it also foreclosed a critical analysis of indigeneity and settler colonialism. A principal example of this dynamic at work is the US military government's argument—ostensibly made in the spirit of racial "tolerance"—that "the Chinese, Filipino, Hawaiian, and various Caucasian people caused no concern because it was known where their sympathies lay. The big question mark were the Japanese with their quaint oriental customs, poorly assimilated into our western civilization."[49] The hyper-visibility of both racial differentiation and anti-Japanese racism within racial liberal statements such as this created a boundary for acceptable loyal behavior on the part of so-called good racialized peoples. The continual inclusion of Hawaiians as a "racial group" in Hawai'i also placed Native Hawaiians alongside immigrants as "assimilable," and it classified them as a racial group rather than an Indigenous people with land and sovereignty rights amounting to a national claim. Further, the militarized caricature of the "Japanese enemy" rationalized the project of martial law as a necessary wartime aberration and obfuscated the ongoing history of settler colonialism and unlawful occupation that formed its conditions of possibility in Hawai'i.[50] This critique of race and indigeneity as distinct yet interrelated categories is essential to halting the reproduction of racial discourse and classifications that are predicated on an a priori assumption of the US nation-state as a white possession—such as that expressed above in the military government's statement.[51] Overall, under martial law, racial liberal biopower simultaneously intensified the codes of gendered white patriotism as a regulatory power, perpetuated the differentiation of racialized peoples, precluded a recognition of indigeneity, and elided the ongoing history of settler colonialism—and thus was *always* also gendered, colonial, and militarized as it stretched to absolve the contradictions embedded in the regime of settler militarism. Yet at the same time, this project and its rationalizations were always unfinished, always unstable, and always failing.[52]

Capitalism and the Social Reproduction of Settler Militarism

During World War II, settler militarism and racial liberal biopolitics operated together in the service of capitalism; collectively, the social reproduction of these structures created the conditions for the late twentieth-century expansion of US military empire. In discussing capitalism and social reproduction in this way, I draw from Cedric Robinson and scholars of racial capitalism, Native American and Indigenous studies, and Marxist, transnational, and Black feminisms: scholars across these fields invoke histories of transatlantic slavery, colonial conquest, and the enclosure of the European commons in order to analyze race, gender, and indigeneity as material relations of capitalism.[53] Building upon these conversations, we can understand how the era of so-called primitive accumulation—that is, the plundering of racialized unpaid labor and Indigenous lands as well as the rupture of non-capitalist social forms such as reciprocal relations between humans and the natural world—never ended, as Marx originally formulated, but continues to sustain capitalist modes of production.[54] This understanding of primitive accumulation further affects how we interpret Marx's theories of abstraction—that is, the equation of objects and labor that are unequal, and the denial of their incommensurability.[55] Marx theorized in the *Grundrisse* that capitalist modernity desires abstraction, arguing that the United States had "truly realized" labor abstraction through its indifferent aggregation of differing types of labor.[56] Yet in spite of this, we know that capitalism has not only abstracted and denied but also has continually *profited from* the specific inequalities and differences produced by histories of race, slavery, and colonialism. In this way, capitalism produces the myth that it accumulates indifferently and homogeneously while profiting materially from the racial, gendered, and colonial differentiation of life: as Federici argues, beyond the appropriation of uncompensated labor and land, primitive accumulation is also the accumulation of these differences that are constitutive of capitalist production and reproduction.[57]

Racial liberal biopower thus aids and abets capitalism's violent dynamic of abstraction via the social reproduction and ordering of peoples, landscapes, and relationships such that relations of capital and property seem rational and inevitable rather than failing, incomplete, and contradictory.[58] For example, both settler militarism and capitalism are dependent upon the accumulation of life, labor, and land to reproduce themselves, yet they are also continually producing their own conditions of austerity through violent and extractive projects that are life and land destroying.[59] Further, this repertoire of settler military, capitalist, and racialized biopolitical mechanisms for dispossession built upon and aligned with colonial discourses of "improvement" and modernity that underlie liberal Lockean theories of property. For example, John Locke's assertion in *The Second Treatise of Government* that it is only improvement via rational labor that can produce valued property is a racial liberal biopolitical logic that devalues and marginalizes Indigenous noncapitalist relations to land while presenting predatory capitalist projects as modern, life-cultivating, and in the service of "public good."[60] We can see this logic of improvement operate across settler military regimes of land acquisition, public health, domestic science, and education.

Further, as capitalism produces unsustainable dynamics of inequality and scarcity that eventually hinder its reproduction, it seeks to remedy its own insufficiencies through military expansion, war, and the colonial appropriation of additional markets, labor, land, and natural resources, as well as through the reiteration of these forms of expropriation within.[61] Thus, as we can see in the case of martial law in Hawai'i and in subsequent US military occupations elsewhere, twentieth-century US empire continually rearticulated and elaborated the primitive accumulation of life, land, and labor as it expanded across the Pacific Islands toward Asia—even as this project was often cloaked within liberal tropes of rescue and rehabilitation, liberation and human rights, or free-market inclusion.

That is, racial liberal biopolitics works to socially reproduce the racial, gendered, cultural, and economic conditions that fortify settler militarism and capitalism. Yet during World War II, these regimes did not have enough willing, healthy laborers to reproduce and expand themselves.[62] At the start of the war, this acute shortage led the US army to unilaterally control labor standards, including wages, working conditions, and the proportion of laborers allocated per wartime industry. Over the course of the war, the US military required workers in public utilities, local and federal government, and government contractors and subcontractors to remain in their positions, while criminalizing absenteeism. Often, laborers were required to work up to seventy-hour weeks. The provost court gave those who disobeyed these regulations punishments ranging from a $150 to a $1,000 fine to jail sentences of up to one year.[63] The military government and the plantations collaborated via a "labor-loan" program, in which plantations forcibly loaned workers to the above industries while continuing to pay them plantation wages and pocketing the surplus from the higher defense wages.[64] This repertoire of labor-control projects increased the number of laborers employed by the federal government eight-fold during the war.[65] These figures speak both to the scale of forced wartime labor and to the immense collective profit that the US military and plantations accumulated during this period. All of these measures—and in particular, the sugar plantations' "labor-loan" program— were examples of the primitive accumulation of labor and, because of the nature of the work, contributed to the primitive accumulation of land. Furthermore, these coercive and punitive responses to labor scarcity are an expression of settler militarism reacting to its internally produced crisis. They reveal the military government and settler military regime's reliance on labor, as well as its fear of the labor unrest that would have occurred had martial law not been declared.

The US military and business leaders sought to rationalize and mask the reality of this inhumane, extractive project: labor-control discourses dovetailed with wartime patriotism and racial dynamics. For example, workers who participated in labor unrest, were frequently absent, or showed a lack of morale were labeled as subversive to the war effort. Many unions were anti-Japanese, and some even explicitly colluded with the military government: for example, the Stevedores Union agreed to surveil its multiracial workforce—many of whom were Japanese, Filipino, Chinese, and Hawaiian—for "security and efficiency on the warfront." In 1943 Military Governor Richardson argued that Japanese labor unrest necessitated the continuation of martial law and blamed the high absentee rate in waterfront work on the alleged "traditional laxity here of the work habits of the Filipinos."[66] Richardson's racialized explanation sought to mask the contradictions of this martial law labor regime built upon a de facto convict labor system. Further, the US military's constant focus on public health not only sought to increase worker productivity but also performed the ruse that the US military government valued life in Hawai'i. Yet labor control would not have been necessary if this wartime project were truly benevolent or life cultivating, rather than extractive, racially exploitative, and colonial.

Beyond the defense industries that the US military government explicitly controlled and surveilled, this book primarily considers the additional forms of racialized and gendered labor required for the social reproduction of settler militarism and capitalism. Social reproduction comprises the myriad biological, physical, and affective labors necessary to reproduce the living worker as well as to reproduce the social, structural, political, and economic relations of production.[67] For example, martial law centralized gendered forms of white patriotism as dominant models for assimilation and loyalty in order to optimize and reproduce the population for war. Just as US martial law harnessed logics of militarized masculinity in the making of patriotic servicemen, defense workers, and blood donors, so too did it necessitate militarized femininity: wartime mobilization depended upon the feminized, affective labors of domesticity and care in its reproduction and maintenance of a multiracial population ready and supposedly willing to serve the war effort. The military government enlisted women of all races—for example, as nurses, mothers, and teachers—in this reproductive labor and in many cases subjected them to increased military scrutiny. Nurses and teachers constituted the principal executors of the wartime registration, fingerprinting, and vaccination of civilians in the islands. Hawaiian, immigrant, and white mothers faced pressure to abide by wartime rationing and nutritional regulations, manage efficient homes, and raise healthy, patriotic children. Teachers were instructed that in the classroom, "*All* prejudices *must* be submerged," in order to help cultivate feelings of patriotism and loyalty among their

16

multiracial students.[68] Because of the specific race, gender, and class dynamics of Hawai'i, it was in many cases Indigenous and immigrant people of color who were enlisted to carry out this gendered labor.

Social reproduction thus recapitulated the uneven and hierarchical conditions of settler militarism and capitalism, which included the contradictory project of cultivating life and labor within a wartime context marked by death, displacement, and dispossession. Reproductive labors, in this sense, not only sought to reproduce the worker in the service of total wartime mobilization but were also tasked with absolving the contradictions of settler militarism and capitalism while reproducing these structures' asymmetrical conditions of emergence, including the differentiated dynamics of race, gender, and colonialism for primitive accumulation in its various forms.[69] For example, chapter 1 examines the federal government's acquisition of land for military purposes via eminent domain cases in the US district court and via leases, licenses, and permits from the territorial government and private landowners. Legal regimes of eminent domain and land leasing employed capitalist logics of property and fair exchange to conceal the reiteration of primitive accumulation and render the US military's unilateral environmental desecration of Hawaiian land as "just." As I discuss in chapters 2, 3, and 4, affective, biopolitical labors of nursing, mothering, and teaching sought to cultivate biological life and produce feelings such as safety, patriotism, or well-being, even as they also fortified settler military conditions of gendered racialization, violence, and extraction. Chapter 2 focuses on how wartime public health projects targeted health and hygiene practices as a means to aid military surveillance, territorial organization, and labor productivity: the mandatory immunization program vaccinated individuals to maintain an uncontaminated military base in Hawai'i and reproduce healthy citizens who could contribute to the defense industry, and the Honolulu Blood Bank stored donations from these healthy citizens for use in the case of another emergency. Chapter 3 examines the US military government's focus on home economics, nutrition, mothering, and child care: these domestic projects included families of all races, while also constructing the "secure" American family home over and against Asian immigrant family practices that did not meet these standards, and masking the persistence of Native Hawaiian food cultures and land-based epistemologies of health. Chapter 4 analyzes wartime education and language projects for civilians in Hawai'i—including primary, secondary, and university education; foreign language schools; the Speak American Campaign; and the recruitment of Hawai'i Nisei to the Military Intelligence Service Language School. These wartime pedagogies were more than simply an effort to educate children about language and citizenship; they constituted a repertoire for the social reproduction of settler militarism.

As Hawai'i became a biopolitical center of the Pacific War, the coercive conditions of martial law, settler militarism, and racial capitalism compelled all people in Hawai'i to cultivate biological health, even as these conditions divided the inhabitants according to invented classifications. This project brought Indigenous and immigrant peoples into its administration of life on the condition that they labored in the service of the US war effort, exhibited patriotism and loyalty, affirmed their position in the settler colonial racial hierarchy, and did not make alternative claims to sovereignty over occupied lands. Furthermore, the productive and reproductive labor of predominantly nonwhite settler and Indigenous peoples fortified a military state that not only did not "include" many of them as full citizens in the liberal sense but that also actively worked to dispossess and incarcerate them—even as it purported to be invested in their health and livelihood beyond the extraction of labor and biological resources.[70] In this way the military state cultivated the health and extracted the labor of those living in Hawai'i for the express purpose of reproducing the security and vitality of *other* lives in the US military, continent, and empire. That is, the military state used the collective product of this wartime labor—the infrastructure of settler militarism—to violently invade and occupy others' lands, often interning them, all under the guise of liberation.[71] Chapter 5 focuses on the wartime internment of Japanese immigrants, Indigenous peoples, and prisoners of war across Hawai'i and Micronesia—and furthermore the circulation of prisoners between these camps and those in the US continent. Decentering the focus on internment as a domestic project of racialized exclusion that took place only in the continental United States, this chapter analyzes how this transnational network of camps used varying logics of racialized military detention, Indigenous displacement, and racial liberal biopolitics as it evacuated and interned Asian and Indigenous peoples across lands acquired for US military projects. This is one example of how techniques of settler militarism were replicated and transformed across the Pacific Islands and Asia, laying the foundation for US military empire in the late twentieth century and today.

Settler militarism is contradictory: as it allegedly prioritized life in Hawai'i, it also elaborated the conditions for violence and death in militarized spaces. Yet, given the long and continuing history of US colonialism and capitalism, it should not surprise us that the "make live" imperative of racial liberal biopower became a tool in the death-dealing context of war: it fortified the burgeoning US military empire and its ambitions to govern which lives it valued, which it extracted, and which it considered disposable. However, this project has never been sustainable, and settler militarism and capitalism sought to mitigate this unsustainability via imperial expansion toward additional sources of labor, markets, and natural resources. Thus, as settler militarism claimed to protect and fortify those lives that it was continually depleting, it was banking on its future absolution and regeneration via imperial war and the plundering of others' lands and livelihoods. Settler militarism—which is necessarily entangled with the relations of capitalism—operates in contradiction to the lives and communities it purports to govern.

As US empire and capitalism tend toward crisis, settler militarism is one imperfect "solution" to this crisis that is always on the brink of collapsing beneath the weight of its own asymmetry. It is also continually faced with opposition and resistance. Significantly, this understanding warns us of the violent lengths that are necessary to mask settler militarism's contradictions. World War II was such a period when many of the structures that intersect with that of settler militarism reached the apex of their contradictory formations: including militarized regimes of security and demands for patriotism, liberal modes of racial capitalism, legal means of property accumulation by Indigenous dispossession, and biopolitical governance and regulation. However, we should not understand this wartime peak in colonial violence and military surveillance as indicative of settler militarism's strength, totalization, or so-called success. Rather, this illustrates the extent to which its mechanisms needed to stretch in order to maintain its ruse of liberal democratic rationality: that is, the myth that settler militarism and this war were just, desired, inevitable, and in the interest of all.

ONE
——

"National Defense
Is Based on Land"

Landscapes of Settler Militarism in Hawai'i

The acquisition of land has played an important part in our national defense program because national defense is based on
land. It must have land for manufacturing, training fields, naval
bases, maneuverings and air fields in addition to housing the increased personnel.—NORMAN LITTELL, assistant to the attorney
general, August 14, 1941

In August 1941, US assistant attorney general Norman Littell stated that
"national defense is based on land," justifying a series of wartime seizures of land and property for a variety of military purposes.[1] Indeed, the
United States had been acquiring land for "national security" in Hawai'i
since its unlawful annexation via the 1898 Newlands Resolution, after
which the US government immediately began to transfer portions of former Crown and Government Lands to the US military.[2] During World
War II, US wartime security was predicated on the continued acquisition, control, organization, and industrialization of land for military purposes. The federal government acquired this land via eminent domain
cases in the US district court and via leases, licenses, and permits from
the territorial government and private landowners. Although landowners had the option to challenge land condemnation in court, they could
contest only the dollar amount of compensation for their land, not the
act of condemnation itself—thus leading to hundreds of court battles
over property values during the war and after. As the defendant trustees'

instructions stated in Civil Case 466, *USA vs 537.2931 acres of land, etc.*, "When property is taken in this manner the owner becomes entitled to receive the full and exact equivalent of it in money. He is entitled to be put in as good a position pecuniarily as if his property had not been taken."[3] In these court cases the settler state declared it a "public good" to transfer land from private or territorial possession to federal—in this case, military—possession. The legal construction of eminent domain as a "just" process assumed not only that the federal government's possession of Hawaiian land was always in the public's best interest but also that the court had the authority to designate the monetary value and the "best and most profitable use" of the property in question.[4]

US property law and legal proceedings such as those pertaining to eminent domain and leasing operated in contradiction to Hawaiian sovereignty and Indigenous noncapitalist relations to land. For example, the egalitarian notion of the "public" in legal assertions of "public good" is a liberal capitalist abstraction that can present as rational only through the erasure of primitive accumulation—including the theft and enclosure of communal Indigenous lands, the expropriation of racialized labor, and the denial of Kanaka Maoli land-based practices of stewardship, reciprocity, and genealogy. As K-Sue Park argues, the settler conversion of land into property that can be possessed or exchanged for currency was one of the principal engines of colonial land expropriation in the United States from its foundation onward.[5] Indeed, Cheryl Harris theorizes in her foundational essay "Whiteness as Property" that US property law is inherently racialized and colonial: the founding of US liberal democracy was premised upon the commodification of Black women and men as objects of property, and it concurrently used Lockean theories of labor and property to rationalize the usurpation of Indigenous land-based relations and to enforce its genocidal regimes of US land acquisition.[6] Significantly, as Brenna Bhandar notes, "In the setter colony the colonial animus is driven by the need to control the land base for the continued growth of settler *economies* and for the *security* of settler populations."[7] In Hawai'i during World War II, these foundational racialized and settler colonial logics continued and were bolstered by martial law's unilateral military orders to occupy land for the purposes of imperial war making.

That is, during World War II the federal government's acquisition, division, and transformation of land were central to the social reproduction of settler militarism. Eminent domain and its accompanying discourses wielded the capitalist regime of US property law to acquire land that would fortify the geographic reorganization of Hawai'i into a landscape governed by logics of militarization—including basing, training, ammunitions storage, and housing, as well as racialized biopolitical surveillance and reproduction. The authority of the federal court to adjudicate claims to Hawaiian lands as property rests upon an unlawful, continuing settler colonial history of Native dispossession and elimination. It is the erasure and denial of this central contradiction that allows for the mythical notion that US possession of land in Hawai'i could in *any* context be perceived as "just." Rather, cases such as these are examples of primitive accumulation sustaining the reproduction of capitalist relations beneath a ruse of fair exchange.[8] As Dean Saranillio argues, capitalism produces profit by envisioning and constructing a "settler future" in which human and nonhuman relations, regarded by Native peoples as interdependent, are ruptured.[9] The legal conversion of land into property creates the conditions for this rupture, and each exchange of this property upholds and reproduces it. Thus, both Assistant Attorney General Littell's assertion and the defendant instructions from the district court illustrate examples of how the federal government concealed this rehearsal of primitive accumulation and portrayed it as "just" through the wartime invocation of "military necessity" and the capitalist logics of value and exchange.

This repertoire of settler military, capitalist, and racialized biopolitical mechanisms for Native dispossession and environmental destruction built upon and aligned with colonial discourses of "improvement" and modernity that underlie liberal Lockean theories of property. At times, the federal government argued that the US military presence was beneficial because it would "improve" upon and industrialize the lands that it acquired, even as these so-called improvements inevitably desecrated natural landscapes for military purposes. Conversely, when the federal government seized land via lease, license, and permit for categorically environmentally destructive activities such as military training and bomb testing, it claimed that the land was too rugged for inhabitation or not profitable for agricultural industry, and thus not worth preserving. This racial liberal biopolitical logic thus conscripted and ordered land such that its partition, organization, hierarchies of access, and desecration seemed rational, just, and in the service of public good, rather than irrational and life destroying. Furthermore, this logic of improvement was always responding to Native sovereignty, as well as anticipated and continual assertions of the right to remain: despite these settler military rationalizations for land acquisition, occupation, and environmental destruction, much of these lands had been inhabited by Kanaka Maoli communities for generations. Hawaiian struggles at Kahoʻolawe and Mākua Valley provide just two illustrative examples of this.

Finally, these federal court cases reified capitalist notions of the undifferentiated individual property owner—an abstraction that contributes to the illusion of equality and justice in land proceedings.[10] Yet we know that liberal capitalist property relations could not exist or reproduce themselves without primitive accumulation, including the racialized differentiation and expropriation of life and the severing of Indigenous and noncapitalist relations to land.[11] In Hawai'i during this period, this figuring of the abstract property owner naturalized white settler possession by intensifying racial and class hierarchies of access to property, land, and natural resources while casting Hawaiian sovereignty as outside of modern conceptions of land use, relations, and knowledge.[12] Further, US land laws during this period incorporated a capitalist regime of remuneration that favored wealthy landowners and unilaterally dispossessed working-class tenants—who were disproportionately nonwhite and Indigenous—with no warning or compensation. Within the myth of fair exchange, a tenant was not a "property owner" who was "entitled to be put in as good a position pecuniarily as if his property had not been taken," and thus these evictions were not legible as a "loss" in the court.[13] Hawaiians who were technically "leasing" the land under the Hawaiian Homes Commission Act were likewise evicted without compensation despite sovereign rights to the land. Overall, regimes of eminent domain and land leasing wielded the commodity logic of abstraction, Lockean notions of improvement, and the ruse of the abstract individual property owner to mask the continual primitive accumulation of land and differentiation of life necessary to reproduce the asymmetrical relations of settler militarism in Hawai'i during wartime.

Land Acquisition in Hawai'i before and during World War II

The conversion of Indigenous land into private property has a specific history in Hawai'i. Prior to land privatization, Hawaiian land tenure operated according to values of reciprocity, in which community members across the social hierarchy collaborated to live sustainably on the land. Maka'āinana (commoners) labored under ali'i (chiefs) across ahupua'a, wedge-shaped sections of land that stretched from mountainous to coastal areas and included the variety of materials needed for all in the community to subsist and share resources responsibly.[14] The Great Māhele—or the division and privatization of Hawaiian Kingdom lands—took place under King Kamehameha III in 1848. The Māhele abolished the existing ahupuaʻa system, dividing communal lands into Crown Lands held by Kamehameha III and his descendants, Government Lands "for the benefit of the chiefs and the people," and lands available for purchase in individual parcels under the Kuleana Act of 1850.[15] White missionaries had pushed for this enclosure of common lands, arguing that the private purchase of land parcels would "improve" Hawaiian farming practices and instill tenets of individuality and industriousness in Hawaiians amid rapid depopulation from epidemic disease.[16] Yet as Jonathan Kamakawiwoʻole Osorio argues, the Māhele's conversion of communal lands into private property was inherently at odds with the ahupuaʻa system, which fostered notions of reciprocity among aliʻi and makaʻāinana that were rooted in stewardship and ancestral relationship to the land.[17] Despite Kamehameha III's intent for the Māhele to protect Hawaiian sovereignty from foreign colonial encroachment, the capitalist conversion of communal lands into private property benefited white settler missionaries and businessmen, who were able to purchase and invest in Hawaiian land for the first time, and only a small number of makaʻāinana were awarded with kuleana land.[18] This facilitated the growth of the plantation industry and the restriction of Kanaka Maoli access to farming, nutrition, healing, and other subsistence practices that had flourished under the ahupuaʻa system. Further, J. Kēhaulani Kauanui argues that Kamehameha III's enclosure of communal lands—even if established in an effort to protect Hawaiian sovereignty—constituted a regime of colonial biopolitical governmentality that "became a basic dimension of social normalization by the Hawaiian Kingdom through its regulation of subjects' customary practices that were commoditized."[19] In this way a private property regime ostensibly intended to "improve" and even protect Kanaka Maoli land relations instead bolstered colonial regimes of primitive accumulation that sought to rupture Indigenous noncapitalist relations to land. The history of settler military land expropriation that followed built upon this initial period of enclosure and privatization.

Furthermore, Hawaiian studies scholars such as Haunani-Kay Trask, Noenoe Silva, and Kyle Kajihiro have already traced how the US military has played an integral role in securing settler claims to land in Hawaiʻi throughout history.[20] After the unlawful annexation of Hawaiʻi via the 1898 Newlands Resolution, which included the seizure of the 1.8 million acres of Crown and Government Lands, the federal government reserved land for the US military by transferring portions of this so-called ceded land from territorial to federal possession via presidential executive order.[21] Over the years leading up to World War II, real estate values steadily increased. There was some market stagnation during the depression of 1930 to 1934, during which time foreclosures and forced sales led the value of properties to drop, but the land available for purchase was very limited. Much of the privately owned land was in the hands of large landowners such as the Bishop estate, the Campbell estate, the Damon estate, the John ʻĪʻī estate, and the L. L. McCandless estate. These huge estates often leased land to tenants and sugar plantations, but it was uncommon for them to relinquish it by selling it. This led to the vast majority of land in the islands being controlled by a small number of large landowners, something that set land relations in Hawaiʻi apart from those in the continental United States. During the years leading up to the war, Hawaiʻi's population steadily increased, which caused the demand for available land to exceed the supply.[22]

As stated in the introduction, during the war the US military occupied an all-time high of 648,666 acres of land in Hawaiʻi, which was more than eighteen times the 35,750 acres that it had occupied in 1940.[23] In the wake of the bombing of Pearl Harbor, discourses of "wartime necessity" against the Japanese enemy permitted the US military to justify its increased occupation of land. The transfer of land via presidential executive order was less common during the wartime emergency, but the US military acquired land fee simple (that is, through an outright purchase), through condemnation cases in the district courts, and by lease, license, and permit. The federal government rationalized this large-scale land control as a military necessity to provide sufficient airfields, training grounds, storage areas, and other necessary installations.[24] On Oʻahu, these acquired lands were mostly concentrated in the areas surrounding Pearl Harbor, Schofield Barracks, Kāneʻohe Bay, and Mākua Valley. This widespread land acquisition perpetuated the militarization of land and the racial and colonial differentiation of peoples: this included the continued dispossession of Kanaka Maoli; the loss of agricultural lands; the displacement of nonwhite and Indigenous tenants, farmers, and plantation workers; damages to land and infrastructure; and the shifting organization of plantations and other industries.[25] Throughout, however, the federal government presented this violent wartime transformation as in the service of "public good."

The federal government's method for land acquisition depended upon who owned the property, how the US military intended to use the land, for how long it intended to possess it, and whether it was necessary for the military to have exclusive use of the property. Whereas the federal government usually acquired public land via executive order during the prewar period, it was more common during the war for it to do so via lease, license, or permit. In these cases the lease, license, or permit often included a "restoration clause" that required the federal government to "return the property in as good a condition as it was when taken over, to restore it to its original condition, or to pay compensation in case of damages."[26] Yet in most cases, the US military completely transformed the land that it occupied, whether by dredging the ocean floor, bulldozing plants and agricultural crops, demolishing homes and community institutions, or decimating the entire landscape via bomb testing and live-fire training. In 1946 the military acquired 62,058 acres by fee simple or by executive order, which was twice the 30,924 acres that it had possessed in 1940. On top of this, records show that during the war the military acquired up to 328,694 acres via 1,500 leases, 1,600 licenses, and 350 permits.[27] The military's wartime land acquisition principally affected Oʻahu, Hawaiʻi, Maui, and Kahoʻolawe, which the US Navy took over in its entirety.[28] Apart from Kahoʻolawe, Oʻahu was the most affected because of its high concentration of military bases and the expanding defense industry: at one point during the war, the military occupied almost one-third of the island, with many of the navy's landholdings concentrated around Pearl Harbor.

This wartime shift in land ownership from territorial or private possession to federal government control coincided with Hawaiʻi's transition from a plantation-based economy to one reliant on industries related to the US military presence and tourism. Significantly, sugar cane lands decreased by 12.3 percent between 1940 and 1948.[29] By 1958, the US Department of Defense reported that the military generated 38 percent of the total income in Hawaiʻi. This was markedly high compared to the 14 percent that the pineapple industry generated, the 12 percent from the sugar industry, and the 10 percent generated by tourism.[30] That year, military-connected civilians made up almost one-third of the total population of Oʻahu.[31] The fact that real estate values for agricultural land in the islands became much higher than those in the continental United States during this period compounded this militarization of the economy and land ownership because the income per acre for the tourism and military industries became proportionally much higher than that for agriculture.[32] Building upon a history in which plantation agriculture catalyzed Hawaiian land dispossession, wartime settler militarism reorganized Hawaiʻi into a landscape governed by logics of militarization. This accentuated colonial and racialized hierarchies of access to land because it created the conditions for postwar economies that allowed local and multinational commercial elites to profit from shaping the Hawaiian economy toward servicing wealthy visitors and consumers.

US Wartime Land Acquisition via Eminent Domain

Just as in the continental United States, the federal government had always permitted itself to acquire land from private landowners in Hawai'i via eminent domain in the name of the "public good." Urban history scholars usually associate the condemnation of land via eminent domain with the history of urban renewal in the postwar continental United States, in which municipal governments perpetuated racial segregation and slum clearance in American cities.[33] Yet large-scale land clearance and demolition also took place during the World War II period in the service of wartime mobilization. Further, it was these war-front land projects that produced the infrastructure, technology, and skilled workers employed in postwar home-front projects of slum clearance and urban sprawl.[34] In Hawai'i—which was both "home front" and "war front"—the federal government acquired thousands of acres of land for military use via land condemnation in the US district court before, during, and after World War II.

In these cases the federal government would first file a "declaration of taking," which allowed the military to occupy the land for a price designated by US Navy–appointed appraisers. If the landowners challenged this appraised value in the district court and the court found that the final stipulation (value) was higher than that initially appraised, then the navy was required to pay a 6 percent interest on the difference, beginning from the date of taking.[35] Between July 1, 1940 and June 30, 1941, the federal government condemned 757 tracts of land, and it took an average of four days, four hours, and twelve minutes for it to acquire the title to these properties.[36] The federal government brought hundreds of land condemnation cases to the district court before, during, and after World War II, and these cases involved both large estates and small individual landowners, in some instances at the same time. For example, the US Navy condemned 977 acres at Barber's Point, O'ahu, in 1943 from the Campbell estate in order to construct an addition to the Barber's Point Naval Air Station.[37] In another case, for warehousing and storage purposes, the US Army Quartermaster Department acquired 68¼ acres at Kapalama that had been owned by the Hawaii Dredging Company.[38] As illustrated below, eminent domain cases such as these employed liberal Lockean discourses of improvement, commodity logics of abstraction, and the ruse of the undifferentiated individual property owner to portray the US military's unilateral acquisition of land as "just."

In a series of eminent domain cases that took place prior to the bombing of Pearl Harbor, the federal government condemned more than one thousand acres of land at Mōkapu peninsula in Kāneʻohe Bay for the construction of a naval air base that is today known as the US Marine Corps Base Hawaii (MCBH).[39] The base at Kāneʻohe Bay would function as an auxiliary base that accommodated additional planes that the US military could not station at Ford Island in Pearl Harbor.[40] It was said that in addition to providing relief for the congested conditions at Pearl Harbor, the construction of a new base at Kāneʻohe Bay would provide facilities for the full-load takeoff of aircrafts, training exercises, and bombing practice. This base included an entrance channel with a turning basin that would be used for tenders or tankers, a cleared operating area for patrol planes, and shore facilities that would allow for the operation of five patrol-plane squadrons.[41]

The US military's condemnation of land at Mōkapu peninsula in Kāneʻohe Bay sharply illustrates the colonial logics of improvement that eminent domain cases employed during this period and throughout the war. In April 1939 the federal government selected a 550-acre parcel of land in the Mōkapu peninsula called the "Heleloa tract," which was owned by Harold K. Castle, one of the largest landowners in the island. This property was reportedly "unimproved," a term meant to indicate that the land had few structures, crops, or industrialized areas currently in use.[42] The terms *improved* and *unimproved*, used throughout land condemnation proceedings during this period, employed colonial discourses of modernity to imply that land held value only insofar as it held potential to be "improved," and thus it could not produce value in its natural state. This is an assumption that goes to the heart of liberal theories of property. Indeed, John Locke explicitly uses the language of "improvement" throughout chapter V, "Of Property," in *The Second Treatise of Government*: "Land that is left wholly to Nature, that hath no *improvement* of Pasturage, Tillage, or Planting, is called, as indeed it is, wast [waste]; and we shall find the benefit of it amount to little more than nothing."[43] This rhetoric not only considered land use and value solely according to its propensity for "Pasturage, Tillage, or Planting," but it also devalued Indigenous land practices in favor of those that reproduce the conditions of capitalism.[44] As Locke infamously argued, "God gave the World to Men in Common; but . . . it cannot be supposed he meant it should always remain common and uncultivated. He gave it to the use of the Industrious and

Rational, (and *Labour* was to be *his Title* to it;) not to the Fancy or Covetousness of the Quarrelsome and Contentious."[45] Locke's assertion that "*Labour* was to be *his Title* to it" implies that it is only *improvement via rational labor* that produces land value, enclosure, and possession: that is, "property." These allusions to "rational labor" in Locke's texts rely and build on a colonial logic of improvement that racializes Indigenous presence and relations as antithetical to capitalist understandings of labor, value, and production. This is a racial liberal biopolitical discourse that not only devalues Indigenous labor but also Indigenous peoples who, in the eyes of liberal capitalism, must themselves also be "improved"—that is, disengaged from noncapitalist relations and assimilated to the racialized expectations of settler society—in order to own and possess property. This colonial notion of "improved" versus "unimproved" land, which is embedded in Locke's foundational theory of property—and, thus, US property law—not only masked the primitive accumulation and destruction of Native land but also rationalized it as destined, logical, fair, and inevitable. Such "improvements" likewise displaced Hawaiian notions of stewardship and disrupted symbiotic relations between Indigenous communities and the land.[46]

In the following eminent domain cases at Mōkapu peninsula in Kāneʻohe Bay, we can see how this precise language and logic contributed to the social reproduction of settler, legal, and capitalist frameworks into the World War II period, for the purposes of militarization and war. The US Navy would use Kāneʻohe Bay to train patrol bombers during peacetime, and it operated as an auxiliary fleet base for Pearl Harbor during the wartime state of emergency.[47] The 550 acres of land on the Heleloa tract cost $250,000, an amount quite small in comparison to the $5,800,000 of "improvements" planned in the construction budget for the Kāneʻohe Bay naval air base.[48] The military's first priority was dredging the bay to support large ships, an environmentally destructive process that involved digging out the underwater environment.[49] Significantly, it is only through settler, capitalist, and military logics that a project such as the scraping of the ocean floor could be seen as an "improvement" rather than as a desecration of land and natural resources. That is, this language of "improvement" also articulated with racial liberal biopolitical logics that portrayed the US military's reorganization and destruction of land as life protecting rather than life destroying. Writing specifically about capitalism's depletion of the natural environment in Hawaiʻi, Candace Fujikane states that "capital expands its domain through the evisceration of the living earth into the inanimacies of non-life, depicting abundant lands as wastelands to condemn them."[50] The pervasive language of "improved" versus "unimproved" land thus sought to rationalize this environmental violence by aligning the theft and destruction of land with military tropes of security, capitalist definitions of property, and the colonial temporality of modernization and progress.

The condemnation of land at Mōkapu peninsula continued in the years before the bombing of Pearl Harbor. On August 3, 1939, Charles Edison, the acting secretary of the navy, began condemnation proceedings for 553.676 acres of land at Mōkapu peninsula in Kāneʻohe Bay, which was a portion of the Heleloa tract.[51] The federal government followed the usual procedure that had been in place before the United States entered the war: the navy made Harold Castle what it considered to be a "fair offer" and then took possession of the land when the condemnation suit was brought in court.[52] The navy initially deposited $115,000 to Harold Castle, but the court later issued a judgment that the land was actually worth $300,000.[53] In this case, Castle cooperated with the US military, and there were not many structures or tenants living on this land. The military condemned an additional tract of 33.9 acres at Mōkapu peninsula on September 9, 1939, for which the navy initially paid $14,650.98.[54] In an additional case, Civil Case 441, *USA v. 464.66 Acres of Land*, the US Navy filed a declaration of taking on January 27, 1941. In contrast to the previous cases, which were litigated relatively quickly and involved mostly unused land owned by only one landowner, Civil Case 441 continued to be contested in court for years because it included more than four hundred parcels, most of which were beachfront lots owned by wealthy individual landowners.[55] As of January 28, 1941, the United States had acquired 1,152 acres in Mōkapu peninsula, for which the federal government had so far paid $61,840.86.[56]

COMMODITY ABSTRACTION AND LAND CONDEMNATION AFTER THE SECOND WAR POWERS ACT

Although the US Constitution had always guaranteed the federal government's right to condemn land in the name of "public good," the Second War Powers Act of 1942—which granted the federal government the right to immediately occupy land for military purposes—built upon and expedited this governmental right.[57] From this point forward, the federal government typically allowed thirty days for property owners to negotiate a selling price with US Navy real estate agents. If the owners could not negotiate a deal during this period, the War Department filed a declaration of taking in court, and a navy-appointed appraiser determined the price of the land.[58] The Second

War Powers Act permitted the navy to occupy land immediately and file a petition in court after the fact. Alternatively, the navy could file an order of immediate possession and settle terms of the payment at a later date. In many cases the condemned land was later valued to be worth up to four times as much as the navy had stated in its appraisal.[59] The Second War Powers Act thus led to unique wartime proceedings in which, to accelerate land acquisition, the federal government negotiated the purchase of land from individual landowners and estates at the same time that it was also preparing a case for the condemnation of this land in the district court. Further, this act allowed the US military to occupy land without purchasing it, which sometimes made it difficult for landowners to receive compensation.[60]

It is vital to emphasize again that US legal jurisdiction over land policy in Hawai'i is itself predicated on an extended military occupation and an unlawful annexation of the islands. All property in this space—whether condemned, purchased, compensated, or uncompensated—is predicated on colonial dispossession. The Second War Powers Act merely reinforced and expedited the settler state's mechanisms of primitive accumulation, and it is the capitalist regime of property and exchange—that is, the conception that if the land were purchased fairly, then US military occupation would be acceptable—that rationalized this repeated act of dispossession as "just." Moreover, the unilateral power of martial law both bolstered these means of primitive accumulation and further concealed them beneath wartime tropes of emergency, sacrifice, and heroism.

The necessity for the Second War Powers Act also underlines the friction between aggregate parties within settler militarism itself: the expedited protection from landowners' resistance to sell their land points to anticipated and actualized disagreement between settler and military desires to possess, use, and value land. Some landowners publicly objected to the intimidating behavior of the navy's land department and what they described as the "threatening" tactics used to occupy land, but left unquestioned the underlying logic of US settler colonial possession in Hawai'i.[61] For example, in May 1943 the US Navy condemned the land of E. J. LeVine, his wife, and their one-year-old son in Pearl City for "security reasons." LeVine was notified that if they did not negotiate a sale with the federal government, the land would be condemned in court. This led him to sell the land for $4,500 after negotiating, but he argued that it could have been worth $9,000 in 1946.[62] Others argued that despite the navy's claim that it was fairly compensating landowners for their land, it failed to realize that "there is only so much land, and to those earning a livelihood from the soil, their livelihood may be irreplaceable."[63]

Thus, within dominant public discourse in Hawai'i during this period, militarism and martial law were often criticized without interrogating the entangled settler colonial and capitalist logics that accompanied them. A clear example of this is mainstream newspapers' portrayal of Restoration Day on March 10, 1943 — when the US government restored many of the functions that the Office of the Military Governor had previously controlled to the territorial government — as a "liberation," even as the territorial government immediately reinstated many martial law decrees, and US occupation of Hawaiian land continued unabated.[64] Thus, it is not surprising that most arguments against land condemnation during the war were expressed through tropes of monetary or property loss. Yet both the acquiescence to land condemnation and its contestation via federal lawsuit reified the myth of fair exchange, upheld the rehearsal of primitive accumulation, and contributed to the social reproduction of settler militarism. This is an example of how liberal resistance performs contestation without disengaging the system of violence: settler colonial property law left space for some forms of injustice to be legible and disputed while it marginalized others — such as Hawaiian dispossession — as a logical impossibility.[65]

We can see some of the implications of this normative assumption in the defendant trustees' instructions for the jury in Civil Case 466. This case, referenced in the introduction of this chapter, involved 537 acres of Campbell estate land at West Loch (which is adjacent to Pearl Harbor), and this land is still used today for naval ammunitions storage. The instructions stated the following: "The amount required to be paid to the owners does not necessarily depend upon the use to which they have devoted the land, but is to be arrived at upon a *just* consideration of all the uses for which you find the evidence to show the land is suitable. . . . You may take into consideration any evidence which indicates the *best and most profitable use* to which the land is adapted and can probably be put in the reasonably near future."[66] Again, it was precisely through the legal invocation of capitalist logics of property value that this unilateral acquisition of land for military purposes could be rendered legible as "just." The instruction that the court will "take into consideration any evidence which indicates the best and most profitable use to which the land is adapted and can probably be put in the reasonably near future" again invokes Lockean definitions of property that figure land as profitable only once "adapted" or "improved." So-called unimproved land held the potential for the future production of value only after the environmentally destructive "improvements" that transformed the land from its original form — whether that be via dredging, building housing or industrial structures, military buildup, or planting.[67] Such "improvements" were not only extractive and land destroying, but they also contributed to commodity logics of abstraction that denied Hawaiian notions of stewardship and disrupted symbiotic relations between Indigenous communities and the land. Yet it was only "improvements" such as these that could signify value to the court because it was these transformations that contributed to the social reproduction of settler militarism and capitalism.

The commodity logic of abstraction is particularly evident in cases when landowners were able to argue in court that they should be reimbursed not only for "improvements" made to their land but also for the profits from any products that would have been produced from these "improvements." This was particularly common in the case of crops on agricultural land. For example, Civil Case 466 included land at West Loch in Oʻahu that was partially owned by the Campbell estate and the Ewa Plantation Company, among others. The United States filed a declaration of taking on December 18, 1941. In this case, Ewa Plantation Company successfully argued that it should receive compensation for both the condemned land and the profits it would have received from goods produced by the sugar cane planted on that land.[68] The jury received instructions that prescribed criteria for evaluating the just compensation of the crops: "In arriving at the value of the crop in question you are authorized to ascertain the gross proceeds of sugar and molasses and the benefit payments payable under laws and regulations in effect at the date of taking."[69] Thus, just as the federal court determined the "best and most profitable use" of land, this passage illustrates the extent to which the court would accommodate commodity logics of abstraction in its calculations of just remuneration. In this case, it is significant that the value of processed sugar and molasses—*a nonexistent future commodity*—was compensated in order to justify the military takeover of the land.[70] This is indicative of how settler colonialism reproduces itself by maintaining the security of future capital. It also illustrates the level of abstraction required for the myth of fair exchange to continue to conceal the primitive accumulation of land and labor that underlies it. More than merely an appraisement of property value, in this case it was plantation owners' reimbursement for the unrealized surplus value of sugar and molasses—which also included the labor that would have produced it and the trade that would have brought it to US markets—that rationalized US legal notions of "justice" in this takeover of land. Yet although this federal case reimbursed the Ewa Plantation Company for the commodities it could have produced and marketed, neither the court nor the plantation accounted for evicted plantation laborers' lost wages in their adjudication of justice. Moreover, the court rendered Hawaiian understandings of land that centralize reciprocity and stewardship as irrational and antithetical to modern calculations of value. According to the fetishized relations of the US settler court, the ghosts of imagined commodities were deemed more substantive than the material thefts of land, labor, and natural resources on which all settler fabrications rest.

RACIAL LIBERAL BIOPOWER AND THE ABSTRACT
PROPERTY OWNER

When the United States entered World War II, Harry and Elizabeth Ching were living in a small three-room house on a quarter-acre lot in Pearl City, Oʻahu. In 1942 the US Navy condemned this property "for security reasons" and gave the Chings $250 in reimbursement—$300 less than the amount for which it was purchased. After Ching and his family vacated their land, on January 1, 1946, they leased a 1.75-acre lot that was owned by the Campbell estate. Once living there, the Chings spent $300 to remove brush and rocks from the property and converted four army houses into an apartment to house their family. Five months later, the navy began district court proceedings to condemn the Campbell estate land where the Chings' lot was located. Not only were they forced to vacate the lot immediately and move once again, but as Ching stated, "Because it is owned by the Campbell estate, I get exactly nothing for my efforts. The navy payment is for the land and goes to the estate."[71]

Harry Ching's dealings with the navy illustrate the different ways in which this land acquisition affected civilians, depending on their class and property ownership. Ching did not have the means to hire a lawyer to challenge the land condemnation in the district court, but the wealthy Campbell estate took part in many eminent domain court cases throughout the war, including Civil Case 446 discussed above, and gained over one hundred thousand dollars in compensation for its many acres of land.[72] Furthermore, once Ching was no longer a landowner and became a tenant merely leasing the land, he and his family were simply displaced with nothing when the US Navy condemned this land.

During World War II, Honolulu attorneys Oliver Kinney and M. B. Henshaw estimated that around 70 percent of landowners did not question the US Navy's assessed price of their land "for patriotic reasons and sometimes through 'fear' of a powerful federal agency." Significantly, Filipino, Japanese, and Hawaiian civilians, who were disproportionately working-class, often did not challenge the navy's offer because of the cost of court proceedings.[73] We might also consider how the intense pressure to demonstrate patriotism and assimilation during this period might have affected racialized peoples' decisions to acquiesce to federal and military requests—particularly if their "loyalty" was in question. This is an example of how racial liberal biopower incentivized immigrant settler desires for rights, property, and inclusion while manufacturing fears of being excluded or interned. This influenced how settlers of color chose to negotiate racial and class hierarchies of access to land as property. Further, these logics of capital and settler militarism perpetuated class inequality because the amount of money that one could gain was directly related to the monetary value of the land in question. There were many who could not afford the costly court proceedings involved in a condemnation case, and entering these cases was not worth the cost of legal fees for those who were working-class and owned an individual lot. For example, a group of farmers entered into an eminent domain case when their land was condemned for two hundred dollars per acre and ended up receiving compensation for four hundred dollars per acre each. Yet after paying their attorney, they had achieved no monetary gain.[74] In another instance, Mr. and Mrs. Robert Waite, who lived in Pearl City Peninsula, decided to sell their land rather than enter the condemnation case because they had two small children and could not face the insecurity of years of court, on top of the uncertainty of the wartime emergency.[75]

Landowners were widely affected by the federal government's condemnation of their land, but these proceedings were far more detrimental for tenants, who were evicted from these properties with no compensation whatsoever. As mentioned above, the wealthy Ewa Plantation Company received remuneration for the labor necessary to produce sugar and molasses from the cane grown on its condemned land, whereas the tenant laborers who were themselves evicted from Ewa Plantation lands and put out of work received nothing. In Civil Case 507, *U.S.A. v. 10.063 Acres of Land*, the federal government acquired land for the expansion of Keʻehi Lagoon in order to provide housing and other facilities for the US National Air Traffic Services and the Naval Air Station in Honolulu, displacing 277 tenants.[76] In another case, the navy condemned 5.9 acres in order to build an addition to the Naval Air Station in Honolulu, which would provide housing for Women Accepted for Volunteer Emergency Service (WAVES) personnel, evicting 128 tenants.[77] In these cases, sometimes the US Navy allowed for tenants to remain when it condemned land, but it would raise the rent to a much higher rate.[78] Further, evicted tenants would sometimes have the option of relocating their "improvements," such as houses or crops, in order to retain them, but tenants were not permitted to do so in other instances.[79] For example, in Civil Case 452, *U.S.A v. 222.142 Acres of Land*, in which the US Navy condemned a tract at North Halawa, Oʻahu, on May 13, 1941, in order to build a naval hospital, Kamato Yonashiro attempted to buy buildings that he had built, but he was unsuccessful and was ordered to leave the property within ten days.[80]

The experiences of tenants as they grappled with the consequences of eviction and the loss of their homes and other possessions demonstrate that eminent domain operated through the administration of racial liberal biopower, which wielded the category of the abstract property owner as a regulatory power while enlisting settlers of color in asymmetrical regimes of property ownership under the guise of due process and fair exchange.[81] This created a threshold of legal legibility that required individuals to abide by liberal capitalist logics in order to fight for their livelihood or the right to remain. In this way, racial liberal biopower disciplined racialized subjects even as it allowed them to contest their oppression by containing the means and logics by which this contestation could take place, and by rendering illegible points of solidarity with Indigenous sovereignty through colonial logics of land as property. That is, even as immigrant settler families experienced oppression and exploitation at the hands of the US military and federal government, their participation in and use of settler and capitalist regimes of property to improve their living conditions contributed to and concealed Hawaiian dispossession, thus reproducing and maintaining settler colonialism.

Not only did this capitalist notion of the abstract, undifferentiated property owner naturalize the white property-owning subject, but the illusion of liberal equality within settler property law and court proceedings also created an alibi for settler land theft and possession by masking violent and continuing histories that sever Indigenous relations to the land. For Kanaka Maoli, land condemnation and eviction constituted a new iteration of settler colonialism enabled by the wartime state of emergency. Hawaiians living throughout the islands experienced displacement, but a principal example of this is that Native Hawaiians who were living on Hawaiian Homestead Lands that had been passed down through families were never compensated when the US military occupied their land because they were technically "leasing" it from the Territory of Hawaiʻi under the 1921 Hawaiian Homes Commission Act (HHCA). In these cases, any remuneration from the federal government would go straight to the Territory of Hawaiʻi.[82] Sometimes, the US Navy would allow Hawaiians to remain living on their land but would require them to pay up to thirty dollars per month, despite the fact that the HHCA stipulates that homesteaders pay an annual rent of "one dollar per year with a ninety-nine year lease."[83] As Kauanui argues, because the early stages of the HHCA initiative for land reclamation centralized Hawaiian rehabilitation as a central element of its platform, this logic of rehabilitation allowed for the territorial government to reconstruct the homesteading program through the logics of "charity and protection" rather than in terms of Native Hawaiians' rightful claim to the land.[84] This racial and colonial discourse surrounding the HHCA aligned with liberal capitalist logics of property ownership that elided Hawaiian sovereignty even as they purported to "help" Kanaka Maoli. This allowed the territorial government to portray itself as a generous landlord rather than an agent of settler colonial land dispossession. We can see these logics still at work in the case of land acquisition during World War II: because the HHCA allowed the settler state to "translat[e] issues of entitlement into a welfare discourse," it also enabled the US Navy to classify Native Hawaiians living on Hawaiian Homestead lands as mere "lessees" who were undeserving of compensation for this reiteration of settler colonial land theft and displacement.[85]

Overall, this repertoire of land acquisition practices via eminent domain illustrates how settler property law governed the horizon of possibilities for a supposedly "just" military occupation, which included establishing a monopoly over Hawaiian lands' "best and most profitable use" and exchange value. These federal court cases cultivated a ruse of equality and justice by employing Lockean discourses of improvement and commodity logics of abstraction while centralizing the individual property owner as the party deserving of remuneration. By these settler military and capitalist logics, the profit losses most legible to the court were those involving plantation agriculture and large wealthy estates, but the federal government did not consider a tenant's loss of property or wages to be one that it should reimburse. Yet in most cases the US military completely transformed the lands acquired via environmentally destructive "improvements" deemed necessary for militarized industrialization.

US Military Testing and Environmental Destruction

As explored above, the US military government often used liberal capitalist logics of property and modernization to argue in court that the land it acquired for military purposes would be "improved" and industrialized—for the benefit of all. This was true in the press as well: for example, in an article on the land debate between civilians and the military, the *Honolulu Star-Bulletin* remarked that "the lands already returned to Hawaii by the services have sometimes contained millions of dollars worth of improvements." The military spent $25,000,000 to build up the Honolulu Airport and others on the neighbor islands, and offered former military housing to the Hawaii Housing Authority for what it considered "a cost considerably less than it would be to 'start from scratch.'"[86] The US military's donation of military housing to the Hawaii Housing Authority shifted focus away from the thousands of acres that it had acquired throughout the war, as well as from the thousands of landowners and tenants whom it had pushed out of homes and neighborhoods. Overall, the federal government used the fact that it had established and funded modern installations such as airfields to rationalize the US military's extended presence in Hawai'i and the transformations of the landscapes that it occupied. But in many cases—such as the dredging of the ocean floor, the storage of explosives underground, or the clearing of land for military housing or installations—these supposedly benevolent "improvement" projects displaced communities and harmed local environments in irreversible ways.

Yet at the same time that the federal government employed capitalist logics of commodity abstraction and Lockean logics of improvement to justify the extractive violence of military occupation, it also twisted this argument to rationalize military activities that were categorically environmentally destructive—including training exercises, military maneuvers, firing ranges, and explosive impact testing.[87] During the war the federal government often occupied this land via lease, license, or permit and in many cases continued to do so for decades after. In order to justify the use of these areas for unequivocally damaging activities, the US military described these lands—many of which included forests, lava fields, or mountainous areas—as being "of relatively low value" or as having "little revenue potential."[88] For example, the US Department of Defense argued after the war that 50 percent of its military training areas—including those at Mākua Valley, Ka'ena Point, Kahuku, Kawailoa, Waikane, and Kapa'a—were not even suitable for large groups to train because they contained "mountain ridges, gullies, and precipitous slopes," so there were few places that vehicles could travel or that helicopters could land. As the report specified, "In all, about 47,000 acres used for training in the areas named above are severely limited by its forbidding topography."[89]

That is, the federal government justified military exercises that it could not feasibly characterize as projects of "improvement" with the argument that the land being destroyed was not profitable in the first place. Per this rationalization, unlike with condemned property, the federal government argued that this land could not *be* "improved" and so was valuable only to the extent that it was disposable. These permits continued to be used for decades as US military endeavors continued to increase during the Cold War. In its explanation of military testing in 1960, the Department of Defense stated that "much of the land is used under non-exclusive use permits and the areas have little or no commercial value. . . . The military service are making the *best possible use* of the limited training facilities available in the Hawaiian Islands."[90] Nonexclusive use permits were a common and relatively inexpensive method for the military to occupy land for a specific use without having to enter into a lease, begin the lengthy legal process of land condemnation, or go to the president for a land transfer via executive order. When the military occupied land via a nonexclusive use permit, it also had no financial stake in maintaining its condition or value. Further, the US military's argument that training exercises were the "best possible use" for this land relied upon the same capitalist logic that undergirded the federal court's process for determining the "best and most profitable use" of condemned land. The military argued that the "best possible use" of land that was of "little or no commercial value" was for it to be subject to environmental contamination and demolition via military training, bomb testing, and live-fire exercises. This is yet another example of liberal Lockean logics of improvement and abstraction rendering invisible noncapitalist understandings of land as anything other than a commodity, including Indigenous modes of subsistence and ways of living. In fact, these supposedly "unusable" lands had been inhabited by Kanaka Maoli for generations. Hawaiian protests against US occupations of Kahoʻolawe and Mākua Valley are two principal examples of how Kanaka Maoli have refused to abide by these constraining and violent logics, and asserted their right to remain via acts of resistance and placemaking that cannot be contained or co-opted by liberal and capitalist regimes.

The US military's acquisition of land for training and bomb-testing purposes at Mākua Training Area, including the north portion of Mākua Valley and Kaʻena Military Reservation, has had far-reaching environmental effects. Military holdings in this area have ranged between 4,000 and 7,000 acres of land between World War II and the present day. The majority of these lands were Hawaiian Kingdom Government Lands that were "ceded" to the territorial government by the Republic of Hawaiʻi.[91] After the bombing of Pearl Harbor, the federal government transferred these lands via permit to the US military. Smaller portions were acquired via condemnation from the McCandless estate and via lease from other smaller landowners.[92]

Significantly, neither the federal government nor the US military considered the importance of these lands to Kanaka Maoli and other displaced peoples, nor did this militarized project of land acquisition recognize competing Indigenous histories, epistemologies, or knowledges. This is indicative of the continuing colonial transformation of land into property and thus the rupturing of relationships between Indigenous communities and the land. Further, it again illustrates the complete unwillingness of the federal government to understand land beyond military and capital use. Despite the fact that the US military and federal government classified land at sites such as Mākua Valley and Ka'ena Point as being "extremely rugged" and as having a "forbidding topography," Hawaiian studies scholarship and archaeological evidence reveal that Native Hawaiian communities had flourished there for generations, living off the land and surrounding fishing areas.[93] Under martial law, the US military evacuated three thousand people in Mākua Valley—including Native Hawaiian families living on kuleana land, Japanese railroad workers, and laborers at the McCandless estate's cattle ranch—thus cutting off access to fishing holes and contaminating the area via bomb testing and waste dumping.[94] In 1943 Revocable Permit 200 granted the US military use of the land for the duration of the war, plus six months after, at which point the US military would supposedly "remove all its property and return the premises . . . [in] a condition satisfactory to the Commissioner of Public Lands." Yet over the course of the war, the US military used houses, churches, and even gravestones for bombing and target practice, thus not only demonstrating a complete disrespect for these prior lifeways but also permanently damaging both the environment and local community institutions.[95]

At Mākua, as at other military training grounds that used local environments and even peoples as stand-ins for enemy targets, the US military's biopolitical claims that it "protected" or "improved" life were laid bare as fiction.[96] In 1960 the Department of Defense argued that "because of the steep mountains surrounding Makua, this is the only area on Oahu relatively safe for live firing of tank guns and infantry assault guns, but limited to high explosive and smoke rounds. Army artillery and mortars fire in this area and it also serves as an impact area for artillery fire from Schofield Barracks." Both the army and the marines used land at Mākua Valley for live-fire training from World War II until 2011, when an environmental lawsuit forced it to close.[97] Military testing at Mākua has endangered more than forty plant and animal species in this area, and wildfires caused by leftover unexploded ordinances have burned thousands of acres in and around the valley.[98] The US military still controls over four thousand acres of land at Mākua today, and this area still has high levels of contamination.[99] This history is a source of suffering for many Hawaiian families who were not only cut off from their source of livelihood but were also separated from a place to which they had had a profound connection for generations.[100] As Kyle Kajihiro's work has shown, throughout this period Kanaka Maoli have continued to use and live on Mākua Beach, despite US military occupation and police raids. There is also a long history of organized resistance to US militarization at Mākua, including the Hawai'i Ecumenical Coalition and Malama Mākua's blocking of a Marine Corps landing on Easter 1997, and a National Environmental Policy Act lawsuit that called attention to environmental justice and health impacts of military contamination.[101] And as Laurel Mei-Singh's work illustrates, Native Hawaiians continue to engage in "place-based counternarratives" via mo'olelo and Hawaiian cosmologies that speak to the "interdependence between humans and the natural world," and remap these spaces via Native memories and practices.[102] It is significant that in many of these cases, Kanaka Maoli insisted on their right to remain while refusing to contain their resistance within the structure of liberal capitalism that fortified US military occupation.

The US occupation of Kaho'olawe is another principal example of this destructive history of land acquisition and military testing. Kaho'olawe was also once part of the Hawaiian Kingdom's Crown and Government Lands, and it was unlawfully seized by the United States in 1898 during the annexation.[103] Under the 1900 Hawaiian Organic Act, Kaho'olawe became the property of the territorial government, which began to lease this land to a series of individual landowners for cattle ranching. In 1910 the territorial government named Kaho'olawe a territorial forest reserve, and it was placed under the control of the Territorial Board of Agriculture and Forestry until 1918. On May 10, 1941, a portion of the island was subleased to the US Army for "unrestricted military operations," and the military occupied all 28,000 acres of the island with the declaration of martial law. A supplemental agreement went into effect on March 1, 1944. The military informed the MacPhee family, which was the last to lease land on Kaho'olawe, from 1919 to December 8, 1941, that their lost years would be added to their lease in 1954, but they were never permitted to return.[104]

Much as at Mākua, racial liberal biopolitical logics masked the destructive nature of US militarization projects on Kaho'olawe. During World War II the military used Kaho'olawe for ship-to-shore bombardment exercises and training for the Gilbert Invasion, as well as ship-to-shore fire-control training. US military submarines also test-fired torpedoes at cliffs along the shoreline from 1943 into the 1960s.[105] The army's sublease was transferred to the navy on November 1, 1945, and this remained in effect until Presidential Proclamation 2487 terminated it on October 28, 1952.[106] During the postwar period, in its analysis of the real estate requirements for training and maneuvers at Kahoʻolawe, the US Department of Defense argued that the island was "uninhabitable" and "heavily contaminated," and was therefore suitable for "air-to-ground gunnery and bombardment and naval gunnery practice."[107] Thus, the military argued that Kahoʻolawe's distance from Oʻahu, the most populated of the islands, and its status as "already contaminated" were the elements that made it most appropriate for this purpose. Yet many of these criteria—including the high level of contamination in Kahoʻolawe and the large concentration of people in Oʻahu because of the defense industry— were in fact produced by the history of US settler militarism in Hawaiʻi. The territorial government canceled the lease of the Kahoolawe Ranch Company in September 1952. On February 20, 1953, Executive Order 10436 placed Kahoʻolawe under the control of the secretary of the navy, stating that it was "in the public interest that the islands . . . would be restored to a condition reasonably safe for human habitation when it is no longer needed for naval purposes."[108] The navy's appointment of itself to oversee the restoration of Kahoʻolawe when it was the navy that had desecrated this land in the first place is an especially contradictory attempt to wield biopolitical logics to render US military occupation as life cultivating rather than life destroying, while again denying and devaluing Indigenous land-based knowledges and modes of relationship.

US military descriptions of Kahoʻolawe as "uninhabitable," like other commodity discourses of abstraction, sought to obscure already-existing noncapitalist and Indigenous relations to this land that fell outside capitalist understandings of labor, value, and production. For example, archaeological studies suggest that prior to the occupation by the United States, Hawaiians had inhabited Kahoʻolawe's coastal and inland areas for more than one thousand years and had thrived by farming and fishing.[109] Native Hawaiians began to urge the US military to return the island as soon as it was occupied in 1941.[110] This movement intensified in the 1970s, when a series of landings on the island took place in defiance of US military occupation. This movement was powerful in that it not only fought for Hawaiians' right to remain but did so in a way that could not be co-opted by liberal capitalist regimes of property and exchange. Kahoʻolawe came to hold large significance for Hawaiian resistance movements during this period, both as land that had been taken away from Native Hawaiians and as a symbol of hope for what the movement could bring for the future.[111] Many activists landed on the island to protest for reparations for lands lost to the military, and others performed religious ceremonies: "The hoʻoponopono—literally, making things right—symbolized the determination of Hawaiians to practice Aloha ʻĀina on the island that symbolized their neglected heritage. Mana was to be restored not only to the island but to the people who care for it."[112] The Protect Kahoʻolawe ʻOhana (PKO) movement began after the tragic loss of George Helm and Kimo Mitchell, two active members of the Protect Kahoʻolawe Association, during one of these landings on March 8, 1977. The PKO continued to mobilize to stop the decades of military bombing on the island, and it eventually played a significant part in Hawaiian sovereignty struggles.[113] In the 1980s the PKO negotiated with the US Navy and the Kahoʻolawe Island Reserve Commission to help with revegetation programs on the island and lobbied for the Hawaiian legislature to fund a water study. Since 1981, Kahoʻolawe has been classified as an archaeological district and was also placed on the US National Register of Historic Places. In 1990 the US military stopped its bombing practice on Kahoʻolawe, yet much of this land is still contaminated today.[114]

Just as with eminent domain cases in the district court, US land acquisition via license, permit, and lease illustrates how the social reproduction of US settler militarism operated across landscapes during this period. The coercive conditions of martial law allowed for the federal government to unilaterally acquire land via lease, sublease, or permit, often without the consent of the landowner, lessor, or lessee. The federal government used capitalist and biopolitical logics to rationalize military activities, even unequivocally destructive ones: it argued that "the best possible use" of land that could not be "improved" was to subject it to environmental demolition via military testing and training. Yet we also know that Kanaka Maoli had thrived on and forged meaningful connections to these lands for generations prior to US occupation. At Mākua and Kahoʻolawe, Hawaiians insisted on the right to remain through meaningful actions that refused the constraints of liberal capitalist logics of property and that insisted upon the importance of genealogical ties to the land.

. . . .

The US military continued to occupy land after World War II concluded, but as property values rose in Hawaiʻi during the postwar period, the territorial government found the military's control over land to be less acceptable. In 1949 some in the territorial government believed that certain military installations were no longer absolutely necessary because the wartime state of emergency had ended and that some military properties should therefore be returned to the territory for alternate use.[115] Some of the lands that the territory hoped would be returned included the 1,505 acres at Bellows Air Base and parts of Mōkapu peninsula, as well as other real estate that the territorial government believed could potentially create more profit as tourist or residential property than as military property because of its proximity to the ocean.[116] In 1960 a survey evaluated property being held by the military and concluded that there was an excess of 3,012 acres held in the islands. Again, the majority of this land was determined to be "of considerable value" because it was located in the city of Honolulu and Pearl Harbor. This report recommended that the US military move facilities located on this highly profitable land to property that was less valuable.[117] Thus, as the state of emergency ended after the war, prolonged military occupation became less acceptable to the settler state when the land could be more profitable if used for another purpose. The US military had historically played a vital role in securing settler claims to land, and this relationship between settler and military governance intensified during World War II under martial law. Yet examples such as this illustrate how the settler and military states have not always agreed on the "best and most profitable use" of land in Hawaiʻi because settler desires for capital can conflict with military desires for security. Once the wartime state of emergency ended and property values began to rise, investors saw an opportunity to profit from purchasing land for high-yielding commercial development of hotels, restaurants, and other tourism-related endeavors.

The federal government likewise continued to occupy land via lease and permit. In 1945 the US military still occupied land via 2,500 leases in addition to that which it had acquired fee simple and via land condemnation. In 1946 a thousand tracts of land were still held by the US Army.[118] In 1947 M. B. Henshaw, a Honolulu attorney, testified in court that the army and the navy continued to own 38.7 percent of the land in Hawaiʻi.[119] By 1949, some of the land that the military acquired via lease, license, and permit had been returned: airfields located at Kahuku, Kualoa, and Haleiwa were returned to the territorial government, and 700 acres at Kipapa Airfield were in the process of being converted back to sugar cane fields for the Oahu Sugar Co.[120] However, at this point the US military still controlled around 117,000 acres, approximately 20,000 acres of which were in the process of being returned.[121] Further, the navy still occupied the 28,000 acres on Kahoʻolawe for use as a target area; 7,042 acres at Mākua Valley, which was supposedly in the process of being "de-dudded"; and 7,140 acres of "lava waste" at South Point, which the US military at Morse Field used as a bombing range.[122] There were also still new lands being requested, as Hawai'i remained a principal US military base in the Pacific Ocean.[123] The US military continued to control much of the land in Hawai'i from the end of World War II into the 1960s. The Department of Defense explained that military-occupied land "must by the very nature of its purpose be land of substantial value, particularly where ocean beach frontage is involved in an area catering to the tourist trade."[124] The martial law period was a time of accelerated US military land acquisition, but its effects could be seen long after the World War II period ended.

Overall, World War II constituted an unprecedented period of US land acquisition in Hawai'i that built upon, rehearsed, and concealed the processes of primitive accumulation that sustain capitalist relations and undergird US settler militarism in the islands. During this period the US military acquired land via eminent domain proceedings and district court cases, as well as by lease, license, and permit, resulting in the displacement of many landowners and tenants. The combination of these methods not only naturalized military activities as contributing to the "public good" but also enabled the federal government to designate the value and "best and most profitable use" of the land in question—whether that be allegedly "improving" it via military buildup or demolishing it for the purposes of military training and testing. The federal government had always had the ability to condemn land via eminent domain, but these settler colonial mechanisms were accelerated by the conditions of martial law, the wartime state of emergency, and the Second War Powers Act in 1942. Beyond the pervasive discourse of "military necessity," capitalist logics of commodity abstraction and property ownership portrayed this extensive unilateral acquisition of land as "just" in federal court. Furthermore, biopolitical logics of modernization articulated with Lockean discourses of improvement to rationalize white settler possession and devalue Hawaiian land-based practices that centralize reciprocity and stewardship. As racial liberal biopower incorporated Native and immigrant settler peoples into the asymmetrical regime of property ownership, nonwhite, working-class tenants faced disproportionate losses as they were evicted without compensation. For Kanaka Maoli, seizures of land and evictions across the islands recapitulated the structure of settler colonialism and the violent dispossession that accompanies it. Yet, as histories of place-based resistance across lands such as Kaho'olawe and Mākua Valley illustrate, we know that Hawaiians negotiated and resisted these regimes during the World War II period and beyond. Kanaka Maoli actions across these landscapes—such as PKO landings and ceremonies at Kaho'olawe—illustrate

Indigenous relations and responsibilities to the land that directly object to the desires of settler militarism and refuse to abide by liberal capitalist logics of property.

The US military used eminent domain and land leasing to unilaterally acquire land that would fortify the geographic reorganization of Hawaiʻi into a landscape governed by logics of militarization. As this chapter illustrates, this included overtly militarized undertakings such as military basing, training, ammunitions storage, and housing. Yet, as the next three chapters of this book discuss, wartime land-based projects also conscripted spaces to fortify militarized biopolitical projects—including those concerning public health, domestic science, and education—that incorporated the multiracial population in order to socially reproduce the uneven racialized, gendered, and colonial relations of settler militarism.

TWO

"Life Given Straight from the Heart"

Securing Body, Base, and Nation
under Martial Law

The first wartime duty of every individual is to safeguard his health.—Office of the Territorial Commissioner of Public Health, April 2, 1942

A photograph published in the *Honolulu Star-Bulletin* in 1943 depicts Pharmacist's Mate Homer H. Elsey as he donates blood to the Honolulu Blood Bank (figure 2.1). Beside him stand two Red Cross nurses: Mrs. Zadoc Brown, who offers him coffee and a sandwich, and Mrs. Thomas King, who tends to his arm. The caption to this staged image, which starts with the phrase "TO SAVE A LIFE," promoted blood donation as a patriotic sacrifice for the nation. This common trope of national sacrifice also occurs in a letter to the editor from four months before, which elatedly describes a man's experience donating blood and the "singular satisfaction" he felt afterward: "After he [the doctor] had pricked that hollow needle into my arm, a pretty nurse sat beside me, and another stood and talked to me. Meantime blood was flowing painlessly out of my arm and up a tube into a cloth covered flask. . . . Then I got up, went into another room, and sat down to eat a delicious sandwich, drink a cup of coffee, and chat with three or four other charming young ladies."[1]

The photograph and the letter present the act of donating blood as a relaxing and enjoyable one during which the donor "saves a life" and is served a free sandwich while socializing with the pretty nurses who treated him. The letter's signature, "DONOR NUMBER 6653," signifies that the author wishes to privilege the act of donating blood and his solidarity with other donors over his own name and individualism. Furthermore, both Donor Number 6653 and the photograph of Elsey connect the patriotic act of donating blood to the gratification of heterosexual masculinity: both male donors save lives, attract the doting affections of smiling nurses, and enjoy their service of complimentary food and drink, thus suggesting a gendered division of labor at the blood bank that contributed to the social reproduction of this wartime project. The exchanges depicted here even suggest an atmosphere similar to that of heterosexual dating—ostensibly, part of the allure of blood donation is the opportunity to meet and interact with these "charming young ladies." Another donor writes that "attractive waitresses circulate constantly around the tables, almost forcing cakes and cookies on the lucky patrons"—shortly thereafter, he reveals he has so far given *thirteen* pints of blood.[2] These gendered tropes were not necessarily specific to Hawai'i. In the continental United States, civilians had the option of attaching a signature tag to their jar of blood before it was sent abroad, thus inscribing the act of donation with the possibility of human connection, gratitude, or reciprocation.[3]

In addition to publishing frequent calls for blood donations, Hawai'i's newspapers also published reminders multiple times per week for civilians to complete a set of mandatory vaccinations.[4] The photograph of Susan Kang discussed in the introduction was published only eight months before the image of Elsey. This image differs from the photographic and written accounts of blood donations above, specifically in its racial and gendered dynamics. If the nurse's feminine care of the soldier Elsey connotes domestic intimacy, Captain Meiz's impersonal grip on Ms. Kang suggests a medical and sterile environment. Whereas blood donors describe their interest in lingering to have a coffee with their nurses, it seems likely that Kang's vaccination will be done quickly and that she will leave the premises upon its completion. The photograph of Kang portrays her as a "foreign" subject, not yet "American," and therefore in need of the immunization that would aid her assimilation; as a white military man and blood donor, Elsey's health and Americanization are not in question.

This chapter elaborates the social reproduction of US settler militarism in Hawai'i by examining the expansion of public health programs under martial law, which functioned in the service of wartime labor productivity. The US military government's wartime public health policies in Hawai'i— including mandatory vaccinations, blood donation, sanitation, and health education—constituted a racial liberal biopolitical administration that

FIGURE 2.1 · The caption of this photograph is "TO SAVE A LIFE: Pharmacist's Mate Homer H. Elsey, USN, of Vinata, Okla., gives a pint of his own blood to the Honolulu blood-plasma bank to repay a 'debt' of three transfusions which recently saved the life of his sister. With him are Mrs. Zadoc Brown, *left*, Red Cross canteen worker, with coffee and a sandwich, and Mrs. Thomas King, of the Red Cross motor corps." *Honolulu Star-Bulletin*, January 16, 1943. Hawaii War Records Depository HWRD 0174, UHM Library Digital Image Collections.

strategically targeted health and hygiene practices as a means of military surveillance, territorial organization, and population control. Public health programs sought to regulate, optimize, and reproduce the heterogeneous population that included Kanaka Maoli, Asian settlers, and white settlers: they provided the language and mechanisms to quantify, evaluate, and differentiate Hawai'i's diverse inhabitants according to the military government's standards for productivity. The mandatory immunization program vaccinated individuals in order to maintain Hawai'i as an uncontaminated military outpost and produce able "Americanized" laboring bodies that could contribute to the US defense industry. The Honolulu Blood Bank collected blood as a resource for military and medical projects while soliciting donations through racialized and gendered tropes of patriotism and loyalty. Discourses of security and scientific rationality legitimated US martial law and universalized corporeal requirements for wartime patriotism in Hawai'i, such as standards for health, productivity, and bodily sacrifices. Accordingly, this chapter explores how scientific rationality — and its monopoly on definitions of "life" and "death" — produces knowledge that legitimizes racial, colonial, and military projects.[5]

Public health projects were predicated on the racial liberal biopolitical logic of improvement: just as eminent domain and land expropriation aligned with Lockean understandings of rational labor and progress, so too did this discourse operate in the realm of public health. Militarized immunization and blood bank projects organized life, affect, and biology such that this racialized and colonial regime of extraction seemed benevolent and life cultivating rather than predatory and life depleting. This biopolitical regime included Kanaka Maoli and Asian settlers on the condition that they exhibited patriotic service, affirmed Hawai'i as a US possession, and did not make claims to Indigenous sovereignty. Furthermore, vaccination and blood donation programs wielded logics of racial liberalism and wartime duty to compel the participation of racialized peoples as an act of loyalty and assimilation. This socially reproductive project fused the primitive accumulation of labor, life, and bodily resources — all in the service of wartime capitalist expansion.

Public Health under Martial Law

In the days after the bombing of Pearl Harbor, Hawai'i's public health, medical, and first-aid stations entered a state of emergency and military control that they had never before experienced. Officials from the US territorial, military, and federal governments collaborated on what they saw as a common cause: the security of an important US military base in the Pacific Theater and the continuing US occupation of Hawai'i. The fact that these various agencies had some of their senior officials and much of their staff in common made this collaboration easier.[6] The Territorial Board of Health met to establish emergency procedures and take inventory of the resources available in the islands, and it placed all of its O'ahu members on twenty-four-hour call for the next two weeks.[7] Nurses, volunteers, and other health-care workers labored day and night in the days following the attack to care for those wounded in the bombing. Residents such as Bernice Hemphill heard about the bombing and the call for blood donations at Queen's Hospital while listening to the radio, hitchhiked downtown to give blood, and volunteered in the blood laboratory there for six days straight without returning home.[8] Hawai'i's public health system underwent drastic changes as its primary management and funding shifted from the hands of the territorial government to the newly created Office of Civilian Defense (OCD), a department of the military government.[9] The Territorial Board of Health remained intact, but it was augmented by federal funds allotted by the US Department of the Interior, the OCD, and the US Public Health Service. Periodic visits from Department of the Interior officials, an increased attention to security, and the rapidly rising population in Hawai'i led to a large recruitment of medical officials, engineers, and inspectors.[10] Further, this expansion of medical services necessitated an increase in the recruitment of feminized medical labor, such as nursing and other hospital staff. For example, the military governor, General Emmons, demanded the registration of all active and inactive nurses in Hawai'i, and began a recruiting program both in the islands and the continent. The American Red Cross supplemented the nursing staff at hospitals and the blood bank.[11] Throughout the war, the Territorial Board of Health worked together with the OCD, the US Public Health Service, and the medical departments of the army and navy to maintain the smooth functioning of health programs in Hawai'i.

During World War II in Hawai'i, settler colonial and military institutions collaborated closely and even shared officials and staff—all under the surveillance of the Office of the Military Governor. The emergency medical program—including the Blood Plasma Bank, first-aid stations, ambulance service, and emergency hospitals—dramatically expanded over the first year of martial law with the addition of 20 aid stations, 365 paid staff, 1,460 volunteer staff, and 63 classes to train new personnel in first aid, nursing, care of chemical casualties, and communicable-disease prevention. These new appointments and courses continued throughout the war.[12] Meanwhile, sanitary inspections and food and water inspection increased and intensified, and new programs expanded dental care, mental health care, child and maternal health, and health education.[13] During this time the US Public Health Service contributed aid by recruiting and training public health nurses to be employed by the Board of Health as health officers, reserve medical officers, and bacteriologists.[14] The Public Health Service contributed an additional $91,000 per year to the Board of Health, and over the course of the war the total budget for the Board of Health increased almost threefold, from $470,232 to $1,266,298.[15] A total of 289 enlisted men from the US Army Health Department assigned to the Board of Health conducted regular sanitary inspections in Honolulu and provided mosquito control. Others served as epidemiologists, county health officers, or nurses. The US Army also supplied the Board of Health with supplies, such as penicillin, typhoid vaccine, and sanitation equipment.[16] The Office of Civilian Defense increased Honolulu's existing hospital facilities by a thousand beds in the first year of the war and also added additional fully staffed and equipped hospitals in buildings.[17] Public health projects such as the immunization program and the Honolulu Blood Bank had high levels of compliance under these militarized conditions, and these statistics did not go unnoticed by territorial, military, and health officials.

Not only did wartime bring a general expansion of scope and volume to territorial health and medical facilities—which required immense amounts of labor and capital—but the expanded management of public health also contributed to a racial liberal biopolitical administration complicit with the reproduction of US settler militarism. These public health projects sought to cultivate life in all its capacities within the population in order to increase wartime productivity during a time of immense labor shortage. Amid punitive regimes of labor control and surveillance that extracted unpaid labor and issued jail sentences for switching jobs or being absent from one's job, public health infrastructures portrayed the martial law regime as "protecting" and "improving," rather than depleting, the lives of people in Hawai'i. Further, although the wartime state of emergency presented martial law–era Hawai'i as an exceptional militarized space and time, Hawai'i was and is a US settler colony in which the US primitive accumulation of capital, land, and natural resources has historically been dependent upon the displacement and devaluation of Indigenous life as well as the racialized exploitation of Asian immigrant labor. Socially reproductive projects such as vaccination and blood donation were therefore not only concerned with cultivating the productivity of laborers and soldiers; rather, they also built upon and maintained asymmetrical racial, gendered, and colonial dynamics of US settler militarism and capitalist expansion.

Vaccination and Wartime Mobilization

In World War II–era Hawai'i, the medical care and surveillance of individual bodies—indeed, "life" itself—was not only a biological resource for social reproduction but also a nationalist metaphor for military security. Biomedical discourses of health and immunity empowered, and were empowered by, Manichaean wartime logics of "the familiar and the foreign" and "good versus evil."[18] Over the course of spring 1942, the Office of the Military Governor mandated that all civilians (other than infants and the elderly) in Hawai'i be vaccinated against smallpox, typhoid, and paratyphoid fevers.[19] In 1943 the military government made vaccination for diphtheria compulsory for children, and it required booster shots in 1944.[20] By August of 1942, more than 90 percent of the target population had been immunized, and over the course of the war at least 363,000 civilians were immunized out of the total population, which grew from approximately 424,000 to 500,000 during that time range.[21] Medical and nursing personnel supplied by the US Army and OCD performed these immunizations, but civilians had the option of receiving their shots from their personal physician. Harriet Kuwamoto, a public health nurse who administered typhoid immunizations, recalls receiving supplies such as syringes, needles, and vaccine from the US military and conducting vaccinations alongside volunteers, military members, and other nurses in the Health Department basement, a process that she estimated took months to complete.[22] In addition to anxieties over smallpox, typhoid, paratyphoid, and diphtheria, the Board of Health worked to combat venereal disease, the bubonic plague, tetanus, and dengue fever.[23] The military government considered the security and productivity of the military bases in the islands to be fundamentally reliant upon the health of local civilians, defense workers, and soldiers. It chose smallpox and typhoid as the mandatory immunizations because they were the most common "war diseases."[24] Therefore, mandatory immunization was not simply employed to decrease death and disease, but rather was part of an effort to cultivate the highest level of life in all its capacities within the population.

Public health policies in Hawai'i have long been intertwined with racial and colonial projects. In nineteenth-century and early twentieth-century

Hawai'i, the Board of Health established racially exclusionary medical programs, such as the Kalaupapa leprosy settlement on the island of Moloka'i and the quarantine and disastrous "controlled burning" of Honolulu's Chinatown.[25] In particular, the practice of forcibly sending leprosy patients, the majority of whom were Native Hawaiian, to the Kalaupapa settlement is an example of how colonial health policies that claimed to "protect" or "rehabilitate" Indigenous people also worked to displace and eliminate them. Yet Kanaka Maoli have always resisted these projects: leprosy patients exercised autonomy over their health practices by refusing to separate from family members, protesting against the Board of Health, voting in Hawai'i's elections, and even using physical force.[26] We continue to see traces of these carceral health policies during the World War II period. Under martial law, the military government asserted, "For the protection of the public health and safety . . . Hawaii must be viewed as an isolated and congested stockade, crammed with a half million men, women, and children."[27] This characterization of Hawai'i as a "stockade" that sequestered its inhabitants in order to protect them combined logics of detention and medical security, and this time incorporated the entirety of the islands out of military necessity. During World War II the pressures of wartime mobilization against the "racist states" of Germany and Japan required the United States to employ a wartime "antiracism," which in Hawai'i promoted the participation of all civilians, the majority of whom were nonwhite. Military policies proclaimed liberal inclusion even as they continued the classification and regulation of racially differentiated groups. Racial liberal biopower strengthened the code of gendered white patriotism as a regulatory power through regimes of health that bifurcated the population into "good subjects" who complied and un-American "others" who refused. These projects created an asymptotic horizon of possibility for inclusion that demanded assimilation without addressing inequalities created by past and present racial violence. Furthermore, the military government's racial liberal logic still relied upon spaces of racial exclusion and imprisonment: during the war, Hawai'i's only quarantine center was converted into an internment camp that segregated Japanese and white internees, thus concretizing the imbricated logics of race, health, carcerality, and military security.

The policy of compulsory immunization was enforced by a military order on December 27, 1941, requiring that the Central Identification Bureau photograph, fingerprint, and register all civilians age six and older under a serial number with personal and contact information. By June 30, 1942, Governor Joseph B. Poindexter reported that the military government had fingerprinted and given identification certificates to 371,500 civilians out of the total re-corded population of approximately 430,000. Governor Poindexter noted that the discrepancy between the number of those registered and the total population was a result of children under the age of six (about 52,000) and war workers who had not yet been contacted (about 25,000 or 30,000).[28] The Board of Health ordered civilians to report to vaccination centers on the day assigned to their serial number, where they would receive their vaccination and mark its completion on their identification card.[29] Officials used this da-tabase to keep track of the vaccinated population, calculate the amount of vaccine still needed, and subject civilians who had not complied to "inves-tigation and penalties."[30] In April 1943 the territorial government increased the maximum penalty for violating a Board of Health regulation from $100 to $500 and one year in prison.[31] Citizens without their identification cards were fined five to ten dollars, and noncitizens were fined twenty-five to fifty dollars.[32] As resident Agnes Eun Soon Rho Chun recalled, "Any time they stopped you at night . . . just about anyplace . . . you had to show your ID."[33] Over the course of three evenings in 1943, more than four hundred residents of Honolulu were arrested for not bringing their identification card with them to a movie theater. These wartime policies and larger fines for noncitizens—along with the threat of potential internment for Japanese settlers—illustrates how this pressure to conform to martial law policies and patriotic norms was harsher for racialized peoples and noncitizens. The US military government claimed that this was the first instance in US history in which it had required the mass fingerprinting and enumeration of civilians, and the first time that it required mandatory vaccinations against both typhoid fever and smallpox for the entire civilian population of a state or territory.[34]

The reduction of individuals to identification numbers with an attached photograph and fingerprint created a carceral taxonomy that organized Hawai'i's population on the terms of the US military government. This lends nuance to Foucault's description of hygiene and medical care as a technology of power that links the "biological," the security and health of the population, to the "organic," the discipline and movement of the body.[35] Vaccinations transformed the immune systems of individual bodies, and the science of immunization contributed to a biopolitical administration that exceeded the realm of bodily discipline and regulated at the level of the population by dic-tating standards of medical care. However, under martial law this so-called improvement of health via mandatory immunization was not a choice or privilege but rather a condition of the state of emergency and US occupation: residents in Hawai'i were "made to live" according to the health and labor productivity standards of the US military government in order to construct and maximize the vitality of Hawai'i's military bases. Although this project optimized life, it did so within a carceral space for the purposes of fortifying US settler military and capitalist expansion. The database of identification numbers, fingerprints, and photographs compelled civilian compliance with military orders: this panoptic system of identification and surveillance enforced the mandatory immunization program and its required patriotism and civil service.[36] The military considered immunization to be an expression of loyalty, and those who did not comply with martial law orders were punished with fines or prison sentences, which were more stringent for noncitizens and racialized peoples.

Furthermore, this wartime program for mandatory immunization illustrates how racial liberal biopower intensified racial differentiation while foreclosing a critical analysis of indigeneity and colonialism. This wartime proliferation of racial fictions built upon settler colonial classifications that absorbed Hawaiian indigeneity into their mythical racial categories. In the introduction I discussed the military government's statement concerning racial tolerance: "The Chinese, Filipino, Hawaiian, and various Caucasian people caused no concern." This statement placed Hawaiians alongside immigrants as an "assimilable" racialized group and ignored that they are an Indigenous people with sovereignty rights and a claim to independent statehood under international law. As J. Kēhaulani Kauanui argues, "Indigeneity is about connection to place and assertions of nationhood, not race and liberal multiculturalism."[37] Yet we know that any acknowledgment of Hawaiian indigeneity or sovereignty on the part of the military government would have contradicted the possessive logics that animated and upheld its settler military project.

Moreover, just as martial law's discourse of racial liberalism absorbed indigeneity and masked settler colonialism, the settler state wielded logics of improvement and scientific rationality to evade responsibility for colonial histories of epidemic disease. The US military government touted the fact that rates of typhoid fever and diphtheria reached an all-time low under its mandatory immunization program to declare that its wartime occupation had actually *improved* and modernized life in Hawai'i.[38] Accordingly, the US military designated itself as "the protect[or] of the public health and safety" of Hawai'i, a territory it described as "untrained, practically unprepared, unorganized, and uncertain."[39] These claims rationalized the increasing US military presence, its continued primitive accumulation of life and land, and its technologies of population regulation and surveillance. That is, just as logics of improvement rationalized the racialized and colonial expropriation of land, so too did this discourse operate in the realm of public health by figuring settler militarism as life cultivating rather than life destroying. Yet, in actuality, it was settlers themselves who had introduced many of the diseases, such as diphtheria, typhoid, and smallpox, from which Hawai'i needed this "protection." The 1853 smallpox epidemic contributed to the rapid depopulation that weakened the Hawaiian land-tenure system and subsistence economy in the wake of the Māhele (1845–1850), which, as discussed in chapter 1, privatized and divided lands and led to the dispossession of the majority of Kanaka Maoli.[40] Thus, the "make live" imperative of this biopolitical health project not only legitimized US military occupation but was also instrumental in masking structures of elimination and histories of mass death.

In this way, even as the wartime mandatory vaccination program included Native Hawaiians within its administration of disease prevention, it was predicated on the denial of Indigenous sovereignty. This biopolitical project built upon a legacy of settler colonial policies that attempted to imprison, displace, or eliminate Native people and disrupt Indigenous reciprocal relations to land. The history of leprosy in Hawai'i is a principal example of this, as is the long history of settler land occupation, including but not limited to sugar and pineapple plantation agriculture in the late nineteenth century and early twentieth century and the US military's unilateral condemnation of land during World War II. These exropriative settler projects cut off Hawaiians' access to land, water, and natural resources, including healing plants and the medicinal practices that accompany them. Under martial law, the US military government claimed to cultivate and improve health by mandating immunizations, when in actuality, military projects voraciously consumed life and labor and accelerated the destruction of Hawaiian lands and their life-giving forces so that new military bases and testing sites could be established.

Beyond this, it is vital to emphasize that Kanaka Maoli epistemologies of health and sovereignty are inherently intertwined: thus, these settler military projects that purported to "improve" Hawaiian health without centralizing Hawaiian sovereignty were inherently contradictory. Noelani Goodyear-Ka'ōpua discusses the concept of ea as one that can mean "sovereignty" or "life": "Unlike Euro-American philosophical notions of sovereignty, ea is based on the experiences of people on the land, relationships forged through the process of remembering and caring for wahi pana, storied places."[41] Reciprocal care and responsibility to the land restores not only landscapes but also the health of Kanaka Maoli communities. Davianna Pōmaika'i McGregor's work illustrates how most Native Hawaiian plants have some medicinal purpose, such as maile hohono, 'ie'ie, 'uhaloa, and noni. Honohono grass and laukahi can be pounded to treat cuts and sores, and laukahi pistil can be boiled into a tea to cure cancer. Pōpolo berry seeds can be pounded and squeezed for juice to treat colds. We know that Kanaka Maoli have continued land-based healing practices such as herbal healing, lā'au lapa'au, and spiritual healing throughout, even as they were forced to adapt in the midst of settler land accumulation and the introduction of new diseases.[42] Thus, we must understand settler military desires to monopolize natural resources as a response to the continuing vitality of Indigenous lifeways and claims to sovereignty as well as the resistance of racialized and gendered communities. Despite settler military attempts to negate Hawaiian sovereignty and epistemologies of the relationship between life, land, and health, we know that Hawaiians could and did resist, and that there have always been moments when, as McGregor argues, cultural kīpuka were maintained and continued.[43]

Blood and the Costs of American Patriotism

As the immunization program expanded in Hawai'i during World War II, military officials also claimed that a large storage of blood plasma could save hundreds of lives in the case of another attack. Practices at the Honolulu Blood Bank illustrate how settler militarism functioned through racial liberal biopolitical projects that universalized American medical science: in the case of blood donation, this naturalization was strengthened by the prominence of discourse that literally equated blood with life. A 1943 article in the *Hawaii Herald* stated that the plasma in this growing blood bank was "guarded as our most precious possession, more valuable than gold or jewels or securities. It represents life itself—life given straight from the heart of members of the community and stored up for use in the future to give life to others." An advertisement in the *Honolulu Star-Bulletin* even referred to the Honolulu Blood Bank as "The Bank of Life."[44] Certainly, the voluntary donation of blood during wartime was, to some, a comforting and patriotic affirmation in the face of uncontrollable violence. The rationalized organization of this blood in a bank enabled the efficient use of this life-giving fluid. Yet, as with the mandatory immunization program, the collection and organization of blood under martial law was not so much a choice, but rather a condition of military control in which bodies and their tissues were subject to heightened regulation and exploitation. The blood bank not only intensified the management of racially differentiated groups, but it also created a regime of biological value that elicited more blood donations, fortified the military state, and reproduced the conditions of settler militarism.

The first blood bank opened in Hawai'i on June 27, 1941. It was located in the City-County Emergency Hospital, was staffed by women volunteers, and was publicized by the Red Cross and Dr. Forrest J. Pinkerton, the director of the blood bank. However, because the Red Cross was unable to fully take over the blood bank when it ran out of funding and became understaffed, it closed in November, storing more than 200 flasks of plasma that would eventually be used directly after the bombing of Pearl Harbor in naval and civilian hospitals.[45] Once this existing stash of plasma ran out, Pinkerton conducted a large-scale call for donors on the radio and in the newspaper to help the military and those injured at Pearl Harbor.[46] There was a huge influx of donors during this period: whereas a total of 253 people had donated blood to the Chamber of Commerce blood bank before December 7, 1941, during the weeks afterward the bank received up to 500 donors per day. After December 7, the Office of Civilian Defense took over responsibility for the blood bank's finances, and the Territorial Board of Health oversaw the bank's laboratory work. Because of its success after reopening, the Honolulu Blood Bank moved into its own building on the grounds of Queen's Hospital on July 10, 1942. Between July 1, 1942, and June 30, 1943, 12,643 donors gave blood in O'ahu.[47]

The Honolulu Blood Bank and its wartime blood donation campaigns exemplify how Hawai'i became a biopolitical center of the Pacific War. As Pinkerton declared in 1943, "Our blood bank here is second to none in the country. . . . The public can be mighty proud of the defense machinery that has been established in the islands."[48] By referring to the blood bank as "defense machinery," Pinkerton cites the superiority of the blood bank as representative of Hawai'i's importance as a secure military base. Further, the Honolulu Blood Bank performed three functions that illustrated Hawai'i's dual position as "home front" and "war front." First, it operated as a wartime blood bank that provided for hospitals that served troops returning to the continental United States, along with residents of Hawai'i. Second, it blood-typed all people in the territory by traveling to schools, businesses, and organizations to take samples, and then bringing them back to the central blood bank laboratory to process. Third, it operated as a reserve for blood plasma that was available to private doctors for nonemergency medical needs through a "lend-lease" program, in which family or friends of the recipient would "repay" the bank with a donation of their own. The feature that made Honolulu's blood bank unique was that it was a procurement center and a plasma-storage unit in one, which was very unusual on the continent. This attribute had significance for military security: bases in Hawai'i would not have to wait for plasma to be shipped in during a medical emergency or attack.[49] In this way, blood donated in Hawai'i not only served those living in the islands, but it also fortified and secured the health of bodies throughout the US military empire and continent.

Moreover, under a table of prices at the Honolulu Blood Bank, body and blood were governed by a capitalist regime of exchange in which members received discounted prices.[50] The bank's membership program suggests that the gift of human tissue can create an imagined intimacy or common identity, and it constructs, as Catherine Waldby and Robert Mitchell argue, a sense of community based on mutual indebtedness.[51] Now an eleemosynary institution, the blood bank relied upon the service charges from blood and plasma withdrawals and cash donations from community members and institutions to procure the necessary funds for it to continue to run.[52] The cost of using whole blood from the blood bank was zero for members of the insurance plan, but there was a $5 service charge for nonmembers who provided another donor to replace their full dose (via the lend-lease program) or a $20 charge for an outright purchase of one dose of blood. For blood plasma, the cost was zero for members but there was a $10 service charge with a replacement donor or $25 for the outright purchase of the dose of plasma. If civilians could not afford their service charge, they were permitted to send in extra donors in exchange for having their service charge waived—thus perpetuating the extraction of blood from working-class civilians. Members of the US military were never charged for whole blood or plasma.[53] These programs of lend-leasing and blood insurance cultivated what Waldby calls "biovalue": they rendered blood as a commodity susceptible to market forces while also producing and capitalizing on bodily criteria for membership in their shared community.[54] Under these criteria, members of the blood bank and their families were encouraged to make regular donations to the bank as a form of wartime service. Much as with the vaccination program, this hierarchy of membership produced and reified wartime tenets of US patriotism, in which those who exhibited loyalty by donating had unlimited access to the blood bank and undesirable "others" who had not made the necessary bodily sacrifices did not. The fact that soldiers always had unlimited access reinforces the idea that bodily sacrifice was necessary for this membership, and therefore for patriotism, during wartime. This regime even assigned a soldier's sacrifice an exchange value: a civilian's "premium" of three blood donations per year granted access to these same benefits.

Furthermore, the blood bank's requirements for donors institutionalized American medical standards of what constituted normative health. As early as 1942, the Territorial Nutrition Committee began distributing pamphlets on foods that were important to attaining the maximum health of blood donors at the Honolulu Blood Bank.[55] Individuals could not donate blood if they had contracted any illness in the past month. An individual who had contracted dengue fever could not donate blood for six months, and a history of having other diseases, such as tuberculosis, disqualified donors for five years.[56] Thus, as the immunization program and other health campaigns prevented disease and cultivated healthy bodies, they also optimized the population available to donate blood to the US war effort. The bank solicited these donations through public venues, including propaganda posters, local newspapers, in high schools through letters home to parents, and through companies via letters to employers.[57] After one was blood-typed, which involved marking the symbol—O, A, B or AB—on one's identification card, newspapers and press releases encouraged individuals to carry some other indicator of their blood type in case of emergency. Some wore metal identification bracelets or necklaces, but Pinkerton and E. E. Black, director of the Office of Civilian Defense, encouraged everyone to have their blood type tattooed on the bottom of their feet. Apparently, metal identification tags were potentially hazardous, could complicate a wound, and would be automatically discarded when the individual arrived at the hospital in an emergency.[58] This suggestion by these medical and military professionals is a rather visceral indicator of the state of emergency under martial law and the importance of blood as a biological resource for war: the blood bank enforced corporeal notions of wartime participation, in which the military state encouraged civilians to engrave their blood type on their skin so that even when incapacitated, they would still be efficiently serving the vitality of the nation.

The blood bank's salience within the community was such that it became common practice as early as December 28, 1941, for provost courts to offer individuals sentenced with crimes the option of donating blood to the blood bank in place of a fine. For example, when Harriet Kuwamoto appeared before the court to receive her sentence for speeding, the judge fined her five dollars and revoked her license, but gave her the option of donating blood instead. On June 18, 1942, the executive to the military governor, General Thomas H. Green, issued a memorandum that gave this practice official recognition in the courts.[59] This ruling occurred at the same time that Oahu

Prison was experiencing overcrowding and prisoners were beginning to be released early if they exhibited "good behavior." This measure was even extended so that those who were currently in prison could donate blood in place of their bail. Green stipulated that one pint of blood donated equaled a thirty-dollar fine or fifteen days in jail.[60] Not surprisingly, this measure was not well received by the general community, and prisoners of the provost court protested via the *Paahao Press*, the prison newspaper, arguing that the military government's measure discriminated against prisoners.[61] The community's criticism of these "blood sentences" eventually led the military government to discontinue the official order on September 3, 1942.[62] Although these blood donations were never made mandatory, they were certainly not voluntary, especially in the case of those who could not afford their fine.[63] Though only established de jure for a short period of time, these "blood sentences" assigned a biological debt to prisoners that again put a price on human tissue under a new regime of biovalue, through which individuals literally gave their blood to the military state in exchange for freedom.

The settler military context in Hawai'i cultivated racialized and colonial conditions for the primitive accumulation of life, labor, and biological resources, all in the service of wartime capitalism. Each of the above blood donation regimes—the table of prices, the lend-lease program, and the use of blood to stand in for prison fines and bail—encouraged people in Hawai'i to understand their own bodily tissues through capitalist modes of commodification and exchange, creating opportunities to quantify corporeal requirements for wartime sacrifice and calculate modes for their expropriation.[64] Compounding this dynamic, the Office of Civilian Defense kept a monthly tally of the number of blood donors, recording statistics of these donations according to age, gender, and "racial extraction."[65] Newspapers such as the *Honolulu Star-Bulletin*, the *Honolulu Advertiser*, and the *Hawaii Times* reported these statistics to the public every month. For example, during the first year of the war, 11,641 people donated blood, and the blood bank recorded their "racial extractions" as such: "54.33% Caucasian; 19.53% Japanese; 9.55% Hawaiian and Part-Hawaiian; 5.49% Filipino; 4.28% Portuguese; 2.23% Chinese; 1.04% Porto Rican; .82% Korean; and all others 2.6%."[66] The list, which mapped on to racial categories used by the Board of Health, always appeared in this order, even when Hawaiians and Part-Hawaiians donated the second-highest percentage of blood, as they did in April, and from July to September of 1943.[67]

I discussed above how the donation of blood connoted membership in a community and how the exchange of blood articulated with capitalist regimes of value; here we also see how the rationalized categorization, measurement, and organization of blood functioned as a metaphor for race and indigeneity. By publishing monthly racial statistics of blood donors, these newspapers contributed to a common liberal narrative of Hawai'i as a "multiracial paradise" in which individuals of all races worked together peacefully and, in this case, donated blood to the cause in World War II.[68] This representation of the United States harvesting military strength from its multiracial volunteers symbolized Hawai'i's "willing" incorporation into the United States and constructed the United States as an "antiracist" liberal power over and against its "racist" enemies, Japan and Germany. However, this discourse of racial liberalism also depended upon the erasure of racial and colonial violence, including settler colonial structures of land dispossession and Indigenous displacement, the internment and exclusion of Japanese settlers, the coercive context of US martial law, and capitalist regimes of exploitation and primitive accumulation.

Furthermore, the statistical categorization of these donations is indicative of how racial liberal biopower reinforced gendered forms of patriotism. In the first year, 9,239 of these donors were men, but only 2,402 were women. This provided a contrast to the continental United States, where the Red Cross specifically recruited women as donors, leading them to contribute approximately half of the blood donations.[69] Because Hawai'i was both home front and war front, this difference is likely a result of the fact that both civilians and soldiers donated to the Honolulu Blood Bank. As discussed above, on the continent, blood donations were feminized as a gift from the home front to the war front, and even sometimes included a note that affectively inscribed this gift with an expression of care or intimacy. A pharmacist's mate at one point remarked that "some romances may develop from this."[70] However, in Hawai'i, where officials explicitly militarized the Honolulu Blood Bank as "defense machinery," this public health project prescribed a different gendered division of labor and service. As visualized in the photograph of Pharmacist's Mate Elsey, the bank recruited men to donate blood as an expression of military masculinity and patriotism, and enlisted women in the feminized labor of feeding and entertaining them in the blood bank canteen to reward them for their bodily sacrifice. Even as each of these projects was structured differently, blood banks in the continental United States and Hawai'i both used dominant gendered and heterosexual tropes to naturalize their enlistment of wartime patriotism and service.

Moreover, the monthly statistics of blood donors by race built upon an already institutionalized US colonial taxonomy that organized and defined human "types" in Hawai'i.[71] These racial fictions not only metaphorized race as biological, and as quantifiable "blood," but this regime of invented classifications and statistics also erased indigeneity and reproduced settler colonialism. Newspapers always listed "Caucasian" as the first category with the highest percentage, thus designating white settlers as the dominant model for assimilation and loyalty and normalizing Hawai'i as a white possession despite its multiracial demographics.[72] Even when Japanese settlers contributed an all-time high of 21.75 percent of the donations in March 1943, an article remarked that the Caucasian group "continued to set the pace with 62.91 percent."[73] The classification of "Caucasian" could encompass many different white races, but here they were all consolidated into one privileged category over and against racialized groups that were separated according to national origin, thus exacerbating their marginalized status.[74] Furthermore, these statistics deployed a settler colonial discourse that again placed Hawaiians alongside immigrant settlers as a racial group rather than an Indigenous people with sovereignty rights amounting to a national claim. It is also telling that "Hawaiian and Part-Hawaiian" was the only category that qualified the purity or mixture of "racial extraction." By the 1940s, American sociologists working in Hawai'i had already focused their research on the high rate of interracial marriage among all racial groups on the sugar plantations in the territory.[75] Surely, donors of other "racial extractions" were also "Part-Japanese" or "Part-Chinese," yet it is only Native Hawaiians who appear as "Part-Hawaiian" in these racial tallies. As Kauanui illustrates, the 1921 legal definition of "native Hawaiian" as "a descendant with at least one-half blood quantum" set a precedent that racialized Hawaiian identity as something that could be measured by US systems of quantification, and that could thus be "diluted" over time via the colonial category of "Part-Hawaiian."[76] Indeed, these statistics of blood donors' "racial extractions" present Hawaiian blood as *already* diluted, whereas other categories such as "Japanese" and "Chinese" remain whole—and, thus, also unquestionably "other."

The racialized logics of assimilation and blood quantum in these monthly statistics also reveal the interconnected regimes of US settler colonialism and military occupation. The continual use of the category "Hawaiian and Part-Hawaiian" racialized Hawaiian blood as diluted and therefore also cast Hawaiians as selectively "assimilable." As Maile Arvin illustrates, the "eugenic pedagogy" of blood quantum has historically racialized Part-Hawaiians as either assimilable and "nearly Caucasian" or "degenerate" others in need of rehabilitation.[77] These are both examples of settler colonial rhetoric that contributed to what Patrick Wolfe theorizes as a structure of elimination, which delegitimized Native sovereignty.[78] In contrast, the portrayal of Asian blood as indissoluble again racialized Japanese and other Asian settlers as "poorly assimilated" and "un-American," and thus potentially disloyal and in need of military surveillance. This juxtaposition of Hawaiian blood as weakening and Asian blood as immutable simultaneously rationalized the erasure of indigeneity and Hawaiian sovereignty, the "perpetual foreignness" of Asian immigrants, and the hyper-visibility of the Japanese as "enemy aliens." This racial liberal biopolitical project thus constructed racialized hierarchies of assimilation, centralized gendered white patriotism, and disallowed recognition of Indigenous sovereignty—in the service of settler militarism.

Furthermore, these monthly racial statistics provide a contrast to the national policy of blood segregation in the continental United States during this time. There, the Red Cross policy separated "white" from "colored" blood, with "colored" blood indicating African American blood and "white" blood indicating the blood of all other races, including Chinese, Filipino, and Mexican Americans.[79] Banks marked blood donated by black donors with "AA" (for African American), but all other blood went unmarked. However, there is evidence that segregation practices were carried out inconsistently and that during battle emergencies all blood was used indiscriminately.[80] In fact, policies for blood segregation often varied from bank to bank: while Irwin Memorial Blood Bank in San Francisco did not segregate blood, Baltimore had two completely separate banks for "white" blood and "colored" blood.[81] Yet despite this policy, African American blood was not the only blood perceived as a "problem." At the start of the war, there was protest and outrage in the continental United States over the inclusion of Japanese American and other Asian American blood with white blood. Yet by the later years of the war, this was not always seen as an issue, with evidence of Japanese Americans' blood donations even being used to support the emerging narrative of the patriotic Nisei soldier. During World War II many civilians, and even Red Cross officials, admitted that they were not sure what the policy was for the segregation of Asian American blood.[82] These inconsistent blood-segregation practices exemplify how Asian immigrant settlers, who were at this point still excluded from US citizenship, have posed a problem for institutional adherents to the black/white binary throughout US history.[83] But unlike in the continental United States, the Honolulu Blood Bank meticulously categorized Asian blood donations, separating them into percentages for Japanese, Chinese, Filipino, and Korean donations. And although there were at least thirty thousand Black soldiers and defense workers in Hawai'i during World War II (mostly men, facing segregation in military units), Hawai'i's racial tallies did not have a classification for African American blood donors.[84] Pinkerton's 1944 study of the Rh factor in blood at the Honolulu Blood Plasma Bank indicates that 25 of the 1,605 individuals tested were of African American descent, yet these percentages were not made public.[85] This suggests either that African Americans were patrons of Hawaiʻi's blood banks but their donations were not included in the racial tallies, or that their donations were included in the racial tallies under the category of "all others." Overall, these varying practices of blood categorization and statistics are examples of regimes of antiblackness operating differently across US colonial landscapes—including San Francisco, Baltimore, and Hawaiʻi—according to the geographically specific requirements of settler colonial racialization and the social reproduction of US imperial war. In Hawaiʻi the palatability of racial liberal biopower—including its hyper-visible accommodation of Asianness and its absorption of Hawaiian indigeneity—was reliant upon the erasure of blackness.[86]

Whereas the gift of blood can create a sense of intimacy, common identity, or community, it can also fortify existing inequalities and power hierarchies because it produces relations of indebtedness.[87] The Honolulu Blood Bank contributed to the primitive accumulation of biovalue by capitalizing on the news media's reproduction of racialized difference: blood donation was mediated by an asymmetrical notion of duty through which racialized peoples, especially noncitizens and those suspected of disloyalty, were forever indebted to keep giving. The monthly racial tallies constructed the category of the "Caucasian donor" over and against the supposedly reticent "Oriental donor." Significantly, these statistics did not note the percentages of each racial group in the population, nor did they reveal that many of the Caucasian donors were not actually Hawaiʻi residents, but soldiers who donated blood on their way back to the continental United States from other bases and battlegrounds in the Pacific Islands. Because the US government classified American citizens of Japanese ancestry as "4-C, enemy aliens ineligible for the military" until 1943, they had an automatic numerical disadvantage in the racial tallies. In fact, as a letter to the editor in the *Honolulu Star-Bulletin* protested, "Since the OCD has seen fit to present blood bank statistics broken down by races, let it be fair to the residents of Hawaii by disclosing the actual percentage of Caucasian donations to the blood bank from resident Caucasians, and the percentage donated by non-resident Caucasians."[88] Despite this letter, signed "non-Caucasian blood donor," many newspapers and civilians in Hawaiʻi invoked the monthly racial tallies in order to pit different racial groups against one another. These racial statistics illustrate contradictions of liberal democratic inclusion: the blood bank claimed to protect all people, regardless of race, yet it simultaneously pointed to certain racial groups as uncooperative because they were not donating enough blood.

Pinkerton, who had already publicly expressed his opinion that doctors of Japanese ancestry should not be permitted to practice in wartime Hawai'i, pointed out that although Japanese made up more than one-third of the population, they had contributed far less than that proportion of blood.[89] This remark and others like it placed public pressure on members of each racial group to demonstrate their loyalty by donating blood, and also betrays an anxiety about the number of Japanese in Hawai'i and their supposedly "questionable loyalties." Another article in the *Hawaii Herald* asserted that "the Japanese have been trying to find ways in which they could convince the people in this community that they preferred our American way of life. . . . But they have neglected one of the most important ways in which they can be of great service to the country they profess to love. This is donating blood for the community plasma bank . . . they have been slackers in this obvious responsibility."[90] This article implies that the desire to donate blood is an important step in the process of assimilation to the "American way of life" and suggests that any racial group, such as the Japanese, that does not donate its share of blood must not be sufficiently assimilated or loyal to the United States.

As discussed above, newspapers promoted blood donation through gendered and racialized tropes of patriotism and loyalty. As Sarah Chinn argues, blood donation showcased the "heroic ordinariness of American citizenship." One man wrote that "it's easier than getting a shave in a barber shop. . . . Your donation may save some young lad's life." Another letter to the editor proclaimed that "America expects every citizen to fulfill his obligations, even to the sacrifice of his life, if required, but contributing to the blood bank is infinitely less than that supreme test of loyal devotion."[91] Much like Donor Number 6653, who extolled his "chat with three or four other charming young ladies" in the blood bank canteen, both of these writers gendered the prospective donor as male, venerating blood donation as a requirement of patriotic masculinity.[92] Further, another claimed, "Racially, donors have not appeared in proportion to their numerical group in the population. . . . The blood plasma bank serves and protects everyone, without racial or any other distinction. It deserves cooperation from all of us."[93] These racial logics are similar to those that compelled Japanese Americans to volunteer for the US military during World War II: as Ronald Takaki argues, Nisei soldiers proved "with their blood, their limbs, and their bodies that they were truly Americans."[94] Blood donation is an additional example of how racially excluded individuals offered their bodies to the military as evidence of loyalty and assimilation. For example, the Emergency Service Committee, a Japanese organization in Hawai'i that worked to exhibit American patriotism and service, organized blood drives for Japanese civilians. Members of the Varsity Victory Volunteers, a similar group of University of Hawai'i undergraduates, each made three donations per year.[95]

Japanese were not alone in feeling pressure to donate blood to show Americanization. For example, the Chinese Research and Education Committee specified that its three major initiatives were "active support for the repeal of the Chinese Exclusion Acts," "aid in naturalization," and "increased donations by the Chinese community to the Blood Bank." Executive Secretary Hungwai Ching reported that after receiving criticism over their lack of contributions to the bank, Chinese found blood donations to be a way to "demonstrate their community spirit by donating more liberally than they had before."[96] At the Kamehameha Schools, the principal wrote home to parents and echoed the Honolulu Blood Bank's call for 50,000 donations, and female students earned pins for serving sandwiches and coffee at the Queen's Hospital blood donation canteen.[97] A ninth-grader, Joshua Akana, wrote in the *Weekly News Review* that "many of our students and faculty members are blood donors for the blood bank at Queen's Hospital . . . they helped save many lives here."[98] At the University of Hawai'i, the YMCA sponsored blood drives, and one student, Elizabeth Num, established the War Council Blood Bank committee, which compiled a roster of students who had not yet donated and elicited thirty-three more pints of donated blood.[99]

While many who donated to the Honolulu Blood Bank did so in a genuine expression of allegiance to the United States, these examples illustrate how the wartime pressure to donate blood was especially acute for racialized and Indigenous peoples. This included Chinese settlers, who exhibited patriotism to prove they were not "aliens ineligible to citizenship"; Kanaka Maoli, whose responsibilities of US citizenship were unilaterally granted by colonial legislation; and Japanese settlers, who were vulnerable to interrogations and internment if they did not exhibit the proper behaviors. Blood donation became a racialized test of loyalty that contributed to US settler militarism: it naturalized gendered white patriotism as the dominant model for assimilation, capitalized on racial differentiation for the primitive accumulation of biological resources such as blood, and created the conditions for productive defense labor and soldiering across unlawfully occupied Hawaiian lands. Furthermore, not all residents were eager to participate: Shigeo Muroda, a Japanese and American dual citizen, was detained and questioned by the

Internee Hearing Board for allegedly leading a group of twelve other workers at Waianae Plantation to claim to be sick on the day of a blood drive. Although he denied all these charges, the hearing board ordered him to be interned.[100]

Rather than acknowledging that most of the Caucasian donors were not actually residents of Hawai'i, civilians and health workers speculated about why Japanese had contributed an "insufficient" amount of blood in proportion to their percentage of the population. Many of these hypotheses relied on racialized assumptions about the Japanese or "Oriental" culture. One example was the stereotype that "Orientals" were superstitious about blood donation and that "the idea of drawing blood out of the human body is repugnant to the Oriental mind."[101] Bernice Hemphill, a supervising technologist at the Honolulu Blood Bank, remarked that "in the islands, where especially some of the Asian groups had superstitions about not giving any part of the body or blood, it was a very, very, big recruitment problem to get people involved doing it."[102] Another common racialization during this period was that "Oriental" and "tropical" blood was naturally thinner than other types of blood. Although this idea had recently been scientifically disproven, it was still commonly believed during the war that different races had different qualities of blood and that tropical climates could thin one's blood. At one point after the war, a news article referred to this as the "tropical anemia bugaboo."[103]

Finally, this wartime regime of biomedical organization and value universalized the language of scientific rationality and its understandings of what constitutes biological "life" and "death." This bank figured blood as a powerful symbol of life and community that could be given via donation, and it rationalized the organization of this vital bodily tissue: by managing blood, medical professionals administered life itself. The ubiquity of this discourse contributed to a racial liberal biopolitical narrative that presented the United States as the "protect[or] of the public health and safety" of Hawai'i and obfuscated colonial histories in which settler structures of land acquisition, gendered and racial classification, industrialization, and epidemic disease had disrupted Hawaiians' access to land-based practices such as herbal medicine, lā'au lapa'au, or subsistence living. The "make live" imperative of this biopolitical project articulated with liberal-capitalist discourses of improvement and marginalized continuing Hawaiian epistemologies that connect life, health, and land. These projects sought to rationalize violent settler military and capitalist regimes—which ruptured reciprocal relations between human and nonhuman—as benevolent and life cultivating rather than predatory and life depleting. In this way, the blood bank wielded the discipline of American medical science to contribute to the social reproduction of settler militarism and capitalism by purporting to "improve" public health while masking the primitive accumulation of life and labor. Yet we also know that Kanaka Maoli have always critiqued and resisted these colonial projects, and that Native land-based healing practices have continued throughout.

Like the mandatory immunization project, the Honolulu Blood Bank structured the boundaries of acceptable wartime health and participation for the multiracial peoples in Hawai'i while foreclosing alternatives to the US possession of Hawaiian land: it institutionalized American medical science, used blood as a quantifiable metaphor for race and indigeneity, prescribed gendered responsibilities for wartime service, and denied Hawaiian epistemologies of health and sovereignty. This project capitalized on racial differentiation for the primitive accumulation of blood: these classifications elicited more donations while naturalizing whiteness as the dominant model for assimilation, demonizing Japanese settlers as "enemy aliens," and figuratively diluting indigeneity. As "defense machinery," the blood bank stored whole blood and plasma as a biological resource for the social reproduction of settler militarism, including the expropriation of labor and land in the service of US wartime capitalism and military empire.

. . . .

American scholars and physicians generally credit medical advancements made for military purposes during World War II with improving the overall health of the civilian population and for making modern health services a priority for the federal government.[104] Dr. Charles Wilbar, president of the Territorial Board of Health at the end of the war, declared proudly that advancements had been made in public health in Hawai'i but that there was still more to do during the postwar period.[105] Reports by the Board of Health, the Office of the Military Government, and the OCD all pointed to the supposedly poor state of health in Hawai'i before the war while providing statistics that boasted of lowered rates of deaths from disease, the large supply of whole blood and plasma available to Hawai'i's hospitals, a decline in infant-mortality rates, and an increase in live births.[106] Even after martial law ended, it remained a medical standard for physicians to vaccinate infants against smallpox, diphtheria, typhoid fever, and other diseases as the vaccines became available.[107] The Honolulu Blood Plasma Bank still exists today and is now called the Blood Bank of Hawaii.[108]

However, this chapter has demonstrated that martial law's medical claim to authority over biological life and death allowed the compulsory immunization and blood bank programs to contribute to the social reproduction of settler militarism while also occluding its central violence and contradictions. These public health projects were predicated on a racial liberal biopolitical logic of improvement that organized wartime relations such that this racialized and colonial regime of extraction seemed benevolent and life cultivating rather than predatory and life depleting. Both of these projects deployed health as a biological tool and metaphor for military security while also denying the role that settler governance and militarization had played in restricting Native Hawaiians' access to land and its life-giving forces. The pressures of wartime labor mobilization led the immunization program to include civilians of all races, even as it strengthened the code of white patriotism as a regulatory power, naturalized the military state as the "protector" of health, and allowed the settler state to evade responsibility for histories of Native death and disease. Building upon the immunization program's optimization of the population, the OCD's classifications at the blood bank deployed the dynamics of racialized and gendered difference for the expropriation of blood as a biological resource, and also absorbed indigeneity into their mythical racial categories. Civilians in Hawai'i had different experiences with these assimilationist health projects depending on their gender, race, citizenship status, and relationship to the US state. Wartime discourse compelled men to donate blood to showcase patriotism, whereas it enlisted women to serve as nurses and waitresses in the blood bank canteen. Asian settlers were obliged to perform evidence of their Americanization, and Japanese settlers faced additional pressure to exhibit loyalty in order to avoid military detention or internment. Finally, these biopolitical projects denied Native sovereignty and contributed to the vitality of US colonial occupation while seeking to mask structures of elimination and Hawaiian epistemologies that challenged US narratives of possession. These projects reveal the contradictions of racial liberalism in that they wielded the logic of inclusivity as a tool for primitive accumulation and population regulation, while erasing past and present narratives of racial and colonial violence—all in the service of settler militarism and wartime capitalism.

THREE

"The First Line of Defense Is Our Home"

Settler Military Domesticity in
World War II–Era Hawai'i

No sphere of life, no home, no child however small, are un-
touched by this war.—Department of Public Instruction, 1943

A bulletin for families living in Hawai'i announced in 1942, "We are at
war. We are also in the combat zone. This war and its outcome will mean
a great deal to all of us. Hawaii, because of its strategic situation and
population of mixed racial backgrounds, has many unusual and unique
problems."[1] Wives, mothers, and homemakers in Hawai'i shared many
experiences with those living in the continental United States, but there
were also many ways that daily life differed when it took place "in the
combat zone." Because Hawai'i existed as both home front and war front
during World War II, the duties and lives of women were intimately
linked to military security, organization, and vitality. Increased anxiety
surrounding family life and working mothers dovetailed with regimes of
governance under martial law, and activities in the home were subject to
military control in ways they were not in the continental United States.
The domestic sciences of home economics, mothering, and nutrition
contributed to a gendered and racialized biopolitical administration that
enlisted women as central to the social and biological reproduction of
healthy and patriotic citizens, laborers, and soldiers.

Wartime domestic projects in Hawai'i organized family life—as
well as Hawai'i's role in the so-called American family—during a period
when the political, military, and cultural incorporation of Hawai'i and

its diverse peoples into the US nation-state was strategically important to American foreign policy. These gendered and racialized projects negotiated Hawai'i's complicated role both as a US settler colony that was included in the US home front and as a vital military outpost of the war front that connected the United States to the rest of the Pacific Theater. As Amy Kaplan argues in her theorization of "manifest domesticity," imperial domestic projects naturalize US expansion by creating a "home" for the colonizer: colonial homemaking renders "prior inhabitants [as] alien and undomesticated" and implicitly "nativizes" the settler.[2] Under martial law in Hawai'i we can observe a logic of settler military domesticity, a particular iteration of patriotic femininity that fused the reproductive and affective labor of settler colonial homemaking with the production of US imperial war. The family, as a central unit of social reproduction, was thus a principal biopolitical site for the fortification and concealment of racialized, gendered, and colonial primitive accumulation.[3] Like the military government's immunization and blood banking programs, these domestic projects operated through a gendered regime of racial liberal biopower that purported to incorporate and "improve" families of all races, yet also constructed the "secure" American family home over and against Asian immigrant family practices that did not meet these standards, and masked the persistence of Native Hawaiian food cultures and land-based epistemologies of health.[4] Thus, settler military domesticity not only operated through the militarization of female-gendered patriotic duties to create hygienic homes, cook nutritious meals, and raise healthy children, but it also strengthened racialized categories such as "loyal citizen," "enemy alien," and "vanishing Native." Further, as domestic scientists institutionalized American standards for the most productive use of Hawaiian lands and natural resources, they naturalized US settler colonial logics of possession. Home economists' campaigns crafted recipes for nostalgic American dishes using Hawaiian-grown ingredients—for example, "mango brown betty" or "taro au gratin"—which masked the life-destroying context of US settler militarism and wartime emergency that had made ingredients common to American recipes unavailable. As part of the military government's administration of public health under martial law, these home economics efforts were central to social reproduction: not only did they contribute to the reproduction of future workers and solders, but they also domesticated the so-called foreign aspects of Hawaiian life, strengthened racial hierarchies, and rendered violent and extractive colonial and military projects palatable. This racial liberal biopolitical project performed a benevolence that articulated with liberal Lockean logics of improvement via its focus on family health and homemaking while reproducing and masking the racialized and gendered primitive accumulation of differentiated life, knowledge, affect, and labor—all in the service of settler militarism and wartime capitalism.

Thus, the gendered heterosexual norms of "domesticity," the "family," and the "home" strengthened racial liberal biopower and its social reproduction of US settler militarism. Furthermore, the labor required to reproduce settler military domesticity in Hawai'i was not only gendered but also racialized and classed. Dominant wartime home economics projects constructed a hierarchy of expertise in which professional domestic scientists, who were predominantly white settler women, built careers on the study of racialized and Indigenous family diets and habits while creating regimes of social regulation that targeted these same peoples. Furthermore, as middle-class women who held jobs and were sometimes unmarried, many transferred the affective and reproductive labor of their own household to immigrant and Indigenous domestic and service workers.[5] Thus, the wartime home economics project in Hawai'i not only contributed to the social reproduction of settler militarism in the service of capitalism, but it was also predicated on the racialized, gendered, and classed extraction of knowledge, affect, and labor from Indigenous and immigrant women and men.

"The First Line of Defense Is Our Home"

Women's experiences during World War II have been described as "simultaneously liberating and limiting": women entered the workforce in much greater numbers, yet women's war work was seen as an extension of domesticity rather than a replacement for it. Wartime culture and propaganda depicted war work as women's temporary patriotic duty, which was performed alongside the duties in the household. This elevated women's labor inside and outside the home without challenging American patriarchal values of family and domesticity.[6] Much as in the continental United States, during World War II in Hawai'i women entered the workforce in record numbers amid the greater demand for laborers, the rise in wages, and the expanding defense industry. Yet, unlike in the continent, there was a shortage of women in the territory because many were evacuated at the start of the war. As a result, the majority of labor needs were located in occupations typically held by women: laundry, domestic work, clerical work, teaching, nursing, and waitressing. In November 1942 the military government called for the registration of all women over age sixteen to determine the number of female civilians available for work, leading many women to enter the work-force for fear of being evacuated and separated from their families.[7] In 1943 O'ahu reached what was then an all-time peak of women's employment, with 43,000 women employed, and after the war in 1946 there were still 33,000 women employed.[8]

These wartime changes to the gendered division of labor led to social tensions in Hawai'i: as more women worked outside of the home, anxiety developed around family health and the necessity of proper child-rearing practices. In 1942 the Department of Public Instruction began to publish a periodical, *Bulletin to Parents*, which called attention to children's health and safety needs during wartime and encouraged parents to consider their protection as their first priority.[9] Regular issues gave tips to parents at their "Home Battle Stations," such as how to prepare healthy meals, save fuel and clothing, keep the house safe, contribute to home-front work, and ration frugally. As a 1943 issue stated, "Always, the first line of defense is our home. . . . Parents 'man' their battle stations in homes often under camouflage! Outwardly, family living is as much unchanged and as serenely quiet as it is possible under existing conditions. Parents spread a protective camouflage screen or net over the lives of their loved ones."[10] The militarized metaphor of the home as the "first line of defense"—common throughout the United States during World War II—proliferated under martial law in Hawai'i, which was itself literally a "first line of defense" for the United States. The newsletter's invocation of "camouflage" connotes the layer of protection that parents should provide for their children during wartime but also suggests the existence of unknown injuries that could be taking place in the home behind the "serenely quiet" exterior. Because Hawai'i was both "home front" and "war front," all children in the territory grew up within the violent context of total war and imminent danger. Just as the military government immediately expanded programs for public health after the bombing of Pearl Harbor, it also focused on family health and psychological well-being as vital to the reproduction of efficient, patriotic soldiers and defense workers. The focus of family campaigns such as *Bulletin for Parents* on cultivating settler childhood during wartime indicates an investment in the success of a settler military future. This vision enlisted mothers in the affective labor of nurturing children to feel at "home" within the context of military occupation.

Much as with the projects of eminent domain, immunization, and blood donation, liberal Lockean logics of improvement had long permeated the domestic sciences of nutrition and homemaking as a means to bolster capitalist expansion while obscuring its predatory repertoires of racialized, gendered, and colonial expropriation. Nils P. Larsen of Queen's Hospital, who would eventually be lauded as a "pioneer in plantation health," urged the Hawaiian Sugar Planters Association to focus on health conditions for laborers: "Scientists have demonstrated that it pays to improve the crops. . . . Let me show you that it also pays to improve human beings." He later added that "improving health will lower the cost of producing cane."[11] In his dehumanizing comparison of human beings to crops, Larsen revealed that his concern for public health was motivated by labor productivity and profit. Indeed, this focus on "improving" the nutrition of plantation laborers is an additional example of racial liberal biopolitics contributing to settler and capitalist regimes of primitive accumulation beneath a ruse of benevolence. Plantation labor does not "improve health"; it rapaciously consumes it.[12] In 1938 Larsen established the Central Nutrition Committee, which provided plantation health care for laborers and their families, and it would eventually join with the Office of Defense Health and Welfare in 1941 to focus specifically on wartime nutrition needs. Renamed the Territorial Nutrition Committee, this organization included health professionals and home economists such as Carey D. Miller, a professor of nutrition at the University of Hawai'i.[13]

Home economics and nutrition had been taught at the university level in the islands since 1908, when Agnes Hunt, one of the founders of the department, was appointed as the first domestic science teacher at the College of Hawaii. This program studied the home as an object of scientific knowledge through a focus on the topics of food, clothing, and shelter.[14] In 1922 the first bachelor's of science degree in home economics was awarded to Mary Ling Sang Li at the University of Hawai'i. Nutritionist Carey Miller, who began working at the University of Hawai'i in 1922, served as chair of the department for twenty-three years, including the duration of World War II. Miller taught college courses in food preparation, nutrition, and home management, and she conducted research at the Hawaii Agricultural Experiment Station.[15] Katherine Bazore joined the department in 1929 and taught courses on food, elementary nutrition, and home management. Bazore established the Home Management House in 1930, where juniors and seniors lived for four to five weeks in order to practice preparing household furnishings, equipment, and meals. She would also go on to publish multiple volumes on nutrition and food preparation in Hawai'i, some of which drew from the work conducted "from observation of, and participation in," learning activities with students in the Home Management House.[16] Food and nutrition courses in the Home Economics Department became especially popular during the war because of the onset of food rationing and the military government's pressures for families to stay healthy. The first master's degree in home economics was awarded in 1942 to Marjorie Abel, who also went on to conduct research on nutrition and homemaking in Hawai'i.[17]

In accordance with the military government's focus on health during World War II, nutrition became a primary concern for researchers of family health and home economics. Anxieties over food scarcity after the bombing of Pearl Harbor led residents to buy as much food as possible, and many grocery stores ran out of stock.[18] Much like the Board of Health and its mandatory immunization program, the Territorial Nutrition Committee explicitly linked the health of Hawai'i's citizens to wartime labor productivity: the committee's principal motivations were to keep workers from missing workdays because of illness and to keep production high on the plantations and in the defense industry.[19] At the start of the war, the committee concluded that the needs of Hawai'i were "unique" from those in the continental United States as a result of the conditions of martial law, the fact that the islands were accessible mainly by water transportation, Hawai'i's role as a military outpost in the Pacific, and the heterogeneous food habits of the various racial groups in the population.[20] When planning for how to mobilize this racially diverse community for better nutrition, the committee argued that "mothers, homemakers, and teachers represent the most important channels in the Community for reaching the largest group of persons in any program falling within the general field of nutrition."[21] This statement enlisted mothers, homemakers, and teachers in the feminized reproductive and affective labor of alleviating Hawai'i's "unique" wartime anxieties surrounding nutrition, racial difference, and military security.

Significantly, although the majority of women in Hawai'i were nonwhite, it was mostly white settler women who were designing and disseminating educational material on wartime nutrition. On December 15, 1941, a volunteer group of home economists began the Home Defense Committee, which focused on educating wives and mothers in Hawai'i on subjects such as nutrition and domestic science.[22] The committee, which included Carey Miller, Katherine Bazore, and Marjorie Abel of the university's Home Economics Department, also included members from the Territorial Nutrition Committee and the Bureau of Maternal and Child Health.[23] The committee claimed that much of the material being broadcast about wartime home-front conditions and rationing in the continental United States did not apply to Hawai'i's landscape and natural resources.[24] The Office of the Military Governor praised the Home Defense Committee for its "very substantial contribution to the war effort," and the *Honolulu Star-Bulletin* called it a "bulwark of home defense, [which] has had much to do with maintaining high morale in the homes of Hawaii." The newspaper's editor praised it as the top civic community project in wartime Honolulu.[25] This committee undertook many campaigns for nutrition, budgeting, and home defense, including a weekly homemaker's radio program, a newspaper series, and home economics demonstrations. At the request of the Territorial Nutrition Committee, a member of the Home Defense Committee served as a consumers' representative for the Food Control Office. This presented the woman and family as central units of capitalist consumption in the wartime market: the objective was for the housewife to assist in food-price control so that she could provide healthy and balanced meals for her family without overspending.[26]

As early as December 18, 1941, the committee began a daily series in the *Honolulu Star-Bulletin* called "Hints for Homemakers." Mostly focusing on nutrition, cooking, and budgeting, this series ran continuously until June 30, 1943, when it was discontinued because of a newsprint shortage. Many of these articles offered recipes using fruits and vegetables that were currently in surplus or provided substitutions for ingredients that were unavailable.[27] One of them included the "Food and Nutrition Code for Women of Hawaii," which was inspired by the US Department of Agriculture's "Consumer Pledge," a document that was first signed by Eleanor Roosevelt:

1. I will inform myself about the nutritive values of food.
2. I will KEEP WELL with the help of a properly selected diet. (Eaten regularly in a calm atmosphere.)
3. I will provide my family with an adequate diet.
4. I will grow some food however little, selecting fruits and vegetables of high nutritive value.
5. I will use local foods whenever possible.
6. I will cooperate with the local food administrators and will buy only enough for present needs when certain foods are limited.
7. I will not complain of food shortages, but will learn to make proper substitutes.
8. I will cooperate in any community program that aims to provide a good diet for all.
9. I will remember that food may win the war and that peace may be permanent only if there are no hungry children in the world.
10. I will remember that my part in the home may be just as great a factor in helping to win the war as building a bomber.[28]

This pledge, which was translated into Japanese the following month, encapsulates many of the tenets of settler military domesticity: to learn about and provide one's family with a nutritious diet; to ration, grow, and make use of local foods; and to contribute to the war effort in any way possible, without complaint.[29] The Home Defense Committee also gave demonstrations for working women on the changes that came to homemaking under blackout conditions and food demonstrations for mothers of schoolchildren.[30] The committee performed about sixty nutrition lectures and demonstrations for parents and kindergarten students per year, with the support from the Free Kindergarten and Children's Aid Association.[31] A specific focus of these demonstrations was to promote the benefits of "unfamiliar foods which have become common on account of the war," such as locally grown fruits: papayas, pineapples, figs, mangoes, and guavas. They also discussed topics such as maternal and child health, the homemaker as hostess, how to prepare holiday meals, and work with clothing and textiles.[32] Honolulu radio stations KGMB and KGU continued the Home Defense Committee's radio program, "Homemaker's Aid," throughout the duration of the war and gave the committee airtime free of charge, stating that the program was a service to "women in the homes."[33] Copies of these talks were also sent to the neighbor islands to be broadcast on their local stations. Press Relations at the Office of Civilian Defense approved all of the committee's radio programs and newspaper articles before they were released.[34]

The racial liberal biopolitics of the home became a tool for the social reproduction of US settler militarism under martial law: homemaking practices and nutritional science served as a gendered and racialized means to "improve" the population and its labor force, and thus became integrally related to military security and wartime capitalist production in Hawai'i. Volunteer groups such as the Territorial Nutrition Committee and the Home Defense Committee allowed territorial and military institutions such as the Board of Health, the Food Control Office, and the Office of Civilian Defense to play an increased role in regulating nutrition, homemaking, and mothering practices for these express purposes. Home economics and nutrition were settler scientific knowledges established in Hawai'i during the prewar period that, through the circulation of "home defense" radio broadcasts, news media, and home demonstrations, regulated the population during the World War II period.

"Good Americans Eat Good Food"

During World War II, institutions such as the Home Defense Committee and the Territorial Nutrition Committee used state and military funds to expand their reach into civilian life. These institutions constructed wartime nutrition as one domain through which to study, discipline, and Americanize multiracial subjects, such as Asian settlers and Native Hawaiians. American domestic scientists conducted research on the vitamin content of fruits, vegetables, and other ingredients commonly found in Hawaiian and Asian immigrant family cuisine. In this way, the professionalization of these mostly white settler women home economists was predicated on the primitive accumulation of Native and immigrant land and food-based knowledges. This extractive dynamic manufactured a false hierarchy of expertise between domestic scientists and nonwhite families: the biopolitical project of wartime nutrition and eating encompassed a racialized and gendered repertoire of cultural customs, patriotic performance, and biological health through which settler militarism domesticated both that which was eaten and those who were eating.[35] Wartime home economics and nutrition campaigns normalized American family and health practices and marginalized Asian settler diets that did not meet these standards, excluding them as "un-American," unhealthy, or impractical during wartime. Furthermore, these projects denied the persistence of Native Hawaiian food cultures and the settler colonial histories that had had devastating effects upon their health and modes of subsistence while contributing to the productivity of the wartime capitalist economy. In this way, just as Larsen's call to "improve human beings" on the plantation belied a drive toward capitalist expropriation, wartime home economics and nutrition projects wielded logics of improvement to rationalize racialized and gendered differentiation and devalue Indigenous modes of relation for the purposes of primitive accumulation.

During the prewar period, it was still the common assumption among white settlers that Hawaiian-grown fruits and vegetables were deficient in vitamins and minerals, particularly iron and calcium.[36] Because of this, many white families relied upon imported or canned produce from the continental United States to satisfy their vitamin quotients. Early on in her career in the Home Economics Department at the University of Hawai'i, Carey Miller noticed that American studies of food had focused only upon white diets and that this scholarship came solely from the continental United States. Arguing that this work ignored the diets of Asian and Pacific peoples, she devoted the majority of her research to the study of foods and diets in Hawai'i.

Nutritional research during this period largely involved testing nutritional values in rats, and through this method she soon determined the high vitamin c content of papayas. Seeing it as an issue of family health, Miller became determined to spread knowledge of the papaya's nutritional value to the larger population by speaking at extension clubs, parent-teacher associations, and the YWCA, and by publishing scholarly and news articles. Meanwhile, she continued to conduct research on the vitamin content of other local fruits and vegetables.[37]

Miller soon became known for her research on the "diets of Polynesians and Asians," and this was the beginning of a long career that Miller built upon the extraction of knowledge from racialized and Indigenous peoples in the name of public health.[38] Miller wrote that she was intrigued by "the stature and fine teeth of some of the Hawaiians," and she decided that the "foods of the ancient Hawaiians seemed worthy of study." She later observed "some very fine physical speimens [sic] of Hawaiian or part-Hawaiian men."[39] Although Miller pushed against contemporary racializations of Hawaiian families as unhealthy and was open to the possibility that local foods were nutritious in spite of their difference from those in the American diet, it is also clear that her academic and social work on nutrition in Hawai'i was motivated by the problematic notion that Native people, their health, and their nutritional habits were objects of study for white researchers.[40] Throughout her work, Miller mainly referred to Native Hawaiians as "the ancient Hawaiians," thus contributing to colonial tropes of the "vanishing Native," ignoring the persistent existence of Native Hawaiian communities, and devaluing Indigenous relations to land. Moreover, as discussed in chapter 2, this characterization of present-day Hawaiians as "Hawaiian or part-Hawaiian men" resonates with colonial discourses of the period, in which blood quantum created a "eugenic pedagogy" that questioned Native sovereignty and enabled the dispossession of "Part-Hawaiians."[41] This all indicates that she was not primarily invested in Hawaiians' contemporary health and nutritional practices but, rather, conducted her research on racialized and colonial "others" for the purpose of improving the health of the settler population, particularly recent white settlers who were unfamiliar with local foods. This is one example of how nutritional science extracted knowledge from Indigenous communities for settler social reproduction.

Yet after deciding that the Native Hawaiian diet had already been sufficiently studied, Miller devoted the majority of her scholarly work to what she considered the understudied topics of "Oriental" nutrition and tropically grown fruits. Miller and her colleagues in the Home Economics Department and the Agricultural Experiment Station at the University of Hawai'i conducted numerous studies on the nutrition of Asian settlers living in the territory.[42] Thus, Miller likewise considered the nutrition of "Oriental" groups as worthy of study and evaluation by white scientists. In 1933 Miller published *Japanese Foods Commonly Used in Hawaii*, which provided practical and scientific information on elements of the diets of Japanese settlers in the islands. It was written for researchers and dieticians, as well as for "the younger Japanese as a source of information concerning the preparation and relative dietary importance of their racial foods."[43] This publication analyzed the vitamin content and preparation of soy-based foods, such as edamame, soymilk, tofu ("a white cheeselike product manufactured from soy beans"), miso ("a better source of iron per unit of weight than are many green vegetables"), and shoyu ("It has a pleasant aromatic odor, and a peculiar taste"). Miller also discussed foods such as nori, udon, sesame seeds ("amounts of calcium, phosphorus, and iron [are] very high compared with other foods"), and dried bonito ("The flavor imparted by bonito to the various food mixtures is especially liked by the Japanese").[44] The last section of the article included "typical" Japanese recipes, as well as a recommended recipe for miso soup made with milk. A second volume by Miller, *Foods Used by Filipinos in Hawaii*, compared the diets of Filipinos in the Philippines and in Hawai'i, finding that those in Hawai'i consumed 500–700 more calories per day, ate more milk products, and consumed less fruits and vegetables. Although Filipinos in Hawai'i consumed more milk, the study concluded that those in the Philippines were healthier because of the higher proportion of fruits and vegetables in their diet.[45] Despite these differences, the study noted that there was an "urgent need for nutrition and health education of this racial group." Suggestions for improving their diet included the replacement of white rice with brown rice and the increased use of sweet potatoes, taro, papaya, milk, legumes, and eggs.[46]

Miller's research not only exemplifies the primitive accumulation of food- and land-based knowledge for the production of cultural and economic capital, but it also illustrates how racial liberal biopower accommodated the racial difference of immigrant and Native families by making them "knowable" through American scientific calculations of nutrition and health. This project included eating practices deemed "healthy" in the wartime repertoire of family nutrition while excluding those deemed "unhealthy" as "un-American." Further, those practices that racial liberal biopower absorbed into its administration of health came to delimit the range of acceptable domestic behavior on the part of "patriotic" nonwhite families. Just as Miller and her colleagues hoped that "the younger Japanese" would read the nutritional study (and perhaps share its findings with their families), the Territorial Nutrition Committee stressed the importance of making nutrition suggestions accessible to audiences of all races. The committee created a series of "Build Health" posters that pictured multiracial men, women, and children smiling, working, saluting, and eating healthily. A list of "Foods That We Need Each Day" was a common refrain on daily nutrition needs that was not only published in the Honolulu Star-Bulletin but was also translated into Japanese and published in Japanese language newspapers.[47] The committee conducted a study on "special problems of low income groups," which stated that "Oriental" groups were having a difficult time adapting to wartime conditions because the territory could no longer import food from Asian countries.[48] The committee also expressed that Asian immigrant groups were not getting enough whole grains because their diets typically included white rice, not brown. This was a common theme during this period: between 1938 and 1950, there were at least three nutritional studies of white rice conducted at the University of Hawai'i.[49] Miller argued that "the consumption of white rice should be decreased," and she concluded that white rice's role as the main grain in Japanese immigrant diets had led to deficiencies in calcium, vitamin A, and vitamin B. This was even emphasized in schools as part of a wartime propaganda campaign in which public school students painted posters, one of which claimed that "Good Americans" eat brown rice and other "good foods" (figure 3.1).[50]

Like the Territorial Nutrition Committee, the Home Defense Committee aimed to reach all racial groups in Hawai'i. Staff members of the Tuberculosis Association translated materials prepared by the Home Defense Committee into Japanese and Tagalog in order to be printed in Japanese newspapers and aired on the Filipino radio hour.[51] Jean Shimamura, the only Japanese member of the Home Defense Committee, wrote one article per week for Japanese newspapers in Hawai'i.[52] The majority of articles that were translated into Japanese were not the same as those published in English because they were "adapted . . . when necessary": for example, many focused on the use of brown instead of white rice or the increased use of milk in cooking, and others aimed to share popular American recipes for Japanese settler families to try. Radio talks that were translated into Tagalog were written specifically for Filipino audiences as well, such as "Vegetables in the Filipino Diet."[53] A radio talk written by Marian Weaver of the Home Defense Committee and translated into Tagalog was titled "Milk Each Day." The broadcast advised that "unless we include milk in our diets we are apt to have a lack of this mineral. But you say, I never use milk and I am strong. But maybe

FIGURE 3.1 · "Good Americans Eat Good Food." Source: Children's posters, undated, Oversized Materials, HWRD.

you are small. People from the Far East are smaller than their children born and raised here in the United States. Diet may have something to do with this fact."[54] The promotion of milk consumption in Hawai'i dates back to early twentieth-century settler colonial projects of cultural assimilation.[55] Wartime home economics projects continued to universalize Western ideals of biological health and personhood—such as the notion that a larger body is a sign of health, productivity, and modernity—over and against those it associated with the "Far East." Yet as Miller's own research illustrated above, "larger" bodies could be the result of diets with more calories from sugar and fat rather than from fruits and vegetables.[56]

Thus, these nutrition campaigns are examples of racial liberal biopower at work in the gendered domain of family health: nutritional research, news

84

articles, and radio broadcasts included all racial groups in their administration of health by disseminating material in languages other than English, but this also became a way to target and regulate the diets of nonwhite families. Further, these nutritional studies, including their conclusions and recommendations for the "improvement" of health, demonstrate a manufactured hierarchy of expertise in which Miller and others built professional standing by accumulating knowledge from the study of racialized settler and Indigenous families. Domestic scientists such as Miller wielded the cultural capital forged by their careers to create racial hierarchies of health that aligned with the colonial asymmetries of settler militarism by marginalizing immigrant diets and denying the persistence of Kanaka Maoli foodways. Again, racial liberal biopolitical logics of improvement contributed to the social reproduction of settler militarism and capitalism: this ostensibly life-cultivating project fostered family health and nutrition, but for the purpose of accelerating the expropriation of wartime life and labor.

Despite the wartime pressures to foster family health according to the racialized and colonial standards of the military government, immigrant and Native families negotiated and resisted these assimilationist regimes, often exhibiting their distaste or neglecting to adhere to them. For example, as Charlotte Wakugawa, a Nisei, recalled of her family nutritional practices, "Instead of milk, tofu was considered the most important food in the diet."[57] Eleanor Maeda, a Sansei, recalled that she was never served milk at home as a child because to her grandmother, "Drinking milk and having food supplements were considered unnecessary and too 'haolified.'" Despite these differences among Asian settler family nutritional practices, it was quite common for children to receive milk as part of a morning snack or lunch at school. As Setsuko Matsubara remembers, "I do remember that in kindergarten we were required to drink milk and I can still see myself holding my nose and gulping down the milk with bites of graham crackers in between." Pauline Apuna, who was Chinese-Hawaiian, remembered that "since my father had little education he regarded milk as an added expense, so I did not have it until I had an allowance with which I could buy milk [I was about 12 years old then]."[58] This memory of saving her allowance to buy milk indicates both her father's ambivalence toward milk and also her desire to abide by nutritional guidelines.

The fact that radio talks and newspaper articles that were translated into Japanese or Tagalog included modified content for their target audience suggests that the Home Defense Committee did not consider the materials written in English to be as appropriate for Japanese and Filipino settler audiences; they were for "mainstream" white settler audiences. Many of these broadcasts included utopian imagery of settler military domesticity or used food as a palatable metaphor to portray or erase violent colonial histories. The majority of the English-language campaigns undertaken by the Home Defense Committee sought to replicate US continental lifestyles, routines, and recipes with the resources available in the islands, or included tips for food storage, proper cooking of vegetables, and emergency food preparation.[59] For example, a radio broadcast about Thanksgiving recommended a variety of recipes for turkey, stuffing, vegetables, and casseroles, with a section on how to use leftovers. At one point the narrator exclaimed, "It's the celebration of a land of plenty—plenty of space, plenty of food and plenty of family."[60] This statement employs a continental settler colonial domestic trope—Thanksgiving—to erase Hawai'i's violent settler colonial history. Katherine Bazore's broadcast, titled "Hawaii's Soups and Stews," began with this statement: "If an ancient Hawaiian should hear this title announced, he might turn over in his cave and wonder just what I was talking about. . . . However, the Hawaiians soon learned from travelers who touched his shores and beef stew is now one of his favorite dishes . . . perhaps the Hawaiian man, who was the cook of the family in those days, may have eaten it on a British ship and decided to try out a stew at home. . . ."[61] Significantly, most of Bazore's invocations of "Hawaiians" in this broadcast occur in past tense, thus writing Native Hawaiians and their eating practices out of current existence in favor of those practices learned "on a British ship." Much as in the Thanksgiving narrative above, this friendly domestic scene of Hawaiians eating stew with missionaries masks the violence of this colonial encounter and the history of environmental destruction, land dispossession, and military aggression that followed it. Bazore's broadcast is indicative of how racial liberal biopower naturalized its incorporation and differentiation of Native and immigrant nutritional practices through a gendered narrative of cultural hybridity and progress, rather than one structured by the asymmetries of colonial and racial violence. Much as this domestic trope rendered colonial narratives more palatable, so too did the wartime focus on nutrition and family health portray settler militarism and capitalism as benignly "improving" life in Hawai'i rather than depleting it via predatory regimes of knowledge and labor extraction.

Furthermore, Native Hawaiians had health and food practices that had been in use for centuries. 'Iwalani R. N. Else writes that "the traditional Native Hawaiian diet of the maka'āinana [commoners] was comprised of poi, taro, coconuts, sweet potatoes, yams, breadfruit, bananas, mountain apples, seaweed and seafood, and occasionally, chickens and pigs. This diet was high in fiber and starch but low in saturated fat and sugar."[62] Many of these eating practices continued and were passed down through families. For example, as Elizabeth Ellis, a teacher born in Hamakua, Hawai'i, recalls of the prewar period, "Everything that we ate came from the land. He [Grandfather] grew our taro, potatoes, bananas, passion fruit, yams, peaches, pineapple, everything came from the land. But my mother sent things for us that came from the store. . . . Some butter, the salt, those things came from the plantation. . . . But we ate from the land."[63] Richard Kekuni Blaisdell's work connects the revitalization of Hawaiians' health to the restoration of their lands and culture, arguing that American changes to Hawaiians' diets, such as the replacement of taro with potato or rice, have had adverse effects upon health and nutrition, such as increased sugar and fat intake.[64] Further, as discussed in chapters 1 and 2, the sugar and pineapple industries' vast acquisition of Hawaiian land and monopolization of water restricted Kanaka Maoli access to noncommercial planting and subsistence living. This process accelerated with the US military's unprecedented acquisition of land via eminent domain and leasing during the World War II period, which also included the increased condemnation of coastal land and water used by many konohiki fisheries in order to expand military bases such as Pearl Harbor.[65] Thus, economic and racial inequality in Hawai'i, along with the history of US settler colonialism, perpetuated a hierarchy of access to land and natural resources that disproportionately affected Hawaiians and disrupted healthy dietary practices.[66] It is ironic that white settlers began to recommend the use of local fruits and vegetables during the war, when it was US settler colonialism that had restricted Native Hawaiians' access to these same foods. It was contact with settlers, their acquisition of land, and the breakdown of the ahupua'a system that led to the decline in Native Hawaiians' health.[67] Research on "healthy" diets and the wartime pressure for all residents to conform to these specifications was simply another aspect of this forced assimilation, which obfuscated a violent history that had ruptured Hawaiian reciprocal relations to land.

At the same time, settler military desires for totality are always incomplete and formed in dynamic tension with Indigenous resurgence and vitality. Kanaka Maoli foodways, farming, fishing, land-based cultural revitalization, and political activism have always persisted and continue today in the islands. For example, the restoration of kalo (taro) farming and poi production in He'e'ia Uli has been a source of ancestral and community pride and revitalization for Kanaka Maoli in the He'e'ia community. Contemporary anti-GMO activism on Moloka'i illustrates the shared political stakes of

Hawaiian movements for land, sovereignty, environmental sustainability, and decolonized food production.[68] In Haleleʻa, Kauaʻi, hukilau (surround-net fishing) and the communal sharing of large catches have continued as a source of subsistence, which Mehana Vaughan and Adam Ayers argue is in large part a result of the persistence of generational ecological knowledge, hōʻihi (respectful reciprocity), and social and cultural ties across the community.[69] The Hāʻena Community–Based Subsistence Fishing Area on Kauaʻi and the Kaʻūpūlehu Fish Replenishment Area on the island of Hawaiʻi are current examples of conservation and sustainability efforts that employ the ahupuaʻa system in a contemporary context to revitalize landscapes decimated by settler colonial expropriation.[70] Kanaka Maoli epistemologies and land-based food practices such as these and others have always sought alternatives to settler militarism, pushed against its prescribed limits, and refused to be interpellated into its projects, thus disrupting the social reproduction of settler militarism, its logics, and its occupation.

The assimilationist project of the Home Defense Committee and the Territorial Nutrition Committee to reach "all racial groups" in Hawaiʻi for the purposes of wartime health and security produced a racialized and gendered biopolitical regime of inclusion, marginalization, and erasure that enlisted wives and mothers in a campaign for military security. Just as Larsen argued that "improving health will lower the cost of producing cane," these wartime nutrition campaigns propagated the ruse that settler militarism and capitalism were invested in the production of life instead of aiding the primitive accumulation of land and labor.[71] The recipes and health recommendations disseminated by these committees—which were predicated on the extraction of food and land-based knowledge from Asian settler and Kanaka Maoli families—claimed to improve the health of people of all races, yet they also centralized settler military domesticity as the dominant model for assimilation, intensified the regulation of immigrant and Native diets, denied the vitality of Hawaiian foodways, and masked settler colonial histories of Native land dispossession.

Domesticating the Foreign: American Foods for the Wartime Hostess

As immigrant and Native diets were becoming the subject of greater scrutiny, wartime rationing policies and food scarcity also led to a shortage of ingredients that were essential to American food and nutrition practices. This included many foods that had been previously imported from the continental United States, such as oranges, apples, oil, sugar, butter, eggs, and milk. Military interests in promoting wartime health and rationing thus led to the increased demand for research on the vitamin content of locally grown fruits and vegetables, to which, significantly, settler projects had already restricted production and access.[72] This wartime rationing and research on foods grown in Hawai'i is an example of US settler militarism seeking to mitigate its internally produced scarcity by extracting natural resources from US colonial territories. Accordingly, much like the "Food and Nutrition Code for Women of Hawaii," this project prescribed criteria for the reproductive labor of settler military domesticity: including feeding one's family nutritious foods, learning about local produce, obeying rationing instructions, and raising healthy, patriotic children. For example, the Territorial Nutrition Committee and the Home Defense Committee encouraged wives and mothers to cook American-style dishes that abided by wartime rationing regulations because of their use of supposed foreign or unusual local produce and ingredients, resulting in recipes such as "taro hashbrowns" with "guava catsup." Further, wartime cookbooks encouraged settler wives to host gatherings that made light of carceral martial law conditions or that aestheticized and performed racial and colonial differentiation in palatable ways. In this way, affective and reproductive domestic projects sought to reconcile and obscure the contradictions of US settler militarism while also recapitulating their racialized, gendered, and colonial conditions of emergence.

Accordingly, Miller and Bazore's *Fruits of Hawaii: Description, Nutritive Value, and Use* became their most widely read publication, which continued to be updated and republished throughout the twentieth century, most recently in 2002. During the war it was even distributed to nutritionists across the United States and to the US Department of Agriculture.[73] This volume included the history and nutritional content of various fruits found in the islands, as well as suggested recipes that were tested by the Home Economics Department at the University of Hawai'i. Similarly, *Ways to Use Vegetables in Hawaii*, by Miller, Helen Yonge Lind, and Mary Bartow, described vegetables in Hawai'i. Particular attention was paid to the many uses of the taro plant: "Taro and the poi made from it were the staff of life of the ancient Hawaiian people. . . . The ancient Hawaiians ate most of their taro in the form of poi."[74] Aligning with the nutritional studies discussed previously, this study concluded that the diets of all racial groups in Hawai'i would be improved if they included more taro and less white rice. Again, the "ancient Hawaiian" was held up as a standard of health, yet not considered a modern subject.

Miller and Bazore's research, along with newspaper articles, advertisements, and radio broadcasts during this period, promoted and described the health benefits of these locally grown fruits and vegetables.[75]

Additionally, the US military government encouraged families to grow their own fruit trees and start victory gardens. For example, Annie Chun remembers that "due to the lack of yard space we did not have a garden except during the war years, because it was necessary then. During that time we grew cabbage, soybeans, string beans and lettuce."[76] The Home Defense Committee and the Territorial Nutrition Committee also participated in a guava-preserving program, sponsored by the Office of Civilian Defense. As Miller wrote, "Our laboratory has shown that 'guava juice' . . . has twice as much vitamin C as orange juice. No one knows if we shall continue to have orange juice, so we are urging everyone to utilize the guavas for juice and juicy pulp for drinks, and for jams, marmalades and jellies."[77] Thus, guava juice was the answer to the US war-produced scarcity of orange juice, and these committees promoted the use of guavas in the diet by calling vitamin C the "War Vitamin." Much as with the mandatory immunization program, this editorial likened the vitamin to a "line of defense" against disease and infection.[78] Similar campaigns took place for island cabbage and Maui onions in 1943, the surplus production of which coincided with unexpectedly large importations of cabbage and onions from the continental United States. Homemakers shared their favorite onion recipes in the newspapers, such as onion soup, creamed onions, and salmon onion casserole.[79]

Thus, as mentioned above, the Home Defense Committee sought to promote the benefits of "unfamiliar foods which have become common on account of the war," such as papayas, pineapples, figs, mangoes, and guavas.[80] Many of these campaigns attempted to invent new versions of classic American recipes with the use of Hawaiian-grown fruits and vegetables, which were less expensive and, as Miller's research showed, often more nutritious than imported and canned varieties. As one of the Home Defense Committee's radio broadcasts stated, "We fuss because we find it hard to get oranges, but the lowly papaya is a better source of vitamin C." In another, two housewives told listeners how they discovered a method to extract oil and syrup from coconuts, and recommended coconut oil for use in American baked goods such as brownies, waffles, and cookies. The Home Defense Committee's recipes suggested adding tropical fruits like papaya or pineapple to American comfort foods such as bread pudding or Kraft minute tapioca pudding. Another suggested making a "milk drink" with banana, guava pulp, poi, or papaya pulp. They also recommended recipes for pineapple or papaya upside-down cake, a guava or mango brown betty, and papaya catsup. Suggested recipes using taro included taro au gratin, taro fritters, cream of luau (taro leaves) soup, and chocolate poi ice cream.[81] As Hiʻilei Julia Kawehipuaakahaopulani Hobart has illuminated in her work on the thermal technologies of ice and cooling, settlers in Hawaiʻi have historically deployed technologies of "comfort" to bolster colonial notions of modernity that normalize settler ways of living and devalue Kanaka Maoli foodways and modes of relation.[82] Similarly, as wartime home economists doctored nostalgic American recipes to include Hawaiian-grown ingredients, they sought to designate the "healthiest" and "most practical" way to use Hawaiian-grown fruits and vegetables while manufacturing artificial hierarchies of expertise that created nutritional standards for the assimilation of racialized and Indigenous families. Recipes that substituted these so-called unfamiliar foods masked the contradiction of promoting Americanized nutrition as the modern route to health when it was US military expansion and war that had rendered American foods unavailable. Further, these recipes that resembled American comfort foods manufactured an affective connection between settlers and Hawaiʻi's natural resources, thus strengthening US logics of possession that justified the unlawful use of Hawaiian lands for settler and military purposes. Moreover, it is ironic that settlers were so enthusiastic about the health benefits of locally grown fruits and vegetables, and even encouraged residents to grow them in victory gardens, when it was settler governance, land acquisition, and industrialization that had historically restricted the cultivation of crops such as taro—and would continue to during wartime and beyond.

And of course, for many civilians who were not white settlers, locally grown fruits and vegetables were by no means "unfamiliar." As discussed above, Native Hawaiian communities had long grown, prepared, and eaten these foods—and these practices continue today. Furthermore, Asian settler families had also subsisted on these foods for generations. Chiko Abe, who grew up in a plantation community during the interwar period, writes that "living in the country fruit like mountain apple, thimble berry, passion fruit, and guava were all common . . . I also learned to like poi, breadfruit, luau leaves, etc." Clara Arakaki similarly remembers that "living in the country with much land area around us, we had quite a source of fresh wild fruits such as guavas, mangos, wild plums, and cultivated fruits and vegetables such as papaya, bananas, oranges, asparagus, spinach, carrots, lettuce, potatoes, etc." Ruth Okahara recalled that poi was one of the first foods she ate as a baby.[83] Thus, although the US military government and local newspapers hailed these wartime nutritional campaigns and recipes as a "bulwark of home defense," the usefulness of and compliance with these campaigns may have varied on the ground, particularly among Asian settler and Native Hawaiian communities.[84] This demonstrates how the palatable performance and circulated imagery of white settler women teaching settler women of color and Native women to use local fruits and vegetables served mostly to enhance the image of the US military as that which "protected" and "improved" — rather than destroyed — life, land, and natural resources.

Sometimes the Home Defense Committee invoked the cuisines of nonwhite peoples as a way to introduce something new and adventurous into the family diet. As a recipe on a KGMB broadcast by Bazore suggested, "With the desirability of extending the meat flavor these days, there are numerous possibilities to try out if we would become cosmopolitan in our tastes and try some of the favorite dishes of our neighbors. . . . Why not get a few ideas from other nationality groups and try out some of their dishes? Variety is the spice of life even in soups and stews."[85] The audience of this radio program is again assumed to be white homemakers: Bazore's references to "our neighbors" and "other nationality groups" centralize the American diet as the dominant model, to which the cuisines of other cultures could be added for "variety" and "spice."[86] Recipes such as these that were "cosmopolitan," yet still Americanized, became popular leading up to the war and expanded to the continental United States during World War II and the postwar period as Hawaiian, Pacific, and Asian cuisines became fashionable elements of military nostalgia.

In Hawai'i the proliferation of cookbooks written for the "wartime hostess" even developed into a cultural genre of its own: in addition to using local fruits and vegetables to make classic American recipes, these cookbooks directed the wartime hostess to hold themed dinner parties that celebrated wartime and martial law conditions. For example, *Hawaiian Hospitality*, a pineapple-shaped cookbook that featured a cover design by the Dole Pineapple Company, provided numerous Hawaiian-style drink recipes "in the hope that it will stimulate Island good-fellowship among all the people, in uniform and out, and add to the pleasure of a tour in this Territory." Another cookbook suggested recipes for a "blackout party," including cocktails that could be made from a week's ration of alcohol under martial law, such as the "7:14'er," which was named for the minute right before lights went out. Yet another, *Cooking for a Crowd*, was written for wartime homemakers who suddenly found themselves hosting large numbers of male defense workers: most of the recipes were designed to serve at least fifty people.[87] By bringing settler militarism into the domestic sphere, each of these texts featured homemaking strategies that made the violent context of martial law in Hawai'i seem enjoyable: tropical drinks made a "tour" in Hawai'i sound more like a tropical vacation, "blackout parties" celebrated military curfews and rationing regulations, and *Cooking for a Crowd* instructed women to provide domestic comfort for war workers who were living far from home.

One cookbook, *Hawaiian and Pacific Foods: A Cook Book of Culinary Customs and Recipes Adapted for the American Hostess,* by Bazore, illustrates yet another facet of settler military domesticity. This guide's explanation of how to replicate "Hawaiian and Pacific" recipes invites the white homemaker to take part in the settler colonial project while it otherizes Asian immigrant cultures as quaint objects of consumption and misconstrues Native Hawaiian culture through tourist tropes. The volume has one chapter on each racial group in Hawai'i and its "typical" cuisine, with a list of common dishes served. It begins with a settler colonial narrative of Hawai'i's transition from monarchy to democracy under the tutelage of the United States, in which Native Hawaiians stopped working on the plantations because they found it "boring," and the United States annexed Hawai'i "at the request of the residents themselves." The passage goes on to describe how in the contemporary 1940s, Hawai'i was a principal example of "the workings of the 'melting pot' of the United States."[88] Much of the section on "Hawaiian Foods and Food Customs" is written in past tense, thus relegating Hawaiians to a no-longer-existing "history," but every other section—on Samoan, Chinese, Japanese, Korean, Portuguese, and Filipino foods—is written in present tense to describe present-day peoples.[89]

Significantly, the "research" for Bazore's book drew from her observations of her own nonwhite students—here coded as un-American—while they were enrolled in the Home Economics program at the University of Hawai'i.[90] Bazore writes that the material for this book "was obtained from observation of, and participation in, meals and customs followed by my students when they were living in the Home Management House at the University." She elaborates that "interviews with the older residents of Hawaii who had come from various parts of the Pacific area were perhaps the most important source of information on the foods, menus, and social customs in their homeland. In most cases, these interviews were conducted by my students who could converse freely with non-English speaking people."[91] Thus, the labor of data collection was carried out by the same students whom she observed in the Home Management House. Again, this and other home economics publications constructed a hierarchy of expertise that centralized white settler women professionals as the "experts" on "Hawaiian and Pacific" cuisine—even as their expertise was built upon the extractive observation and labor of immigrant and Indigenous students of color.

Moreover, volumes such as this produced dominant notions of proper racial liberal femininity, coded here as white, while trivializing nonwhite food cultures as objects of curiosity and consumption. Accordingly, there is no "Caucasian Foods and Food Customs" section but rather a section called "Haole Hospitality" that includes modified, Americanized menus drawn from each of the previous sections. These menus that selectively incorporated foods from racialized cultures are emblematic of how settler military domesticity accommodated racial difference to naturalize US logics of possession and make settlers feel at "home" in Hawai'i. Bazore claims that "a food experimentalist welcomes foods that are different—but not too different; strange—but not too strange. It is a wise hostess who leads guests slowly from the known to the unknown in foods and flavors." She specifies that her menus include "foreign or unusual combinations" but that the actual foods themselves are fundamentally "well known, tried and true—the kind of foods the traditionalist wants." To encourage the hostess to adjust recipes according to her guests' needs and tastes, the book includes a "Substitutes Which May Be Used in the Recipes" section with suggestions for American ingredients that can be included in place of Asian or Pacific foods, such as the use of bananas instead of poi or taro root, or the use of salami instead of lap cheong.[92] This combination of "known" and "unknown" ingredients resonates with the settler military discourse of the recipes above: by converting "foreign" ingredients into "traditional" foods, the haole hostess "domesticates the foreign" while abiding by wartime rationing guidelines and masking the violence and destruction of US settler militarism and war.

Furthermore, this cookbook implies that these new dishes will also be part of a festive, culturally themed dinner party: in its suggestions for decorating and serving each of these menus, *Hawaiian and Pacific Foods* encourages the hostess and her guests to "play" members of each racial group—such as Hawaiian, Portuguese, Japanese, Chinese, or Korean. As the hostess was instructed to cook Americanized versions of various Asian, Pacific, or Hawaiian meals, she was also to provide the proper decorations and dress so that guests felt they were participating in a new and adventurous culture. For example, suggestions for a Hawaiian meal included tips for decorating the dining table, and those for the Japanese meal recommended costume and decorum:

Suggest Waikiki beach by using a mirror plateau on which you put white sand, crêpe paper palm trees, brown skinned dolls, miniature out-rigger canoes, surf boards. . . .

In true Japanese style, stiffly starched blue and white kimonos and straw sandals should be worn by all the guests. As hostess, you provide them, asking the guests to take off their shoes before entering the dining room.[93]

We can understand these hostess instructions as racial scripts that used domestic scenes to erase the politics of violence embedded in racialized and colonial encounters.[94] Within the context of wartime Hawai'i, these role-playing dinner parties served to alleviate anxieties produced by US settler militarism within the privacy of the domestic sphere. By eating dinner around a display of "brown skinned dolls, miniature out-rigger canoes, [and] surf boards," settler women masked the violence of Indigenous displacement and land dispossession, and acted out an uncontested fantasy of what they wanted "Hawaiian culture" to be. By politely taking off their shoes and eating Americanized versions of sukiyaki or miso soup, both host and guest shifted focus away from wartime racializations of Japanese military aggression and redefined "Japanese culture" as a nonthreatening object of amusement and consumption. Instructing American women to play with these racial identities within the confines of their homes, this handbook encouraged white settlers to naturalize themselves as "native" over and against Kanaka Maoli—here figured morbidly as "brown skinned dolls"—while domesticating nonwhite immigrant cultures that were racialized as "foreign" or "dangerous."

Thus, this genre of cookbooks for the "wartime hostess" worked to mitigate the anxieties, asymmetries, and scarcities produced by US settler militarism, Hawai'i's changing role in the "American family," and the inclusion of racialized peoples within the US nation-state. Institutions such as the Office of Civilian Defense, the Home Defense Committee, and the Territorial Nutrition Committee enlisted mothers and homemakers to mask the contradictions of wartime rationing by transforming tropical fruits into classic American dishes, thus inventing new "patriotic" wartime foods. This logic of settler military domesticity created criteria for reproductive labor that blended the "domestic" and the "foreign," creating an affective connection that made Hawai'i seem like "home" to American settlers during a time when Hawai'i's political and military importance to the United States was rapidly increasing. Further, these projects, which extracted knowledge and labor from nonwhite families and students, contributed to a hierarchy of expertise that artificially positioned white settler women professionals as the authority on proper nutrition, family health, and femininity in the islands.

Settler Military Domesticity in the Life of Carey Miller and Ada Erwin

Dominant wartime home economics projects constructed a hierarchy of expertise in which professional nutritionists and domestic scientists, who were predominantly white settler women, built careers on the extraction of knowledge via the study and observation of racialized immigrant and Indigenous family diets while perpetuating regimes of social regulation that targeted these same peoples. Building upon a racialized and colonial "cult of domesticity" that differentiated "good" or respectable women, who participated in proper child rearing, from "bad" or undesirable women, who practiced sexual promiscuity, wartime domestic scientists produced a mid twentieth-century ideal of racial liberal femininity that was coded as white and that contributed to US settler military projects. Furthermore, as "liberated" middle-class women who worked and were sometimes unmarried, many did not perform the reproductive labor of their own household, transferring it to immigrant and Indigenous domestic and service workers.[95] Overall, the wartime home economics project in Hawai'i not only contributed to the social reproduction of settler militarism in the service of capitalism, but it was also predicated on the racialized, gendered, and classed extraction of knowledge, affect, and labor from Indigenous and immigrant women and men. The lives of Carey Miller and Ada Erwin provide one instructive example.

In 1958, upon Carey Miller's retirement from the University of Hawai'i, the Home Economics Department building was named in honor of her. Having served as chair of the department for over twenty years, Miller was credited with developing the program from its modest beginnings, with one student major in 1922, to at least 190 majors upon her retirement.[96] Miller had also become widely known for her many published articles on the diets of Polynesians and Asians and on Hawaiian fruits and vegetables, which many considered especially timely during World War II. One year before, her former students had established the Carey D. Miller Award, which would go to one undergraduate per year in home economics at the University of Hawai'i. Eventually, Miller would go on to leave the majority of her estate to student scholarships and nonprofit organizations, including the Hawai'i Dietetic Association, which she cofounded.[97] In 1958 a dinner was held to honor Miller and Dean Harold Wadsworth, who would also retire from the University of Hawai'i that year. After receiving leis and gifts, Miller gave a speech that, according to her personal notes, began with a message of thanks: "Few people achieve anything in this world alone. The success of some men is due as much to their wives as to their own efforts. I should like to take this opportunity to pay tribute to a few of those who have greatly aided me in my work at the University of Hawaii. My companion of many years came to Hawaii for a year's vacation and has also been here for 36 years. She has seen me through my ups and downs and I would like to ask Miss Erwin to take a bow."[98] The "Miss Erwin" is Ada B. Erwin, who was also a home economist: she founded the Home Economics Department at Punahou School and taught there from 1923 to 1946.[99] In her message of thanks, Miller implies that Erwin is her metaphorical "wife" who has seen her through her "ups and downs," without whom she would be "alone," and to whom she owes her "success." This is not to say that their relationship literally mirrored that of husband and wife, but it is noteworthy that this was how Miller chose to render their relationship legible to the audience at the University of Hawai'i. Further, the fact that Miller and Erwin privately shared their life together despite their public involvement in the regulation of the ideal nuclear family household is significant, allowing us to continue to complicate the production of settler military domesticity in Hawai'i.

Miller and Erwin traveled from San Francisco to Hawai'i together in 1922 and shared a home for more than fifty years in Honolulu. Miller was forty-seven at the start of World War II, and Erwin was fifty-three. Although Miller's speech seems to be one of the few times that she publicly acknowledged Erwin, the latter is often referenced in Miller's personal papers, whether that be through her descriptions of their activities at their house or the retelling of a vacation that they took together. Personal letters written to Miller often end with messages such as "Mother joins me in sending aloha to both you and Ada" or "I hope to see you and Ada when you come to Washington," thus suggesting that they both socialized and traveled together. In her yearly Christmas cards, Miller gave friends and family updates on her and Erwin's life in their Honolulu home, the changes to their daily activities during the war, and the success of the "Erwin-Miller garden." Miller referred to Erwin varyingly as her friend, housemate, or companion.[100] In the 1940 census, Erwin is listed as their "head of household," whereas Miller is listed as her "partner," even though "partner" is not one of the recommended answers for this question. Neither Miller nor Erwin ever married, and they continued to live together from the day they arrived in Hawai'i in 1922 until Erwin's death in 1983. A photo taken by a friend in 1933 depicts them having tea together in their garden (figure 3.2).

FIGURE 3.2 · This photograph is captioned "Tea in the garden with Ada B. Erwin [*left*] and Carey D. Miller [*right*]." Source: People—Chick, Harriette (1933 Hawaii), cm.

There is not much more detail in the archives about the lives of Miller and Erwin other than what is recounted here. They moved to Hawaiʻi together, shared a home for sixty-one years, identified themselves to the state as "partners," and socialized and traveled together. Lilian Faderman's work illuminates the history of what we now think of as "lesbian" lifestyles and experiences from the late nineteenth century onward: from "romantic friendships" in the Victorian era that were not necessarily sexual, to the growing stigmatization of close female companionship in the 1920s and 1930s, to a period of relative "freedom" during World War II, and to the intense surveillance and condemnation of homosexuality during the Cold War. For many women who chose other women as partners during the early twentieth century, it was access to middle-class status, white privilege, and a respectable reputation that allowed them to support their nonnormative life choices without arousing suspicion.[101] Contemporary accounts portrayed Miller as a "little old-fashioned lady" from Boise, Idaho, who was "small in stature, only 5' ½" tall," "of slight build," and "very conservative in her attire." And poignantly, despite the fact that Miller and Erwin granted each other their power of attorney, were the executors of each other's wills, and share a gravestone, Erwin was never mentioned in Miller's many eulogies and obituaries.[102]

It is impossible—and not necessarily important—to discern for sure whether these women, who came of age in rural communities during the decline of the Victorian era but spent time in New York City during the 1920s and onward, identified as homosexual.[103] What is significant is that Miller's nonnuclear, nonheteronormative domestic life did not keep her from embodying and constructing the ideal of white racial liberal femininity or from engaging publicly in empire-building projects throughout her lifetime. For example, much of Miller's writings reflected her participation in dominant racial liberal discourse that specifically bolstered and rationalized the social reproduction of settler militarism: as she wrote in a 1940 letter, "[Hawai'i] is not merely the most important military outpost of the United States, but one of the beauty spots of the world where one may live a quiet but interesting life among friendly people of various races."[104] Furthermore, beyond merely employing US empire-building discourse, Miller oversaw the development of a state-funded Home Economics Department that created institutionalized standards for homemaking, mothering, and domestic science, and that directly collaborated with the military government under martial law to "improve" family health during World War II. As a white nutritional scientist from the continental United States, Miller positioned herself as an authority on family health over and against the racialized immigrant and Indigenous people whom she studied. Her publications marginalized Asian settler and Kanaka Maoli nutritional practices, and positioned the white settler as the dominant model for health, patriotism, and loyalty. US military interest in domestic science during World War II enabled Miller to build up her department and expand the audience for her own research. Miller trained students and colleagues, such as Bazore and Abel, who produced similar work as members of the Home Defense Committee and with whom Miller often collaborated in her published works.

Furthermore, a closer look at the life of Miller and Erwin reveals the racialized domestic labor that allowed for this nonheteronormative couple to contribute to US nation building during a time when homosexuality was still disallowed in the public sphere. Despite Miller's prominent role in the field of home economics in Hawai'i, she did not do the domestic work in her own home, describing it as "a real burden in addition to professional duties and the extra-professional and community activities that one is expected to perform."[105] Miller prioritized her career and the social responsibilities of her class position over the ostensibly menial labor of housekeeping and cooking:

in a 1943 letter she wrote that "I am interested in having a full time maid, as my hours are long and I am very busy. . . . We would expect the girl to do all the work."[106] These remarks reveal the racialized and gendered labor that is forgotten in dominant narratives of Miller's ascendance as a home econo-mist, illustrating in yet additional ways how the social reproduction of settler militarism was dependent upon the invisible racialized and gendered repro-ductive and affective labor of Indigenous and immigrant women and men.

Specifically, Miller and Erwin employed immigrant or Indigenous do-mestic servants throughout their life in Oʻahu. These individuals did their cooking and cleaning, washed their clothing, designed and installed their interior furnishings, and aided with garden work.[107] Miller's personal archive contains momentary mentions of these individuals: she imitates the Pidgin English of her masseur, speculates about the whereabouts of her seamstress, or jokingly wonders if she and Erwin have offended their gardener.[108] The 1940 census describes Erwin and Miller's home as including a third resident: Alice Yamamoto, born in Hawaiʻi in 1912, whose relationship to the head of household is described as "servant" and whom they paid thirteen dollars per week.[109] Miller and Erwin preferred that their maids be familiar with the lifestyle to which they were accustomed: in her request for a new maid in 1943, Miller wrote, "I am interested to know if you have had any experience in working in a haole home."[110] Furthermore, the fact that Miller and Erwin were able to afford a housemaid is a significant marker of their economic and cultural capital. This was rare both in Hawaiʻi and in the continent during World War II, when new jobs were suddenly available to women of color who previously had been able to find work only in domestic service.[111]

This racialized and gendered division of reproductive labor enabled Miller and Erwin to preserve a private life that differed from the institution-alized discourse that they espoused: it was the employment of racialized domestic workers that allowed them to cultivate an image of respectable white femininity while remaining unmarried, continue full-time work in home economics and nutrition, and participate in the community activities expected of their middle-class position during the war. Further, as Evelyn Nakano Glenn's work demonstrates, racialized domestic labor has through-out history made possible both the ideal of "white femininity" and that of the "American home": accordingly, many families in Miller and Erwin's neighborhood likewise employed housemaids who were of Japanese, Puerto Rican, or Hawaiian descent.[112] Therefore, this example of the Miller-Erwin household not only continues to nuance the dynamics of gender, sexuality, and race embedded in the social reproduction of settler militarism during the period of martial law in Hawai'i, but it also connects this complex narrative of settler military domesticity in the islands with the longer continental history of the United States forging the "family" of the nation through the invisible reproductive labor of enslaved, immigrant, and Indigenous women of color.

....

This chapter traces the logic of "settler military domesticity" in Hawai'i, whose location at the intersection of "home front" and "war front" during World War II perpetuated the convergence of the reproductive and affective labors of settler colonial "homemaking" and the production of US imperial war. As central to the social reproduction of future citizens and soldiers, the gendered security of the home was considered integral to the vitality of the American nation. Housewives in Hawai'i "manned their home battle stations" by promoting wartime domestic projects such as "home defense," family health, and nutritional science. Even after the war, books on motherhood suggested that mothers should not go back to work and continued to describe mothering as a nation-building project: in 1952 *A Guide to Mothers in Hawaii* cited a recent secretary of labor stating that "it is important to remember that mothers of young children can make no finer contribution to the strength of the Nation and its vitality and effectiveness in the future than to assure their children the security of home, individual care, and affection."[113] Furthermore, much as with the mandatory immunization program under martial law, many even went as far as to argue that wartime military control had improved mothering and homemaking practices in the territory of Hawai'i.

Settler military domesticity enlisted women in Hawai'i to contribute to the racial liberal biopolitical administration of health, family, and social reproduction: as with wartime eminent domain and public health projects, nutritional and home economics campaigns that proclaimed to "improve" the population in Hawai'i organized regimes of racial, gendered, and colonial differentiation such that settler militarism presented as benevolent rather than expropriative. Wartime organizations such as the Home Defense Committee and the Territorial Nutrition Committee used research on racialized and Indigenous families and students in order to institutionalize regulations for the "secure" and "healthy" wartime American family home for the purposes of wartime labor productivity while marginalizing immigrant diets, masking the history of settler colonialism, and denying the continual persistence of Hawaiian land-based health practices. Furthermore, home economists and nutritionists in these institutions encouraged families to make use of local fruits and vegetables when making American dishes, thus contributing to a feminized culture of cooking and hostessing that extracted locally grown natural resources in order to resolve settler militarism and wartime capitalism's internally produced dynamics of scarcity and life depletion. Finally, a closer look at the life of Carey Miller and Ada Erwin nuances our understanding of the racial, gendered, and colonial dynamics at work in the reproduction and maintenance of settler military domesticity. Overall, these racial liberal biopolitical domestic projects ostensibly worked to cultivate and improve healthy civilians, laborers, and soldiers while also negotiating Hawai'i's place in the "American family" during a time when this supposed inclusion was strategic to US military strategies for war and empire.

FOUR

"A Citizenship Laboratory"

Education and Language Reform
in the Wartime Classroom

A curriculum study of Hawaiian public schools during the academic year 1944–45 includes two photographs of students at McKinley High School in Honolulu. In one, young women students sit at desks using typewriters and filing equipment, and in another, boys and girls complete tasks in a science class. The caption states, "Pupils in a citizenship laboratory act as office staff to maintain school government records."[1] The term *citizenship laboratory* explicitly illustrates the biopolitical nature of education as a martial law project. Wartime schools instructed pupils in academic subjects while also socializing young people of all races in the responsibilities of patriotic US citizenship during wartime and beyond. The project of wartime education also included the repurposing of schools for the state of emergency: from the occupation of school buildings for military activities to the preparation of students for various jobs associated with the war effort and the defense industry. But as the curricula, teaching materials, and school policies examined in this chapter demonstrate, the primary imperative of education under martial law was a socially reproductive one: teachers inculcated the tenets of American citizenship in children across the territory and sought to cultivate Hawaiʻi's diverse civilians as a population of civil subjects ready and willing to sacrifice and labor for the US nation. This project focused especially on the teaching of English language curriculum. Further, wartime schooling was not limited to instruction in the grammar and mechanics of what was referred to as "American" speech and writing, but was also a medium for teaching and normalizing the superiority of American civic culture and values within the gendered, racialized, hierarchical space of the classroom.[2] That is, wartime pedagogy articulated with racial liberal biopolitical imperatives to curate the speech, bodily comportment, and epistemological and civic priorities supposedly inherent to a civilized American population by cultivating these behaviors in the classroom and encouraging students to model them in daily life. In addition to English language instruction, educational policies aimed explicitly to censor Japanese language and culture, and to eliminate the speaking of Pidgin both in and outside the classroom. On December 7, 1941, all foreign language schools in the territory, including Korean and Chinese language schools, were closed.[3] Further, such efforts to standardize "American" English language use in Hawai'i built upon the longer settler colonial history of attempts to eradicate the Hawaiian language and suppress Kanaka Maoli cultural traditions.

Just as the US military considered the cultivation of life in all its capacities within the population as integral to the wartime capitalist vitality of its military bases, so too did it centralize the project of teaching the proper forms of knowledge, language, and sensibilities to US citizens and civilians. Like nursing and homemaking, teaching was a form of gendered affective and reproductive labor that contributed to settler militarism within the wartime context, including its hierarchical and racialized dimensions that upheld and naturalized the primitive accumulation of land and labor. Teachers were to provide care for children of all races, cultivate their growth as American citizens, and normalize the violence of martial law and settler militarism. Furthermore, much as with the liberal Lockean logics of eminent domain, public health, and nutrition, wartime curricula's biopolitical ambitions to "improve" the written and oral English language skills of students wielded racialized and colonial logics of modernity to reinforce an epistemological hierarchy that subordinated immigrant and Indigenous racial differences to Americanized standards while perpetuating the erasure of Hawaiian language practices. Furthermore, schools were expressly invested in inculcating wartime tenets of patriotism and civic duty among their pupils: as an officer of the Hawaiian armed forces stated, "Schools are responsible for the internal security of the nation, just as the armed services are responsible for external security."[4] Overall, the broader repertoire of education and language projects for civilians in Hawai'i—including primary, secondary, and university education; foreign language schools; the Speak American Campaign; and the recruitment of Hawai'i Nisei to the Military Intelligence Service (MIS) Language School—was more than simply an effort to teach children about citizenship and language. Rather, these wartime pedagogies were racial liberal biopolitical agents of social reproduction, capitalist mobilization, and military empire.

Teaching in a State of Emergency

In January 1942 the superintendent of the Department of Public Instruction, Oren E. Long, wrote to teachers as schools were preparing to reopen after the bombing of Pearl Harbor: "We are opening school under conditions that are different from any we have ever before experienced. In the first place, we are at war with Japan, another world power of the Pacific area. We live in a combat zone of that war. This means that everything we do and say—*even our very thinking*—will be affected by war conditions."[5] Because of Hawai'i's wartime location as both "home front" and "war front," education and knowledge production—"even our very thinking"—were considered a line of defense in the "combat zone" of the Pacific War. Notably, at the end of 1942, 80 percent of teachers in the territory of Hawai'i, or 3,107 out of the 3,890, were women.[6] There were roughly equal numbers of male and female students, with 83 percent of the 99,773 students enrolled in public school.[7] Furthermore, 99.58 percent were US citizens. In contrast, only approximately 80 percent of Hawai'i's 423,300 residents were US citizens in 1940.[8] The American Council on Education portrayed the management of the diverse students in Hawai'i's schools as a unique "challenge."[9] In its description of its policies toward nonwhite students, a 1944 education report cited Military Governor Emmons, who stated that "Hawaii has always been an American outpost of friendliness and good will and now has calmly accepted its responsibility as an American outpost of war. . . . It is important that Hawaii prove that her traditional confidence in her cosmopolitan population has not been misplaced."[10] The education report's use of Emmons's remarks is yet another example of how racial liberal biopower wielded the fact of Hawai'i's diversity as a mode of social regulation by prescribing a bandwidth of acceptable patriotic behavior on the part of this "cosmopolitan population." As with the racialized pressures to contribute to the Honolulu Blood Bank, we can see how this statement about education suggests that white Americans' tolerance of nonwhite peoples in Hawai'i had produced a debt that could be repaid via contributions to the US war effort.

Superintendent Long presented schools and teachers as being responsible for cultivating both racial tolerance and morale during wartime: he instructed them that "you must be a *builder of morale*" and also asserted that "*all* prejudices *must* be submerged and under no circumstances appear in action or speech."[11] Further, Long argued that teachers must ensure that Japanese who faced wartime prejudice did not "lose what enthusiasm [they had] for American institutions and that [they] be made to feel that discrimination is not personal."[12] Thus, in the life-cultivating space of the school classroom, teachers' use of the rhetoric of "tolerance" performed the feminized affective labor of incorporating wartime children of all races into a patriotic and loyal population while denying the reality that the education project itself was fundamentally gendered, racialized, and colonial. This gendered racial liberal biopolitical project incorporated peoples in order to differentiate them while masking the ongoing history of structural inequalities and colonial dispossession, thus perpetuating and obscuring the dynamics of US settler militarism.

Under martial law, the US military occupied school campuses to be used as emergency hospitals, fingerprint and registration centers, vaccination centers, and training centers. After the bombing of Pearl Harbor, all public schools were closed for almost three months from December 8, 1941, to February 2, 1942. During this period most teachers and students did voluntary work for the military government. Some assisted with fingerprinting and registering, others aided Red Cross activities such as vaccination and blood donation, and some volunteered for fire patrols and as wardens.[13] At the Kaiulani School, schoolteachers housed and provided food for Filipino evacuees who had been removed from Iwilei, which had been designated a military area. At Washington Intermediate School, they sewed Red Cross uniforms and knit sweaters for the navy.[14] In June 1942 the Department of Public Instruction reported that a total of 878 "units"—including classrooms, cafeterias, labs, storerooms, garages, dispensaries, restrooms, gyms, and auditoriums—had been given up for the military or war effort. Twenty-six schools across Oʻahu, Hawaiʻi, Kauaʻi, and Maui gave up nearly all of their facilities to the US Navy, Army, Marine Corps, and Office of Civilian Defense. In Oʻahu, all eight schools that gave up their entire campus were located in Honolulu, Pearl City, and Wahiawā—locations that were close to US military installations at Pearl Harbor and Schofield Barracks.[15] These agencies primarily used these school buildings as barracks, military schools, bases, and training centers.[16] The military's occupation of campuses reached a peak in 1942, then gradually ebbed during the course of the war. Eight schools remained closed for the duration of the war in order to serve as hospitals.[17] The US military occupied some private school buildings as well during this time.

During the period that schools were occupied, teachers taught in temporary classrooms located in places such as private homes, churches and temples, social halls, and storerooms.[18]

The emergency war work of teachers during this period is another example of how women were enlisted to perform the labor of racial liberal biopower, including fingerprinting, registration, and vaccination programs. The US military government redirected the reproductive labor of schoolteachers toward the militarized incorporation of—and collection of data on—peoples of all races in the settler landscape, thus providing the means to calculate and implement strategies for primitive accumulation in its various forms. Voluntary war work put these teachers, many of whom were middle-class, into contact with working-class nonwhite people whom they had not yet encountered. A project called "Hawaii and the War—Schools Aid" asked teachers at the Kaiulani School to fill out a survey to describe their performance of emergency duties between December 7, 1941, and March 1, 1942, and then also to recount "several comical incidents." Although many teachers commented that they did not experience any "comical" incidents, others did relate some, many of which involved their encounters with individuals or families of a different race or class. These women's reactions to this experience varied. Elise M. Quinn recalled that "they [Filipinos who were evacuated from Iwilei] were in every nook and corner of our school— each family having from 6 to 10 children and some more. . . . Their food is so different from the American food that there just was not a thing they liked, even lovely creamed turkey went in the garbage can. . . . When they once got in here we had quite a time to get them out, they said this was better than what they had left."[19] Here, Quinn emphasized what she interpreted as the ungratefulness of the Filipino evacuees that she served rather than the injustice of their displacement for military purposes. Her comments that the Filipino evacuees "were in every nook and corner," that each family had "6 to 10 children and some more," and that it was hard to "get them out," resonate with longtime militarized and capitalist racializations that present Asians and Asian immigrants as an unclean "infestation."[20]

Teacher Mae S. Akina wrote that "my next job was to enumerate all the mixed races of people. . . . I called on a Chinese mother who through her hard work in tailoring managed to raise a family of four. After a little difficulty in getting her to understand my mission, she said before dis dam Jap bump us meaning (bomb) me and my chiren (children) very happy. You think we going get another bumping (bombing). It was very funny, for she was toothless and weighed over 225 lbs."[21] In another story, Akina recounted how "a

Filipino woman . . . quietly told me that the man in the house was *borrowed* pending her divorce with her husband. I have often wondered through these experiences how some people are able to live under such filthy conditions I found in the district, not only in sanitation but morally." We can see how this settler military project obliged women of all races to take on the gaze of white racial liberal femininity via this enumeration project that registered people of all races while differentiating between so-called respectable and promiscuous women. In the first instance, Akina, who was likely an Asian settler, imitated the Chinese accent of the woman with whom she spoke and remarked on her weight and "toothless" appearance as another element that made this interaction "funny." In the second passage, she also invoked logics of race, gender, and sexuality to racialize a Filipino woman as "immoral" and "filthy." Both teachers' accounts of their interactions with people during the war emphasized the racial and class difference of those that they encountered, thus consolidating their own privileged class position.

Other teachers' responses included mentions of cross-racial and cross-class interactions, but their stories used racial liberal rhetoric to praise the ability of many people of different backgrounds to work toward a collective goal during the war. For example, another teacher wrote the following: "What seemed to be a wild nightmare turned out to be an experience of a lifetime—all barriers torn down!—principal, teachers, children, layman working side by side for a common cause—that of security—we respected man as man and not for his or her position!"[22] "Security," here, is portrayed as the mechanism through which multiracial individuals of different class positions came together. Overall, the above accounts of wartime experiences illustrate how, despite the US military government's official call for racial tolerance and inclusion, individual responses to contact with those of different races varied on the ground. Yet in all cases this registration project wielded the gendered reproductive labor of settler militarism to categorize, define, and surveil racialized peoples who would be enlisted as laborers and soldiers. The fact that it was teachers doing this labor signals that the military government viewed them as having an aptitude for this kind of work because of their experience in the classroom.

The Militarization of Wartime Curriculum

In 1945 the American Council on Education credited the public education system in Hawai'i with many of its wartime successes, including the development of a stable democratic community in the islands, the patriotism and loyalty during the war, the ability of its citizens to conduct wartime labor, and the possibility of Hawaiian statehood.[23] As the council stated, "The schools have helped Hawaii to meet war conditions successfully through developing a stable American community out of diverse racial strains. In spite of the many ancestries represented by the population, Hawaii moved on without any overt disturbance of any kind whatsoever."[24] As mentioned above, both the US military government in Hawai'i and the federal government argued that education was fundamentally different in the islands because of their location in the combat zone and the diversity of the students. Officials tasked schools and teachers with the responsibility of directly contributing to the war effort and also forced them to make many sacrifices when buildings and personnel were diverted to military use.[25] The racial liberal statement above that schools created "a stable American community out of diverse racial strains" credits wartime education for the lack of "overt disturbance" that could have resulted from the supposed "challenge" of this racial diversity. Moreover, Hawai'i's location as both home front and war front directly linked school activities and curricula to military security. As the Department of Public Instruction declared in 1942, *"Schools in any country today are on a battle front, for in those schools are shaped the citizens of tomorrow. What those citizens believe, what they are, and what they can and will do, is of vital importance. . . .* The schools of Hawaii are a front line of national defense; they are developing an intelligent citizenry, proud to be Americans."[26] Long's statement that *"what those citizens believe, what they are, and what they can and will do, is of vital importance"* reveals a racial liberal biopolitical calculus preoccupied with cultivating and surveilling children's minds, racial makeup, and physical capacity to labor according to the specifications and desires of settler militarism. Schools sought to reproduce a multiracial population with Americanized sensibilities and patriotic behaviors while naturalizing and masking the continued primitive accumulation of racialized labor and Indigenous land, all for the purposes of imperial war.

Even after schools reopened in the islands on February 2, 1942, both the military's physical occupation of school campuses and the larger project of wartime labor mobilization under martial law in the islands greatly affected the public school system in Hawai'i. Further, many teachers left their positions in order to pursue employment in wartime industries, the military, or other agricultural or commercial work as a result of the wartime need for laborers skilled in industrial work and the higher wages for defense work.[27] Many students also left school during the war: older children quit school to work, allegedly because of a "patriotic urge to help with the all-out war effort and also because of the exorbitant wages which are now offered." Many underage children were also evacuated to the continental United States.[28] During the war, intermediate and high schools met only four days per week, and the fifth day was reserved for student work in sugar, pineapple industries, and other essential labor. Many school buildings and facilities were still occupied for military and defense purposes even after schools were allowed to reopen. Teachers had to improvise new classrooms and devise new teaching materials in temporary buildings, occasionally forcing classes to meet for only a half-day at a time.[29] Overall, schools and teachers contributed to the social reproduction of settler militarism by accommodating wartime policies that affected school practices and schedules.

As the education project in Hawai'i morphed to accommodate military needs for space, infrastructure, and labor, Superintendent Long enlisted teachers in the project of cultivating moral and patriotic citizenship among all students, which entailed the responsibilities to keep calm during the wartime emergency and to instill in students an appreciation for American loyalty and heritage.[30] Long claimed that "the public school program is more concerned with good citizenship than with any other single objective. Through school experiences the pupil learns of his rights and privileges under the American government; at the same time, he learns of his duties and responsibilities to his country."[31] This imperative to focus school curriculum on patriotic citizenship, which incorporated and differentiated racialized students while denying the asymmetrical relations of the education project, reveals the operation of racial liberal biopolitics within wartime pedagogy. For example, the fact that the vast majority of students in Hawai'i were US citizens but many had noncitizen parents increased the schools' focus on indoctrinating children in American ideals because officials doubted that these children would receive lessons in Americanization at home.[32] For example, both University of Hawai'i president Gregg M. Sinclair and Superintendent Long argued that high schools and universities in Hawai'i should require a course in the causes of World War II so that students "would have this information to convey to their alien parents."[33] In this way, similar to the home economics campaigns that considered the family as a primary unit for social reproduction in the realm of nutrition and health and enlisted mothers in this reproductive labor, racial liberal biopolitics worked through wartime schooling to enlist young citizens of color in the cultivation of patriotism among members of their family unit.

Furthermore, wartime educational policy reorganized schools to aid the reproduction of the militarization project by augmenting curricula to suit military needs, encouraging student participation in wartime fund-raisers and campaigns, and preparing students for wartime emergency scenarios. For example, many schools created new math and science courses that aimed to train students to enter into the armed forces or other defense work. Some expanded their social studies courses so that assignments included students' engagement in emergency wartime activities such as war-bond sales and other community-defense projects.[34] Additionally, schools added a "war-activities period" to the regular schedule to encourage all students to contribute to the war effort by, for example, selling war stamps and war bonds. Many campus vocational agricultural departments started school gardens, which contributed food crops worth an estimated $286,087, including 552,832 pounds of vegetables. Homemaking classes devoted time to Red Cross activities and made slippers, surgical dressings, hot-water-bottle covers, Christmas gifts for hospitals, wheelchair covers, "ditty bags" for military men, children's toys, clothes, and sweaters.[35] Schools trained their students in emergency first aid and even staged "first aid drills" in which they acted out wartime emergency situations. In a photograph of one of these drills at Liliʻuokalani School, a student pretends to have suffered a grave injury while his classmates and teacher tend to his wounds, and other students watch while "hiding" in an adjacent war trench (figure 4.1). Some schools established "School-at-War" programs, in which the entire campus would set a sizable fund-raising goal in order to purchase a large piece of military equipment, such as a jeep, field ambulance, bomber, duck, or plane. Some schools made it their goal to raise funds for a constructive, rather than destructive, wartime contribution, such as the equipment for a 1,500- to 2,000-bed hospital or for a laboratory in a military hospital.[36] This signals schools' participation in the social reproduction of settler militarism via biopolitical projects that—even if they were ostensibly life cultivating—still worked to fortify the wartime capitalist project and its violent ends. The above are all examples of how the education of patriotic minds in the public schools produced tangible results for military buildup.

In the classroom, teachers performed the feminized affective labor of caring for students and supporting their development into young citizens who would be ready and willing to contribute to the American war effort. Some worked to provide students with educational or creative outlets to make sense of violent and stressful wartime conditions. For example, Caroline Curtis, a teacher at Hanahauʻoli School, described her work with a sixth-grade Japanese student who had witnessed a woman killed in the bombing on December 7 and in the aftermath refused to eat or speak for days. This student,

FIGURE 4.1 · The caption of this photograph is "FIRST AID DRILL: Getting set for any emergency, Liliuokalani school is teaching students the technique of first aid, as pictured here. First aid kits have been provided the pupils to hold demonstrations. In the picture, left to right, are Abigail Ching, Eva Castro, Lila Lee, Mrs. Edith Chang, instructor, and Richard Choy. The 'victim' is Johnson Wong." *Honolulu Star-Bulletin*, March 3, 1942. Hawaii War Records Depository HWRD 0352, UHM Library Digital Image Collections.

whom Curtis noted was quite artistically gifted, returned to school when it reopened in 1942 but was still recovering from this incident and was at first unable to paint as he usually did during his first period. However, she stated, "At the beginning of the second period he asked, 'Can I paint the war?'—then worked with his usual abandon. The group left but he continued to work. The result was a well-integrated, beautiful, but horrible picture—a chaos of fire and smoke, whirling fragments, injured people, blood."[37] Curtis noted that this student never again drew a wartime scene, but she suggested that it was this artistic breakthrough in the classroom that allowed him to return to his daily routine. Furthermore, students at Robert Louis Stevenson School and Hanahau'oli School created calendars illustrated with block prints that contrasted tropical or ocean scenes with military images of barbed wire, battleships, and cannons, or wartime activities such as spraying for mosquitoes and starting victory gardens.[38] The practice of these therapeutic activities in the classroom illustrates how teachers, in their effort to comfort students or help them to acclimate to wartime conditions, also contributed to the normalization of war trauma and violence. By encouraging students to print war scenes on an everyday object such as a calendar, teachers allowed martial law conditions to seem ordinary rather than exceptional. These logics are also at play in the image of the "first aid drill." Although the staging of the photograph suggests a militarized scene—an injured body surrounded by medical supplies and a recently dug trench—the faces and postures of the students reflect a lack of interest in, and perhaps even boredom with, this "emergency" situation, as if it were a common occurrence. These school activities illustrate how education functioned as an institution of social reproduction: wartime pedagogies rendered militarized violence as quotidian and enlisted teachers in the affective labor of nurturing children to feel comfortable in the context of total war.

In some cases, schools directly enlisted students to artistically engage with wartime issues via the production of wartime propaganda. Schools of all levels encouraged their students to create propaganda posters using paint, crayon, and construction paper, such as the one discussed in the previous chapter, which proclaimed that "Good Americans Eat Good Food." These projects were often part of a series of school poster contests sponsored by the Junior Civilian Defense Corps, the High School Victory Corps, and the Honolulu Community and War Chest, which were displayed across thirty-two public schools. Other posters had slogans such as "Bonds Will Buy Bombs," "Speak American," and "Work for Victory." One included an image of a red cross and a giant hand holding a syringe, with the message "DONATE YOUR BLOOD." Some included explicitly anti-Japanese messages, such as one depicting General Hideki Tōjō with a pineapple-shaped head and a giant ear listening to people in Hawai'i. In this poster, Tōjō is holding a sign with the words "Notes for Tokyo" and is saying, "'IMFOMATION' PLEASE," implying the presence of Japanese spies in the islands (figure 4.2).[39] Through these school art projects, teachers and students wielded the affective power of childhood innocence toward the production of racist wartime propaganda. This use of militarist imagery within the sentimental genre of children's art is unsettling in its potential to normalize wartime racism as a "universal good."[40] Even as Superintendent Long directed teachers that "*all* prejudices *must* be submerged and under no circumstances appear in action or speech," it is clear that this racial liberal statement belied the reality of wartime racial hierarchies and violence. Because most students during this time were nonwhite US citizens,

FIGURE 4.2 · "'IMFOMATION' PLEASE." Source: Children's posters, undated, Oversized Materials, HWRD.

these classroom activities also illustrate how the gendered project of education sought to discipline racialized children into loyal American subjects by instructing them to take on the wartime white racial gaze. Further, beyond the explicit racist messages of "'IMFOMATION' PLEASE," we know from chapters 2 and 3 that even less explicitly racialized directives such as "Donate Your Blood" and "Good Americans Eat Good Food" themselves fortified racial liberal biopolitical projects that socially reproduced the racial hierarchies and expropriative dynamics of US settler militarism.

The Focus on English Language in the Classroom

In 1944 Superintendent Long argued that one positive outcome of World War II had been the "improved mastery of the English language" on the part of schoolchildren in Hawai'i. He argued that "an intense public interest has been created in the exclusive and improved use of the English language throughout the community—at home, on the street, in stores, on the playground."[41] During the war this imperative that public schools increase their emphasis on English language reading, writing, and speaking targeted language practices in both the classroom and daily life. As with education in US citizenship, the Department of Public Instruction stressed English language teaching as vital to students' understanding of American civic culture, ideals, and traditions.[42] Furthermore, Long's use of this "improved mastery of the English language" as an example of wartime success again sought to justify violent racialized regimes of Americanization, military occupation, and settler colonialism by aligning English language education with Lockean understandings of rationality and progress. This curriculum reproduced racial and colonial hierarchies of knowledge that subordinated Asian, Indigenous, and creole languages to English while building upon the historic erasure of Hawaiian language practices.

This emphasis on Americanization and English language instruction during World War II was a US militarization project that built upon decades of settler colonial policy and Kanaka Maoli dispossession. Since the late nineteenth century, the US government had enforced English-only instruction in public and private schools in Hawai'i as a part of colonial Americanization efforts. Most significantly, Act 57, Section 30 of the 1896 Laws of the Republic of Hawaii designated English as the only language of instruction in public and private schools. Not only did this law classify Hawaiian as a "foreign" language in Hawai'i, but its regulations also prescribed that any school that did not comply would stop receiving government funding. This caused the number of Hawaiian language schools to fall from 150 in 1880 to none in 1902. This decree was reinforced when Hawai'i became a US territory in 1900, despite the fact that the majority of people living in Hawai'i, both Native and non-Native, spoke Hawaiian at this time. Although some Hawaiian language instruction did take place at the University of Hawai'i starting in the 1920s and at the Kamehameha schools beginning in the 1930s, overall there was little access to education in this language during the territorial period.[43] Furthermore, any interest in learning Hawaiian was often stigmatized as "backward and foolish," whereas English became coded as a mark of high educational and economic status. As with other racial and colonial logics of assimilation, the oppressive notion that speaking English "improved" Hawaiians was a eugenic discourse that contributed to structures of elimination by eradicating the Hawaiian language and obstructing access to meaningful Indigenous epistemologies, land and familial genealogies, and communal ties.

As Katrina-Ann R. Kapāʻanaokalāokeola Nākoa Oliveira argues, "One of the best ways to disempower a people is to burrow into their minds, infecting and incapacitating them at every level of consciousness, while simultaneously stripping them of their language—thereby erasing their historical memory and undermining their traditional knowledge systems." In this way, Long's heralding of the "improved mastery of the English language" in Hawaiʻi belied contemporary and historical settler colonial violence and compounded it by employing education as a primary means of social reproduction during wartime. Yet as both Oliveira and Noenoe K. Silva have illustrated, Hawaiian resistance to this settler colonial project continued throughout the territorial period and beyond, whether through families who continued to teach the language to their children, the small number of Hawaiian language classes that were taught beginning in the 1920s, the persistence of Hawaiian language newspapers, or the Hawaiian language revitalization movement that began in the 1970s and continues today.[44]

In addition to this settler colonial history, English-only Americanization campaigns have long been part of American war culture: for example, during World War I, campaigns targeted Germans, Italians, and Eastern Europeans. Education efforts that encouraged Asian immigrants to improve their English language skills began in the 1920s and increased during World War II. Furthermore, like wartime nutritional studies that sought to study the diets of Asian settler families, there was a proliferation of educational studies during this period that predetermined their discovery of English language "deficiencies" among bilingual students by making them the continual subject of investigation. There were at least two studies of the English and Pidgin use of children conducted at the University of Hawaiʻi during the war, one of which sought to analyze the speech patterns of nonwhite peoples and deduce how to Americanize these practices. Another study determined that in their homes, Japanese families spoke English the least frequently and with the highest percentage of Pidgin use, whereas Caucasian families spoke English the most frequently and with the lowest percentage of Pidgin use.[45] A third study compared the "mental maturity" and "achievement" of third graders and sixth graders in Honolulu public schools to that of students in California, concluding that students in Honolulu scored lower as a result of differences in language sophistication.[46]

These language studies and performance tests examined the rates of foreign language use in the islands in order to acquire data through which to analyze the racially diverse population, thus contributing to racial liberal biopolitical curricula that sought to "improve" English language skills by studying, surveilling, and modifying the knowledge, daily habits, and even the private familial relations of nonwhite students. As Foucault theorizes, the biopolitical apparatus of security establishes a statistical understanding of the "normal" versus the "abnormal" in order to "bring the most unfavorable in line with the more favorable."[47] Here, the categories of "normal" and "abnormal" are explicitly racial and colonial. Studies of bilingual students not only designated a certain level of English language proficiency as "optimal," but they also constructed an epistemological hierarchy that stigmatized the language skills of nonwhite students attending schools in Hawai'i as "backward" or "lacking." Research on children in Hawai'i recorded statistics through which to administer, manage, and consolidate Native and immigrant peoples into an Americanized population that had colonial and racialized expectations for normalization and assimilation. Further, as an ostensibly benevolent project, English language teaching sought to make these hierarchical relations seem rational and natural even as they fortified settler military logics that justified land dispossession and Indigenous erasure, the colonial suppression of the Hawaiian language, the marginalization and forced assimilation of Asian settlers, and anti-Japanese racism.

Furthermore, English language curriculum not only focused on written components such as grammar and syntax, but it also placed a large emphasis on speech proficiency—including rhythm, accent, and pronunciation—skills that, if mastered, would signal successful dedication to the standardization of English in both the classroom and daily life. As with other linguistic studies, research on English speech in Hawai'i supported colonial educational discourse that sought to manage the "foreignness" of nonwhite citizen students. For example, a community report on education in Hawai'i during the years 1940 and 1941 determined that the majority of children who came from immigrant families and did not attend kindergarten were two to three years behind in English speech by the time they began first grade. To ensure that children began school at an earlier age, the 1943 legislature authorized funds to establish twelve more kindergartens throughout the islands and to procure teaching staff and equipment. Teachers were instructed to grade each student's quality of speech based on their ability to use proper sentence structure, omit dialect errors, have a "normal" speech rhythm, and display correct enunciation. In 1943 the Department of Public Instruction established a campaign to teach students to practice better oral English skills, a departmental committee for English, and a committee for the study of "speech problems" during the war. The goal of this "speech problem" committee was to create a "standard program" for instruction in

English language speech and also to provide "standard materials" with which to teach good speech patterns at every grade level.[48] This colonial, racialized, and military discourse negatively portrayed any resistance to English use as a "speech problem" and thus standardized English as the "normal" language to which peoples deemed "abnormal" should assimilate. The goal was for these increased programs in English writing and speaking to bring all schools to meet the criteria for English Standard schools.[49] The University of Hawai'i also created a speech program during this time that sought to train English language teachers to understand speech "difficulties" that it deemed specific to students in Hawai'i. Further, the committee argued, "This problem should be studied continuously. The English used by our pupils is both a community problem and a challenge to the schools."[50] This focus on English speech as a "community problem" illustrates again how wartime education encompassed a biopolitical project of social reproduction concerned with "improving" and surveilling the language and culture of Hawai'i's diverse peoples—in the classroom, the home, and the broader society—in order to prepare them to properly contribute to the nation.

There were many ways that schools and their teachers placed the blame for so-called speech problems on the students themselves. The Department of Public Instruction specified that factors that led to students' English "problems" included speaking Pidgin at home, a lack of confidence in English, a poor vocabulary, and a feeling that speaking English was a chore rather than a natural habit. The department focused on reminding teachers to always use correct English in the classroom, to encourage students to come to them with questions about English, and to assign speaking English at home as part of students' English homework.[51] In this way, schools sought to directly discipline the habits and communication of families in the intimate sphere of the home. A report directed to all intermediate schools' principals argued the following: "Is there one seventh grade child in this Territory who has not repeatedly been *taught* how to say "hit" and "this" and "did not"? Of course there is not. It is not inadequate teaching that is responsible for "heet" and "dees" and "seent." It is resistance to change, indolence and indifference that cause those errors to persist."[52] Much like the racial liberal rhetoric that encouraged Japanese to showcase American patriotism and ignore racial discrimination in the classroom because it was not "personal," the Department of Public Instruction individualized the problem of English language deficiencies and placed the burden on the student to resolve the contradictions of colonial educational policy by showing enthusiasm for English. The statement claimed that it was students' "resistance to change, indolence and indifference" that was at fault for this pattern, rather than the forced assimilation to English speech, the settler colonial education system, and the history of racialized labor exploitation. Racial liberal biopolitics manufactured a linguistic hierarchy that centralized English as the standard and portrayed the preference for any other language as a "speech problem" — despite the fact that multilingual and creole language communities had thrived in Hawai'i for generations amid US occupation and racialized labor exploitation. Rather, students' "resistance to change, indolence and indifference" to speaking English would be better understood as an exercise of autonomy that challenged the dominance of this colonial education regime.

That is, we can understand this singular focus on the English language as a tool of assimilation and "improvement" to have been an effort to secure the wartime project against local resistance by eliminating the possibility of alternative epistemologies, languages, and communities that existed in contradiction to settler militarism. For example, the Department of Public Instruction racialized Pidgin as an immigrant, working-class language and centralized English skills as required for social, cultural, and economic success: "English is the language of America. Above all, local residents and employers should feel ashamed to speak 'pidgin' to maids, yardboys, and other employees."[53] This racial liberal biopolitical statement purports to be concerned with the so-called improvement and success of racialized peoples while denigrating their language traditions — which were forged communally on plantations in the face of racialized labor expropriation — as supposedly shameful. Chapter 3 referenced how Carey Miller, an educated white professor of nutrition, imitated the Pidgin of her masseur in her annual Christmas card: "Haru, my 64 year old masseur, who for almost 20 years has rubbed the cricks out of my tired shoulders and soothed my headaches with her strong and supple fingers has expressed the feelings of many of us when she says, 'I tink God verry sorry see his children fight. Erry morning I say, Aloha God, please, war pau.'"[54] Similarly, a teacher at the Kaiulani School who helped with civilian registration recalled a "comical incident": "In enumerating the oldest woman in our district, 'Maikai' was her reply for practically every question asked."[55] In these instances, settlers explicitly signified racial and class difference by relaying impressions of Pidgin or Hawaiian speech, whereas proper English use signified Americanization, education, and upper- or middle-class status.

Furthermore, the Department of Public Instruction found the idea that students proficient in English would *choose* to speak Pidgin in their everyday life to be particularly threatening because it signaled a pride in racialized difference that contradicted colonial logics of deviance and ineptitude: "The chief language problem, however, is, and will continue to be, the elimination of pidgin unless marked changes in attitude are developed. Sometimes children who can speak perfect English will revert to pidgin on the playground because that is the common vernacular and those who depart from it are likely to be dubbed as 'sissies' by their playmates."[56] Pidgin, a language unfamiliar to most Americans from the continental United States, was a linguistic expression of autonomy that resisted colonial assimilation and was subversive in its possibilities for collective insurgency.[57] Trying to combat student preferences for Pidgin, the department proposed that schools make proper speech a requirement for graduation in order to put "on the spot" the child who "sneers" at learning English, thus suggesting an institutionalized shaming of this resistance to the colonial education project.[58] In this way, racial liberal biopolitical education requirements compelled assimilation to the colonial standard of English by constructing an epistemological hierarchy that presented autonomous or subversive language use as indolent or inferior, rather than an expression of agency or collectivity.

Although the US military government, education officials, and teachers continually marginalized Pidgin, this language is a product of immigrant and Indigenous communities' negotiation of the history of US settler colonialism, immigration restrictions, and racialized labor exploitation.[59] Pidgin was a common language on American plantations that had historically employed laborers of different nationalities and languages in order to keep them from organizing collectively.[60] In this way, Pidgin has always been an autonomous language forged in the face of racial and colonial oppression. Moreover, the immigrant settler population in Hawai'i is multiracial precisely because of US racialized immigration laws such as the 1882 Chinese Exclusion Act, the 1907 Gentleman's Agreement, the 1917 Asiatic Barred Zone Act, and the 1924 Johnson-Reed Act, all of which progressively restricted immigration from different Asian countries and led American plantation owners to seek laborers from other parts of the continent.[61] Although many refer to this language as Pidgin in the vernacular, linguists now consider it to be a creole language called Hawaiian Creole English, which, along with the languages of Asian immigrant laborers, draws mostly from Native Hawaiian grammar and language, including words such as pau and maikai.[62] The disciplining of Pidgin use during World War II was thus a form of racialized, capitalist, and settler colonial violence that endeavored to destroy opposition and resistance to military occupation.

At the end of the war, US officials connected English language education to the overall "progress" of the islands, arguing that the community could either assimilate to US national language standards or else signal that they would prefer to be "held in contempt in other parts of America."[63] This racial liberal biopolitical education project included racialized peoples to consolidate and supposedly "improve" Hawaiʻi's diverse population into docile Americanized subjects. By aligning this linguistic hierarchy with racialized and colonial temporalities of modernity and progress, education officials rendered this forced assimilation as benevolent and inclusionary rather than racial and colonial: this racial liberal logic bolstered US military projects while naturalizing the history of US settler colonial policies that had prohibited Indigenous and creole language practices. Yet at the same time, the persistence of languages such as Pidgin and Hawaiian illustrates how communities continued to cultivate subversive modes of communication and understanding that were less legible to the colonial and military administrations.

The Militarization of Japanese Language Censorship and Translation

This effort to improve English language instruction and discourage the use of Pidgin in Hawaiian schools coincided with the increased focus on the censorship, translation, and militarization of the Japanese language. In 1940 more than 230 Japanese language schools existed in the islands, with almost 43,000 students enrolled and more than 700 teachers employed. Yet the US military government forcibly closed all of these schools directly after the bombing of Pearl Harbor.[64] Concurrently, the Emergency Service Committee established the Speak American Campaign, which discouraged the use of Japanese in public and in one's home. Yet despite these wartime efforts to censor Japanese language, the US military simultaneously recruited Japanese to serve as translators in Pacific Theater operations. This selective censorship and enlistment of Japanese language nuances our understanding of how schooling socially reproduced the uneven and hierarchical relations of settler militarism during this period. In the realm of education and language instruction, not only did the US military government centralize the teaching of English, but it also endeavored to neutralize the so-called threat of Japanese language use in the local community and redirect it toward US military expansion.

Public discussion in favor of and against Japanese language schools employed racial liberal biopolitical logics to delineate encouraged versus undesirable behaviors on the part of Japanese, thus contributing to the social reproduction of the ideal American citizen and laborer. Although all foreign language schools were closed on December 7, 1941, and Japanese language schools did not reopen for the duration of the war, these schools had faced marginalization and public scorn since the interwar period. For example, Superintendent Long argued that the abolition of Japanese language schools was another positive outcome of the World War II period.[65] Leading up to the eventual closing of Japanese language schools on December 7, 1941, there were many attacks against them in the local newspapers. A letter printed in the *Honolulu Star-Bulletin*, signed "an Observer," accused the schools of being anti-American and of seeking to convert students to Shintoism, and asserted that Japanese language teachers could be spies or linked to subversive activities. A response to this letter, signed "FAIR PLAY," included the following: "Apparently Mr. Observer is ignorant about the subject he wrote. . . . First of all, I'd be very happy if he could tell me of any language school conducted by Shinto temples. And if he ever uncovered any subversive and unmoral activities run by the teachers. . . ."[66] Another editorial argued that all of the foreign language schoolteachers were in line with "the highest type of true Americanism." It argued that Japanese language classes specifically focused on American citizenship, patriotism, and loyalty; that most of the students were born in the United States; and that almost all of the students were American citizens: "Those subjects, loyalty, patriotism, democracy, citizenship . . . are taught against a background of Japanese home life and from the Japanese point of view. They thus become more vital and real to the children, more practical and easily understood than when presented academically in a language and from a standpoint that is essentially haole and to a certain extent racially different."[67] Thus, this article argued that the language schools were actually an *Americanization* tool.

Others suggested that Japanese language school students begin to salute the American flag on the school grounds or that the students refrain from bowing to their teachers at the beginning of class: "Some might regard it as unbecoming the forthright and independent behavior of young Americans. . . . Although the custom was innocent and in many ways an admirable one, it might be well in view of current criticism and the strained international situation to substitute a simple and less deferential occidental greeting such as the ordinary salutation of 'Good morning, teacher,' or 'Good afternoon.'"[68] This suggestion to change the greeting at Japanese language schools was part of the larger racial liberal biopolitical education project that policed not only language and speech but also bodily movements, habits, and interactions between teacher and student. Some even suggested that the Japanese language schools had detrimental health effects for their students. Mrs. Katharine F. Genest, the director of hygiene at the Free Kindergarten and Children's Aid Association, conducted a study that analyzed one thousand students of kindergarten age and determined that the 17 percent who attended a foreign language school in addition to a public school were "generally less healthy" and needed "special care" because they were fatigued from spending more time in the classroom after a full day of public school.[69] Thus, wartime discourses concerning the eradication of foreign language use even permeated the biopolitical regimes of health and wellness — suggesting that a bilingual education and lifestyle was too taxing for young children. Overall, the wartime censorship of Japanese sought to eliminate not only the language itself but also the cultural difference, community cohesion, and potential resistance or rebellion that this language represented to American government, military officials, and white citizens during the wartime emergency.

Even after all Japanese language schools were closed in Hawai'i on December 7, 1941, efforts to encourage English language use and discourage foreign language speaking continued to take place outside of the classroom. The Emergency Service Committee, a Japanese group that worked to showcase American patriotism, established the "Speak American Campaign" on October 12, 1942, as part of its larger project to improve the community's perception of Japanese.[70] The Speak American Campaign included news articles and editorials; endorsements from important community members; the display of posters at businesses, public areas, and school campuses; and the distribution of stickers. Furthermore, the campaign held group meetings at local schools, clubs, and businesses to discuss the importance of establishing English as the standard language in Hawai'i. Alongside this campaign, the Emergency Service Committee organized and increased the number of English language classes for adults in the community, and some served on the Adult Education Council. The increased focus on adult education in English during this time led the YMCA, the YWCA, the Friends Service Committee, the Palama Settlement, the Salvation Army, and the University of Hawai'i to increase the number of English language classes that they offered as well.[71] Furthermore, all foreign language newspapers were ordered to stop printing on December 12, 1941. The US military government permitted the *Nippu Jiji* and the *Hawaii Hochi*, two Japanese language newspapers, to resume printing in early January 1942 under the new names *Hawaii Times* and *Hawaii Herald*, but still censored their content and specifically required them to support the Americanization effort and the Speak American Campaign. During this time, the US military government had detained and interned Yasutaro Soga (the editor of *Nippu Jiji*) and other prominent members of the Japanese language press. Throughout the war the US military government also pressured these newspapers to refer to the Japanese enemy as "the Japs."[72]

As with the wartime campaigns focusing on blood donation, homemaking, and nutrition, we see the ways that the Speak American Campaign became a means to incorporate civilians while intensifying racial differentiation. Many of its cartoons gestured toward the multiracial citizenry in Hawai'i yet at the same time also prescribed a set of regulations for acceptable behavior on the part of these racially diverse individuals, while erasing Kanaka Maoli indigeneity by not acknowledging Hawaiian as a language spoken in Hawai'i. One cartoon included a photograph of children of various races and stated, "Speak American, the one language for all of us loyal Americans" (figure 4.3). By characterizing the "American language" as "the one language for all of us loyal Americans," this campaign centralized "American" as the desirable common tongue among multiracial peoples who were to be, despite their racial difference, "loyal Americans." Another said, "Pidgin is better than nothing, the American language is best. But nobody wants to hear foreign tongues — especially the enemy's. Use and encourage others to Speak American." Another cartoon demanded, "Don't speak the enemy's language! The Four Freedoms Are Not In His Vocabulary. Speak American!" This cartoon depicted caricatures of Adolf Hitler, General Tōjō, and Benito Mussolini, all of whom were saying "We must destroy democracy" in German, Japanese, and Italian.[73] The use of the term *American language* alongside racist anti-Japanese propaganda is indicative of the climate of hyper-patriotism during this time. Furthermore, much like the focus on American "speech" and language in the classroom, this project built upon a settler colonial history in which English had supplanted Hawaiian as the dominant language in the islands.

Thus, the eradication of Japanese language schools and the Speak American Campaign during World War II illustrate how the US military government viewed the encouragement of the English language and the forcible elimination of Japanese language and culture as necessary to assimilation and Americanization in Hawai'i. Yet even as these wartime projects emphasized English language instruction in the public schools, forced Japanese language schools to close, and established propaganda campaigns, the US military simultaneously recruited Nisei as translators. The MIS students were deployed to areas throughout the Pacific Theater, including Guadalcanal, Attu, New Georgia, Okinawa, the Mariana Islands, the Philippines, Burma, India, and China. Most of the students at the MIS Language School were

FIGURE 4.3 · "Speak American" poster. Source: Speak American
Campaign, Folder 9, Box 52, HWRD.

Nisei from Hawaiʻi or the west coast of the continental United States, but
there were also some Nisei from other locations, such as Connecticut,
Texas, and Michigan.[74]

Participation as an officer in MIS became one way for Japanese men to
exhibit militarized masculinity and American patriotism during a time when
there was immense wartime pressure to do so. For example, inductee Kenichi
Murata, who was thirty-four and an associate economist with the Agriculture
Extension Service in Honolulu, had one brother in the US Army and another
brother who was a pro-Japanese radio broadcaster in Tokyo. He stated that "I
am ashamed to admit . . . that I have a brother dishing out Jap propaganda.
But both Jack, who's in Louisiana, and I will try to wipe out that shame by our

record in the army. We're going to shove all that propaganda back down the throats of Tojo and the emperor and their militarists." Masaji Marumoto, another volunteer from Oʻahu, was a chairman of the Emergency Service Committee and an attorney in Honolulu.[75] Throughout the war, the Emergency Service Committee "actively aided" the army in its campaign to enlist more volunteers in MIS.[76]

There were stories often told about specific battles that showcased Nisei MIS officers exhibiting extreme heroism, and these narratives circulated in conversation and in the newspapers. One story in particular told of a Japanese American translator, Sergeant Heichi Kubo of Lāhainā, Maui, who ate a bowl of rice with three Japanese soldiers inside a cave during the Battle of Saipan and within half an hour had convinced them to surrender to US forces. This story was printed in both the *Arizona Republic* in Phoenix and the *Gila News-Courier*, which was the main news publication of the Gila River Relocation Center.[77] Another story in the *Washington Post* described the risks that MIS translators took: "One of them allowed himself to be lowered by a rope into one of those huge caves on Saipan which the Japanese had utilized as centers of resistance: then by a combination of wit and bluff and bravery he contrived to obtain the release of all the civilians whom the Japs had herded there."[78] Thus, MIS translators were lauded not only for their military heroism as soldiers but also for their intellectual and strategic cunning in dangerous situations. The program continued to operate even after World War II ended, and MIS translators were employed as part of the US occupation of Japan.[79]

The MIS, much like the drafting of Japanese American soldiers—and other health, domestic, and education projects under martial law—is yet another example of a racial liberal biopolitical project that enlisted racialized peoples while prescribing the proper patriotic behaviors required for wartime inclusion. Even though the US military government closed all Japanese language schools in Hawaiʻi and censored the use of Japanese in school and daily life, the recruitment of Japanese language translators to the MIS illustrates how the military also required individuals with expertise in this language to advance the US war effort. Furthermore, the military's decision to relocate Japanese students from Hawaiʻi and California to the MIS Language School in Minnesota mirrors the larger project of Japanese American internment: this project rendered the Japanese language "unthreatening" by separating those who spoke it from their social networks and local communities. In this way the United States sought to incorporate the Japanese language into the social reproduction of US military expansion and occupation: this racial liberal biopolitical project surveilled and cultivated the habits, practices, and knowledges that were deemed beneficial to military security while censoring those considered subversive, unhealthy, or unproductive for the war effort.

. . . .

A postwar study of education in Hawai'i stated that "there has been a wielding of this social miscellany, with all its abrupt differences, into a democratic community. Various agencies, private schools, press, church, industrial and business management, and many others, of course, have contributed to this end. But the instrumentality, effective beyond all others, has been Hawaii's program of public school education."[80] This statement illustrates the racial liberal biopolitics of wartime education and teaching: much like public health, domestic science, and nutrition, education projects cultivated patriotism, racial tolerance, and morale among children and adolescents who were to labor in the service of the war effort in Hawai'i. The statement concerning the public schools' "wielding of this social miscellany" celebrates schools in Hawai'i for consolidating a diverse student body into loyal Americans. This phrase also implies that it was the logic of racial difference itself that was wielded to compel assimilation—much as it was via other martial law projects such as the military government's statistics of blood donors by race or the Home Defense Committee's multilingual recommendations for Asian settler family nutrition. Further, teachers carried out this gendered and racialized reproductive labor whether by performing emergency war work and civilian registration, administering English language instruction, or fostering a classroom environment that comforted multiracial children and normalized martial law conditions.

Education was thus a principal means for the social reproduction of settler militarism and wartime capitalism. Not only did the US military physically occupy many school campuses, but schools explicitly recruited students as defense laborers while soliciting the purchase of war bonds and other wartime donations. Furthermore, wartime curricula's biopolitical ambitions to "improve" the written and oral English language skills of students wielded liberal logics of modernity to reinforce a racial and colonial hierarchy of language. These educational projects were accompanied by campaigns that sought to discourage or censor those activities and languages—such as Japanese language teaching and the use of Japanese and Pidgin in everyday life—that were deemed detrimental to wartime Americanization and assimilation. Furthermore, the hyper-visibility of these anti-Japanese and pro-English campaigns worked to naturalize and mask the settler colonial history that had outlawed the teaching of the Hawaiian language in schools, thus naturalizing Hawaiʻi as a US possession. In this way, educational curricula that promoted US citizenship and English language skills reinforced settler colonial knowledge production in the service of US militarism. Yet even as the US military government forbade Japanese to be spoken, it also recruited Nisei to continue their study of the language as MIS translators: the US military encouraged Nisei to become fluent in "the enemy's language," but only if they used it on behalf of the American war effort. Overall, as the US military government, the Department of Public Instruction, and schoolteachers accommodated the racial difference of nonwhite peoples and their families, they wielded this tolerance as a tool for wartime regulation in the service of settler militarism.

FIVE

Settler Military Camps

Internment and Prisoner-of-War Camps
across the Pacific Islands

A typical US map of World War II–era internment camps often centralizes the states on the US continent located west of the Mississippi River
or, if including Department of Justice and military camps, might feature
a full continental map that includes Alaska and Hawai'i offset in the corner. However, a complete map of US camps during this period would be
much more expansive, encompassing over half the globe and including
internment and prisoner-of-war camps strategically placed across the Pacific Islands, Asia, and Latin America.[1] During World War II the US military constructed a network of camps throughout the Pacific Islands and
Asia in locations such as Hawai'i, Alaska, the Northern Mariana Islands
(NMI), the Marshall Islands, and Okinawa—all of which were also sites
of US military bases during World War II and the Cold War.[2] By the end
of World War II and into the postwar period, the United States possessed
an expansive military base system in the Pacific Islands, with Hawai'i serving as a principal base that connected this network to the US continent.[3]
This intertwined history of wartime racialized incarceration and military
basing expands our understanding of the World War II "camp." This final
chapter analyzes internment and prisoner-of-war camps together as a
differentiated yet linked transnational project through which the United
States organized peoples and land along a military geography of occupation that extended from the continental United States to the Pacific
Islands and Asia, with Hawai'i serving as a hub in this system of bases.[4]

A relational analysis of camps across these spaces—specifically for
this chapter, in Hawai'i, the Marshall Islands, and the Northern Mariana
Islands—gives us a lens through which to consider how US and Japanese
settler militarism and capitalism have affected the experiences of Asian

and Pacific Islander communities and their diaspora since the late nineteenth century.[5] Both Japan and the United States had colonial and capitalist interests in the Pacific Islands prior to World War II. After World War I, the League of Nations transferred the previously Spanish territories of the Marshall Islands and the Northern Mariana Islands to Japanese colonial control.[6] During the interwar period, Japan utilized lands in the NMI for agricultural production, employing primarily Japanese and Okinawan migrant laborers in these industries.[7] With the start of the Pacific War, Japan recruited some of these laborers to construct military bases in both the NMI and the Marshall Islands while also forcefully conscripting Korean, Chamorro, and Marshallese laborers in these projects.[8] Two decades prior, and as discussed in the introduction, the United States illegally annexed Hawai'i via the 1898 Newlands Resolution, which was a domestic US Congress resolution not recognized by international law and included the seizure of 1.8 million acres of Crown and Government Lands. Kanaka Maoli widely protested against this resolution and US annexation through petitions that were signed by more than 38,000 of the population of 40,000.[9] As in the NMI, the sugar plantation industry in Hawai'i employed migrant laborers from Japan and its colonial territories, as well as other parts of Asia, leading to an extensive history of multiracial settler migration and racialized labor exploitation in the islands.[10] Significantly, US militarism had been intertwined with the sugar plantation industry even prior to the annexation of Hawai'i: the 1876 Reciprocity Treaty, which allowed for the duty-free trade of sugar between the islands and the US continent, also ceded Pu'uloa (now Pearl Harbor) to the United States for use as a military base upon its renewal in 1887. After annexation in 1898, the US government quickly began to transfer portions of former Crown and Government Lands to the US military for base construction.[11]

Thus, even before World War II—when Hawai'i, the Marshall Islands, and the NMI would become linked by a network of US military bases and camps—these lands were already connected by circuits of US and Japanese colonial and military expansion, labor migration, and capital. Significantly, the immigration of Japanese, Okinawans, and Koreans to Hawai'i and Micronesia was a direct result of Japanese colonial strategies of settler expansion across the Pacific Ocean in the late nineteenth and early twentieth centuries.[12] The concurrent project of US settler colonialism in Hawai'i benefited from these different groups of workers because the plantation industry produced wealth for a growing white oligarchy in the islands. The simultaneous rise of the US and Japanese empires was thus predicated on the acquisition of land, water, and natural resources necessary for plantation agriculture and militarization, as well as the displacement of Indigenous peoples across these spaces. Indeed, it was the intertwined histories of US and Japanese settler colonialism, Asian labor migration, and military buildup during this period that led non-Indigenous peoples to outnumber Kanaka Maoli and Chamorros in their own lands by the start of World War II.[13]

In Hawai'i and the Pacific Islands, settler militarism continued to intensify during the World War II period. Just as the United States placed Hawai'i under martial law from 1941 to 1944, it also invaded and occupied the Marshall Islands and the Northern Mariana Islands from 1944 onward.[14] All three locations were sites of immense US land acquisition and military buildup during the war. As I discussed in chapter 1, the US military occupied more than 600,000 acres of land during the World War II period. In the Marshall Islands, the US military government took unilateral control over land transfers, and in the Northern Marianas militarized land acquisition allowed for the construction of the airfield on Tinian that launched the *Enola Gay*, the B-29 aircraft that dropped the atomic bomb on Hiroshima. And—as this chapter will primarily discuss—in these spaces chosen for military base construction, battlegrounds, and training areas, settler militarism also required projects of wartime racialized incarceration.

By exploring the understudied history of internment and prisoner-of-war camps in Hawai'i and the Pacific Islands, this chapter decenters the focus on internment as a domestic project of racialized exclusion that took place only in the continental United States and reframes it within this longer transnational history of settler militarism and capitalism. The complex repertoire of internment and prisoner-of-war camps across these locations used varying logics of racialized military detention, settler colonial dispossession, and liberal governance to legitimize the evacuation and internment of Asian and Indigenous peoples across lands selected for US military projects. Wartime racialized incarceration, in this sense, was not only a means to contain the so-called enemy but also displaced Indigenous peoples from lands chosen for new bases, expropriated internee and prisoner-of-war labor for their construction, and bolstered US military expansion toward Asia. In this way, these settler military camps reiterated the racial and colonial primitive accumulation of lands and labor—which had begun in the nineteenth century—for the purposes of US wartime mobilization and military empire. The first section of this chapter illustrates how in Hawai'i the US military established internment and prisoner-of-war camps at the Honolulu Immigration Station, Sand Island Quarantine Center, and Honouliuli Internment Camp. This detainment project included civilians in Hawai'i who were of Japanese, Italian, and

German ancestry; enemy soldiers and officers captured in battle; and civilian noncombatants captured in Japanese colonial territories. The second section analyzes the imprisonment of Indigenous peoples and Japanese prisoners of war—including combatants and noncombatants—in the Marshall Islands and in the Northern Mariana Islands. The final section analyzes how security regulations in the Pacific Theater led to the circulation of internees and prisoners of war between these camps across the Pacific Ocean and the continental United States.

Internment and Prisoner-of-War Camps in Hawai'i

I have discussed throughout this book how under martial law in Hawai'i, settler militarism operated through a regime of racial liberal biopolitics that proclaimed to "improve" the life and labor of Kanaka Maoli, Asian settlers, and white settlers, even as it perpetuated militarized racial logics that demonized Japanese settlers, and settler colonial structures that denied Native sovereignty. Yet this ostensibly inclusionary wartime mobilization project still relied upon spaces of racial exclusion and incarceration, which strengthened its biopolitical optimization of the population to serve and labor in the militarized economy of the islands. Moreover, internment camps in Hawai'i were not only central to wartime racialized strategies that defined and segregated the "enemy alien" from the "loyal citizen," but they also formed a crucial piece of military strategy to acquire land and organize the islands as a base for combat in the Pacific War. Unlike in the continental United States, where camps were administered by the Department of Justice and the War Relocation Authority (WRA), internment camps in Hawai'i and other islands in the combat zone were organized by the Department of War.[15] As a result, internees and prisoners of war in these locations were held in adjacent compounds within the same camps and were governed by the regulations of the 1929 Geneva Convention.[16] Under martial law in Hawai'i, the Office of the Military Governor (OMG) was responsible for all administrative issues related to the internment of civilians, such as apprehension, interrogation, release, and parole. Thus, in contrast to camps in the continental United States, internment and prisoner-of-war camps in Hawai'i were closely connected in both administration and custody matters.[17]

The vast majority of those held in camps in Hawai'i were prisoners of war who were captured by the United States during Pacific Theater operations such as the Gilbert and Marshall Islands Campaign, the Battle of Midway, the Battle of Saipan, and the Battle of Okinawa, and who were imprisoned in Hawai'i on their way to being transferred to the US continent. Approximately 17,124 prisoners of war were held in the islands between December 7, 1941, and September 2, 1945, and the maximum number held at one time was 11,351.[18] Over the course of World War II, prisoner-of-war compounds in Hawai'i contained Japanese (4,766), Italian (5,000), Korean (2,692), and Okinawan (3,723) prisoners, as well as 36 prisoners who were Chinese, Indo-Chinese, Manchurian, or Formosan. Most Japanese and Italian prisoners were enlisted servicemen, but the majority of the 6,415 Koreans and Okinawans, and all 36 Chinese, Formosan, Indo-Chinese, and Manchurian prisoners of war, were noncombatant civilians.[19] Significantly, the racialized logics of military detention in Hawai'i and Micronesia were complicated by US and Japanese colonial histories, which blurred the Manichean distinction between "ally" and "enemy." For example, many Okinawan prisoners — civilian and soldier — had direct relatives living in Hawai'i on the other side of the barbed wire. Further, after the arrival of Korean civilian prisoners of war, it became necessary to construct a new compound to separate Japanese prisoners from Korean prisoners, who did not want their names reported to the Japanese government and often treated Japanese prisoners of war as their enemy. Military Governor Robert C. Richardson even specified that it was "highly desirable" for Korean prisoners of war to remain in Hawai'i as long as possible because they were especially productive laborers.[20] Here, the military government's regime of racial liberal biopower selectively incorporated so-called enemy prisoners of war whose behavior it deemed acceptable enough to contribute to wartime capitalism via militarized labor projects.

During this period of martial law in Hawai'i, civilians were already subject to a range of surveillance measures, including fingerprinting, travel bans, nightly curfews, and blackouts, which were intended to maintain "internal security." Yet Japanese settlers faced surveillance and restrictions beyond these measures. After the bombing of Pearl Harbor, the provost marshal immediately established the Alien Registration Bureau: under the regulations of this bureau, noncitizens were forced to register, request permission to change residence or occupation, disclose any history of foreign military service, and report all property holdings. The bureau also closely monitored all community gatherings of noncitizens. The 1940 census recorded 157,000 people of Japanese ancestry (including 35,000 noncitizens and 68,000 dual citizens) living in Hawai'i, constituting more than one-third of the islands' total population.[21] For comparison, this was more than the total number of Japanese and Japanese Americans interned in the entire continental United

States. Further, these stringent martial law measures and additional restrictions for noncitizens were apparently not enough to quell US military anxieties surrounding the threat of Japanese "alien enemies." On December 29, 1941, President Roosevelt established thirteen security regulations specifically for Japanese located in the combat zone via Proclamation 2533. One of these regulations specified that no Japanese citizen could enter or leave any US territory, and the secretary of war would intern any who violated this regulation. The proclamation also gave military commanders the power to prescribe restricted zones that noncitizens could not enter, as well as unilateral powers to arrest, detain, and intern noncitizen civilians. US martial law in Hawai'i complemented the secretary of war's authority in the territory by permitting the military governor to expand upon any of the above powers. This included the ability to intern citizens of "friendly" countries, such as American citizens who were of Japanese, German, or Italian descent, as well as the administration of curfews, civilian evacuations, and morale and censorship programs.[22] The administration of internment camps thus created an additional level of security within a carceral landscape already regulated by extreme surveillance policies.

The US Department of War originally planned to evacuate all Japanese from Hawai'i, but Military Governor Emmons argued that this would have deleterious effects on wartime productivity in the islands, stating that "the skilled labor in Hawaii is approximately 95% Japanese and there is no available soldier or civilian replacements."[23] This concern—which is a stark contrast to racialized discourses surrounding internment in the continent—speaks to the role of racial liberal biopower in accommodating racial difference in its social reproduction of settler militarism and capitalist expansion. For these reasons, the military government in Hawai'i detained only civilians who were suspected of disloyalty. In order to decide who would be interned and who would remain free, each civilian detained in Hawai'i received a trial in front of the newly created Internee Hearing Board (IHB), which included three citizens and one army officer. The IHB met for the first time on December 16, 1941, at the Honolulu Immigration Station.[24] The FBI, the Naval Intelligence Division, and the G-2 section of the Hawaiian Department reviewed the findings of each hearing and either agreed or disagreed with the board's decision. All papers from the case were then forwarded to the Office of the Military Governor, which made the final decision on whether or not to intern the individual.[25] Even as this selective logic of internment differed greatly from the mass incarceration of Japanese and Japanese Americans in the continental United States, it still strengthened the boundaries of acceptable wartime behavior for Japanese settlers through the military government's unilateral power to detain, interrogate, and intern any individual whose loyalty was questioned.

Several hundred people in Hawai'i had been under surveillance by the G-2 division of the Hawaiian Department and the FBI prior to the bombing of Pearl Harbor, and many of them were detained right away by the military police. Most of these individuals were prominent local Japanese settlers, including Thomas Sakakihara, a representative of the Hawaii District; Senator Sanji Abe, the president of the Japanese Chamber of Commerce; and approximately two hundred consular agents.[26] Next, the military government conducted broad-scale investigations of Japanese community leaders and others considered "dangerous," including Buddhist priests, Japanese language schoolteachers, Japanese businessmen, and Kibei."[27] The military government stated that internee hearings "were granted to suspected persons as a matter of justice in order that innocent persons should not suffer. . . . It was a means whereby persons disloyal to the United States were segregated from the loyal population so as not to influence the loyal ones."[28] These hearings were ostensibly ordered in the service of "justice," yet, as noted above, they were also accorded as a matter of pragmatism by a government dependent upon the labor of its potential prisoners for the construction and maintenance of its bases and plantation economy. Hearings also adhered to many of the same logics that organized the WRA loyalty questionnaire used in the US continent. Much like questions 27 and 28 of the loyalty questionnaire, the questions asked in the IHB hearings were often contradictory or very difficult to answer for individuals who had spent time in or who had family in both the United States and Japan.[29] The hearing board interrogated detainees at length about their personal background, family, time spent in Japan, military service in Japan, property holdings there, and whether they were loyal to the United States or Japan. The board also asked detainees about their activities between December 5 and 8, 1941; whether they had ever had contact with enemy soldiers; and whether they listened to Japanese radio broadcasts.[30] This is indicative of how the internment program in the Pacific Theater not only incarcerated Japanese settlers but also sought to gather information about these internees in order to define and "segregate" the disloyal from the loyal. Like the nutritional and educational studies discussed in chapters 3 and 4, these internee hearings in Hawai'i are another example of how settler militarism operated through logics of racial liberal biopolitics, which incorporated and differentiated racialized peoples in order to render them "knowable" through rationalized systems of data collection and categorization.

Harry Urata, a Kibei born in Honolulu in 1917 who would become known for preserving and teaching holehole bushi, folk music sung by Japanese settler plantation workers in Hawai'i, was one such internee who faced this type of interrogation. When asked if he would prefer the United States or Japan to win the war, Urata answered: "That is a most difficult question. I don't care—win or lose, just both countries negotiate." The hearing board asked Urata a series of other questions along these lines, such as "Isn't it a fact that you would rather see twenty American ships sunk in the Bismarck Sea, [than] you would twenty Japanese boats sunk by the Americans?" Urata's answers did not indicate that he would like to see either ships sinking. After the board continued to question him, he clarified that he was hesitant to answer in any way because he knew that the government was suspicious of him.[31] In another case, Shigeo Muroda, who was detained and brought in for questioning after allegedly leading a group of twelve other workers at Waianae Plantation to claim to be sick on the day of a blood drive, was asked similar questions about his background and loyalty to each country. After he denied these charges, the board asked why he had never expatriated from his Japanese citizenship. Muroda explained that the twenty dollars required to expatriate was too much for him to pay.[32] Neither Urata nor Muroda ever declared allegiance to Japan, and Muroda had never even been to Japan, despite being a dual citizen. Yet their apparent ambivalence led the board to conclude that they were disloyal, dangerous, and should be interned for the duration of the war.[33] As the military government stated, "In a vital and strategic outpost, like the Hawaiian Islands, it was felt that there could be no divided loyalty between the United States and Japan; a man of such divided loyalty was a disloyal man." Yet despite this zero-sum logic, many detainees, such as Urata and Muroda, refused to conform to the bipolarity of this wartime racial discourse.[34]

Approximately 1,444 Japanese settlers were interned in Hawai'i during the war, about half of whom were American citizens.[35] Three major camps were constructed in O'ahu during this period: the Honolulu Immigration Station, the Sand Island Quarantine Center, and the Honouliuli Internment Camp. Two of these, the immigration station and the quarantine center, were already-existing state institutions that the military took over under martial law and converted into camps. Planning for these two camps began months before the bombing of Pearl Harbor, and in some instances the takeover and transformation of these spaces relied upon the declaration of martial law.[36] In addition to prisoner-of-war compounds at the Immigration Station, Sand Island, and Honouliuli, there were additional camps in O'ahu at East Range

Schofield, Kahili Valley, Kāneʻohe, Fort Hase, Hauʻula, and Waikakaula. There were also two compounds on the Big Island, in Hilo and the Kilauea Military Camp.[37]

The military chose the Honolulu Immigration Station as a primary internment location because it already had facilities for detention, interrogation, and administrative duties—yet it also made significant changes to this structure in preparation for its wartime functions. The architectural changes made to the Immigration Station in order to make it into a camp included the addition of nine-foot man-proof fences around the station that were topped with three strands of barbed wire and included two gates. Additional barbed wire divided the administration building, where the military government offices and record books would be located, from the detention building, where detainees would be held and interrogated. The military also constructed barracks for both internees and officers, a dormitory for fifty internees, an alarm system, and at least four fifty-foot-high guard towers equipped with floodlights. The US military increased the capacity of the Immigration Station from 254 to 400 internees by building two 106-person barracks, a kitchen and mess hall for internees, increased utilities, two 63-person barracks for guards and officers, and a kitchen and mess hall for guards and officers.[38] Throughout the war the Immigration Station was mostly used as an administrative center for receiving and interrogating detainees, and only officers and internees "of a better class" were interned permanently in the dormitories there.[39] The administration building of the immigration station also included an area where three hearings could take place at once, a reception office, a large room for stenographers, a processing room, an office for file storage, and space for administration officers. The detention barracks, which formerly held immigrants waiting on admission decisions, now held detainees awaiting the decision of the Internee Hearing Board and the OMG.[40] In July 1944 the Prisoner of War Base Camp Headquarters was established in the immigration building, where it would govern the regulations of camps throughout the Pacific Islands, including the Northern Mariana Islands. The 810th and 623rd Military Police Companies and Operations Office of the 724th Military Police Battalion were also located at the Immigration Station.[41] The fact that the very building used to admit immigrants was also inherently capable of imprisoning them is emblematic of how this internment project was part of the longer history of racialized immigration control in the United States. As scholars such as T. Fujitani, A. Naomi Paik, and Kelly Lytle Hernández argue, internment and other forms of racialized incarceration should not be analyzed as anomalies within US liberal democracy but rather should be understood as complicit with the administration of state violence against and confinement of racialized peoples both inside and outside of US borders.[42] This history is embedded in the design and transformation of the Immigration Station's structure.

At the beginning of the war, all detainees were processed at the Immigration Station for their hearing, and then they were transferred to Sand Island Quarantine Station to await the board's decision.[43] The military government argued that Sand Island was ideally suited to be an internment camp: it was a small island close to Honolulu that was already equipped with housing, mess halls, and administrative facilities. The camp was divided into four compounds, two of which were for male Japanese internees and held two hundred fifty detainees each, one of which was for females of all races and held forty detainees, and the last of which was for male Germans and Italians and held twenty-five detainees. Each compound had its own mess hall, sanitary controls, and internal administration, which ensured the complete separation of groups.[44] This quarantine station, which was now functioning as an internment camp, segregated its prisoners as if race and disloyalty were diseases, which, eerily, resonates with an October 1942 letter circulated by the White House press secretary stating that the Japanese were "infected": "Let us face the fact now that these people are infected—just as surely and as dangerously as if they were carrying plague germs. We must treat them so. . . . We must have the moral guts to render the Japanese in Hawaii impotent for treachery and evil."[45] Again, as in chapter 2, we can see how discourses of medicine and disease can dovetail with the militarized, carceral logics of detention and security. This camp contained minimal community facilities for internees. There was a canteen where internees could purchase cigarettes, tobacco, magazines, vitamins, and phonographic records. Civilian internees were permitted to write two letters per week of twenty-four lines each and a postcard. Civilians held in the camps often gardened or undertook carpentry projects to maintain the camp's grounds.[46]

The Red Cross reported that there were good exercise facilities and that the sanitary conditions were excellent. In accordance with the Geneva Convention, Gustaf W. Olsen, vice-consul of Sweden, the country in charge of Japanese interests during the war, and the International Red Cross were required to inspect Sand Island periodically. After a visit in October 1942, Olsen specified that the camp was in good condition, the buildings were new, and there were garden plots outside with vegetables, which he stated many internees tended voluntarily "with zest and evident delight." Olsen reported on a visit on December 19 that "from my observation and contacts I am satisfied that the evacuees are well treated. No complaints have been heard; rather there have been many expressions of appreciation and thanks to the officers and personnel."[47] Further, the Red Cross reported that the food at Sand Island was the same quality as that of the army. Although there was a complaint that the food lacked vitamin content, the Red Cross deemed this unfounded: "All the internees are unanimous in affirming that the authorities treat them well and they express only praise and sentiments of respect for the commander of the camp."[48]

These favorable reports from the Swedish legation and the Red Cross are starkly contrasted by the accounts of Japanese internees in their oral histories and memoirs, many of which recall experiences of exploitation and discrimination during wartime internment in the islands. Dan Nishikawa characterized his experience in the camps as one in which malnourishment, the refusal of medical help by officers, and incidents of internees going mad were common occurrences. As he remembered of Olsen,

> I recall he visited the island once every two month. At his very first time, he refused us saying, "You were Americans, and I could do nothing for you." Shortly after . . . only five minutes later as I recall, when we went back accompanying Issei [Japanese citizens] to see him, he had gone already. At his next visit, we rushed to his office with our Issei, but he had gone already . . . in less than one minute. After we moved to Honouliuli, he had never come to visit our camp. However, according to a recent newspaper article, he was awarded the second order of merit [from the Japanese government] for his various efforts helping Japanese during the war. We could not understand at all what he did to help Japanese.[49]

Because the experiences of Japanese American internees contradict the reports by Olsen, we can conclude that Olsen's report did not capture the totality of conditions at the quarantine station. As Nishikawa wrote in his diary, "Our life at the Sand Island was worse than the jail for villain. We were treated like in hell—no disregard for human rights with extreme racial discrimination."[50] Furthermore, this points to wartime contradictions within the international legal frameworks of the Geneva Convention: there was no state body assigned to protect American citizens of Japanese descent held in camps in the combat zone because these individuals were ostensibly protected by the very state government that was imprisoning them.

The War Department completed the construction of the Honouliuli Internment Camp in early 1943 and moved all internees from Sand Island to this new location in March of that year. Like Sand Island, it used barbed wire to separate male and female Japanese internees, and all white internees, and each compound had its own kitchen and mess hall. By the middle of September 1943, all white internees were either released or paroled. The prisoner-of-war compound was divided into separate areas for Japanese officers, enlisted men, and noncombatant civilians captured during battle. There was also a tailor shop, a dental office, a dispensary for medical treatment, a recreation field, and a room where a motion picture was shown two times per week. Internees and prisoners of war at Honouliuli also tended gardens with vegetables and fruits such as beans, corn, cabbage, carrots, tomatoes, and watermelons.[51]

Scholars such as T. Fujitani have described how internment camps in the US continent were ostensibly designed to cultivate internees as democratic civil subjects, in that they mimicked the setup of a small town, stressed Americanization in schools, and even sought to recruit internees as soldiers. The US government later used this as evidence that internment was a democratization project that assimilated Japanese Americans and prepared them to resettle in American communities.[52] The government enforced this assertion with the sanitized language that it used to describe the camps: government documents referred to internees as "evacuees" and used language such as "relocation center" or "resettlement community" instead of "internment camp" or "concentration camp."[53] Fujitani argues that this illustrates how technologies of racialized incarceration in the camps were complicit with the administration of US liberal governance in the continent.[54] However, camps in Hawai'i were administered and organized differently, and did not attempt to replicate settlements, towns, or communities. The Department of War separated men and women in different compounds, did not intern children, and provided minimal community facilities. In fact, the Military Governor's Review Board stated that it would be administratively impractical and unwise for security to allow families to be interned at Honouliuli: "There is not only insufficient space available, due to anticipated increased numbers of Prisoners of War, but the problems relating to Family Internment [such] as schooling, recreation, and cooperative endeavor of mutual benefit to all would be difficult to handle."[55] Those imprisoned were explicitly called "internees of war" or "prisoners of war," and the camps were called "internment camps" or "concentration camps" in military documents. Chapter 3 analyzes how domestic campaigns in Hawai'i cultivated the nuclear family formation as a central unit of settler military and capitalist social reproduction, yet here in the camps we can see the literal separation of families deemed to include so-called enemy aliens. Further, whereas camps in the US continent stressed

Americanization and allegedly sought to prepare evacuees for eventual re-settlement, the context of martial law made camps in Hawai'i more analo-gous to prisons within a prison.

That is, these camps formed an additional level of imprisonment within an already carceral landscape meant to bolster settler colonial land acquisi-tion in the territory and maintain US military security in the combat zone. The different administration of camps in Hawai'i suggests that World War II racialized incarceration did not only contribute to US state power in the continent; rather, these projects were imbricated with the liberal governance of a growing US military empire that reiterated racial and colonial modes of primitive accumulation as it expanded beyond the continental west coast toward Asia.

Camps in the Marshall Islands and the Northern Mariana Islands

During this period, settler militarism and racial liberal biopolitics operated together in the service of wartime capitalism; military expansion rearticu-lated these expropriative projects via the administration of camps and the construction of bases across Indigenous lands in Hawai'i and the Pacific Islands. In addition to the camps located in Hawai'i and the continent, the US military invaded, occupied, and established camps in Japanese colonial territories throughout the Pacific Ocean. In the Marshall Islands and the Northern Mariana Islands, the navy organized and governed internment and prisoner-of-war camps, with the army also contributing facilities and per-sonnel. The first military occupation of a former Japanese territory in the Pacific Islands took place after the navy's invasion of the Marshall Islands in January 1944 and was administered by Military Governor Admiral C. W. Nim-itz. The US occupation of the Northern Mariana Islands began in June 1944 after the Battle of Saipan, when the military interned Indigenous Chamorros, Carolinians, and Japanese prisoners of war on the islands at Camp Susupe.[56] The plans for and operations of these camps were not isolated or aberrational endeavors; there was a circulation of expertise in military occupation, im-prisonment, and labor conscription throughout these locations in the Pacific Islands. Admiral Nimitz communicated frequently with the military gover-nor of Hawai'i, Robert C. Richardson, about the military occupation of the Marshall Islands, and he also sent regular reports on its progress. Further-more, Major Spillner of Hawai'i's Prisoner of War Base Camp organized and trained administrative staff for camps in Saipan.[57] These military projects replicated and adapted techniques of martial law and internment and in this way socially reproduced settler militarism across the Pacific Ocean: as projects of land acquisition and Indigenous displacement, these carceral projects contributed to US settler colonialism, yet as part of a broader US militarization project in the Pacific Islands, they were also agents of US empire and expansion.

Just as in Hawai'i's "laboratory for the study of martial law," supposedly benevolent biopolitical regimes operated in tandem with settler military camps in Micronesia, where tropes of rescue and rehabilitation obfuscated the primitive accumulation of land and labor that propelled US wartime military expansion. The racialized logics of these camps and their techniques of incarceration varied depending on the racial, colonial, and military context in which they were located. As in Hawai'i, the US military largely depicted Japanese prisoners of war and detained noncombatant civilians, many of whom were Korean and Okinawan, as a dangerous threat to US operations. Unlike in Hawai'i, the US military justified internment in the Pacific Islands by depicting the interned Marshallese, Chamorros, and Carolinians as peaceful yet primitive peoples who were incapable of modernization without American aid.[58] According to the US military, these camps allegedly "improved" life for Native peoples after their liberation from Japanese colonialism, even as they were part of a military occupation in the service of US imperial war.[59] Admiral Nimitz described the US occupation in the Marshall Islands as one of "humanitarian treatment" and presented the Marshallese as an inexperienced yet friendly and cooperative people. He also stated that the principal goals of the US occupation in the Marshall Islands were to contribute to military security in the Pacific Theater, maintain the international credibility of the United States, and to gain knowledge that could be useful for future US occupations of former Japanese island territories.[60]

As the Battle of Saipan ended in the NMI, the US military constructed "safe areas" that segregated Japanese nationals from Chamorros and Carolinians.[61] The US military specified that although Japanese soldiers and civilians were being held as prisoners of war, Chamorro and Carolinian internees were being "protected" for their own good. For example, a navy account describing Japanese prisoners of war in the medical center included a picture of an injured young boy with this caption: "This haughty son of Japan appears to disdain the care he has so far received. Yet he has much to be thankful for." On the other hand, the tone of US military interactions with Chamorros was paternalistic, if still suspicious of whether their loyalties lay with Japan or the United States.[62] The navy described how Americans nursed Chamorro children back to health, improved their diet and exercise regimens, and taught them to garden in an orderly fashion. Chamorro living spaces were nicer than the Japanese barracks: some Chamorro barracks included room dividers and almost always had some tin exterior walls. Over the course of the war, the navy reported that the camps in the Northern Mariana Islands held around 1,350 Koreans, 3,000 Chamorros and Carolinians, and 13,800 Japanese, of whom 78 percent were Okinawans.[63] Camp Susupe was divided into three separate compounds: one for Chamorros and Carolinians, one for Koreans, and one for Japanese and Okinawans.[64] In the Marshall Islands, where there were fewer Japanese settlers, the US military government sent at least 21 Japanese and Korean civilians and soldiers to be held as prisoners of war in Hawai'i.[65] In both the Northern Mariana Islands and the Marshall Islands, the portrayal of internment camps as modernization projects helped to justify US military occupation and expansion in locations that were strategic to the building of US global empire and national legitimacy on the global stage.

The US military's attention to internees' health contributed to this narrative of humanitarian internment: public health projects in the Marshall Islands and the NMI were an example of how racial liberal biopolitical projects employed under martial law in Hawai'i could be adapted in the service of US settler military expansion into others' lands. In the Marshall Islands, US military forces evacuated and interned those who were living in areas that they deemed unsafe, and endeavored to improve sanitation, hygiene, and communicable-disease prevention by establishing a licensing system for Marshallese medical practitioners, as well as two hospitals complete with limited medical supplies, a pharmacy, a laboratory, a dental dispensary, and an examining room. US officials educated the Marshallese community in what they considered to be the proper disposal of waste and sewage, insect control, and food and water sanitation.[66] As in Hawai'i, the military also mandated the vaccination of the entire Marshallese population over the age of one against smallpox, arguing that these immunizations would protect the soldiers stationed there and ensure that the Marshallese were as productive in defense labor as possible. The military penalized those who violated any of these public health regulations with a fine of up to ten dollars or six weeks of labor.[67] The US Navy in Saipan recounted that Chamorro civilians received "a standard of medical attention which is superior to any the people of Saipan as a whole have previously enjoyed," indicating that the navy felt that it was doing a service for a people unfamiliar with modern medicine and hygiene.

Much as in Hawai'i, these wartime biopolitical projects in the Marshall Islands and the NMI combined logics of detention and medical security: even as internment officials optimized and "improved" the health of their prisoners, they simultaneously excluded them as a racialized people in need of modernization. Interestingly, in Saipan the US military specified that the internees' teeth needed a phenomenal amount of attention and that the dentistry office at the camps was one of the most necessary dispensaries.[68] The extraction of and care for teeth is usually not a vital medical necessity that saves lives, like medical care for broken limbs, gunshot wounds, or disease. Rather, in the context of the wartime violence that Chamorros, Carolinians, and Marshallese had endured before receiving this medical care—often at the hands of the US military itself—this aesthetic attention to teeth highlights the assimilationist nature of this biopolitical health project.[69] Much as in Hawai'i, as these medical efforts accommodated the racial difference of newly occupied peoples, they did so in order to constitute a productive population to labor in service of the American war effort.[70] As settler militarism expanded across landscapes in Hawai'i, the Marshall Islands, and the Mariana Islands, these varying technologies of biopolitical incorporation, racial differentiation, Indigenous displacement, and incarceration contributed to US empire building.

The racialization, detention, and evacuation of Asian and Indigenous peoples during this period were also integral to the US military's acquisition of Native lands in locations that were crucial to US wartime strategy. As discussed in chapter 1, in Hawai'i the US military occupied more than six hundred thousand acres of land during the period: this took place unilaterally via lease, license, and land condemnation—all of which were expedited via the Second War Powers Act in 1942.[71] In the Marshall Islands the US military government evacuated and interned the Marshallese who were living in areas that it had chosen for base development. It also forbade the Marshallese to transfer, sell, or give land without its permission, a policy directly at odds with longtime Marshallese practices of ri-pālle (planting) and imōn aje (land gifts).[72] The US military employed the Marshallese as laborers in the construction of these bases: Marshallese had the option of moving to US military bases for six months at a time, where they lived in labor camps and worked eight-hour days for six days per week, and were paid between forty and eighty cents per day. The United States called this system "humanitarian" in contrast to former Japanese labor policies of forced conscription for military construction, and about four hundred Marshallese participated in this work during the first year.[73] Yet significantly, this labor-camp program aided in the reorganization of local people for the social reproduction of settler militarism and wartime capitalism: the US military enlisted the Marshallese in defense labor, housed civilians in areas that did not obstruct military operations, and created an increasingly dependent relationship between the local economy and the US defense industry. During the Pacific War, the US military government also unilaterally acquired land in the Northern Mariana Islands to build bases, including the airfield on Tinian that launched the *Enola Gay*.[74] During the postwar period, the United States would go on to conduct a series of military tests in the Marshall Islands, including sixty-six nuclear bomb trials between 1946 and 1958, which are estimated to have yielded the radioactive fallout of over seven thousand Hiroshima bombs.[75]

Thus, biopolitical regimes of incarceration that purported to rehabilitate and rescue obfuscated the acquisition and desecration of Indigenous lands, the expropriation of Indigenous labor, and the violent disregard and abuse of Indigenous health and lifeways. Jenise Domingo Takai, a Chamorro resident of Saipan, captured the contradiction of US wartime "humanitarian" occupation when she wrote of her family history, "There were two worlds on Saipan during World War II. The world outside with soldiers filled with pride and love for their country fighting for their cause, and the world inside the stony basin with locals praying to end the war, praying to stop all the hatred, praying that it would all soon end."[76] That is, after the United States achieved victory in the Battle of Saipan, it continued its project of settler military expansion in an imperial war against Japan rather than assisting in the decolonization of lands and peoples who had endured decades of Japanese colonialism. Moreover, after conducting nuclear testing in the Marshall Islands in the postwar period, the US government allowed the Marshallese to return before the area was safe and, via Project 4.1, enrolled at least 539 individuals (including children) in nonconsensual medical experiments on the effects of radiation contamination on the environment and human body. Not only did Project 4.1 neglect to actually treat any of the debilitating effects of radiation exposure but the confidential nature of this study allowed the United States to evade responsibility for Marshallese concerns about the acute medical problems they were experiencing.[77]

These histories of wartime incarceration and its violent aftermath in the Marshall Islands and the NMI again lend nuance to our understanding of how US settler militarism, which claims to protect and cultivate life and land, actually operates in contradiction to the life and health of those it purports to govern. US projects of military occupation in Saipan and the Marshall Islands governed to optimize, in that they brought Native peoples into their biopolitical administration, yet they did so through a racialized administration of military detention that was only invested in life to the extent that it could be leveraged for international diplomacy or expropriated for labor. Moreover, these settler military camps, which were predicated on land acquisition and the dispossession of Native peoples, also contributed to US military expansion as part of a project of military basing in the Pacific Theater. Thus, as these extractive carceral projects rearticulated and amplified racial and colonial modes of primitive accumulation—which in Micronesia, built upon histories of Japanese colonialism—they created the conditions of possibility for the ascension of the United States as a postwar global empire.

Circuits of Camps across the Pacific Ocean

As this network of internment and prisoner-of-war camps replicated and transformed modes of settler militarism across the Pacific Ocean, these camps were also connected by the circulation of prisoners between locations in Asia, Micronesia, Hawaiʻi, and the continental United States. In Hawaiʻi, after the Internee Hearing Board evaluated internees throughout the war, the US military government then moved them accordingly between the Honolulu Immigration Station, Sand Island, and Honouliuli, depending on their loyalty status. Additionally, the secretary of war and the secretary of the navy arranged for, and even encouraged Japanese families to be "released" from internment in Hawaiʻi and evacuated to the continental United States for "resettlement."[78] The US military presented this option under the guise of freedom and family reunification, despite the fact that individuals were merely being transferred from an internment camp in Hawaiʻi to a relocation center in the US continent.[79] This led family members who had previously not been interned to choose to be held in camps in the United States, sometimes without realizing the consequences. For example, Tsukasa Setogawa transferred to the continental United States believing that when he arrived he would be free, and did not understand why he was sent to yet another internment camp.[80] Another individual, the son of former internee Sam Nishimura, recalls his family's attempt to reunite with their father in a "relocation center": "I remember preparations were being made for us to go to the mainland. Mom . . . sewed woolen outfits for us because we were to go to a cold place. To me it sounded pretty exciting to be able to go to a place across the ocean and best of all we'd be with pop. Little did I know that we were lucky not to have gone."[81] Some internees found conditions in the camps in the US continent to be better than in Hawai'i, but they continued to encounter new hardships: "[We] have lived in a much more difficult environment than here. So we are thankful to be with our families, although some of [us] have had some financial difficulties. Everyone is astonished at the lowness of the monthly compensation. Each family has had to spent [sic] from $200 to $400 to prepare for the winter. Thus savings have been depleted."[82]

Some internees did not want to relocate to the continental United States and hoped to stay in Hawai'i to remain with family. After being interned at Honouliuli for over a year and initially applying for "repatriation" to Japan, Harry Urata wrote to Major Springer in August 1944 to request that he remain interned in Hawai'i because his mother did not want him to separate from her "for the welfare of our family unity." In the following weeks, Urata learned that because the provost marshal had already received his request for repatriation, this could not be ensured.[83] He wrote again to Major Springer later that year: "My mother being old and not having anyone to lean on have asked my [sic] to stay in the Islands until my brother comes home from the Army, so that in case there should be an accident, I can be near to help her." Still, although the hearing board reviewed his case, he was evacuated to Tule Lake on November 7, 1944. Evidence that contributed to his hearing decision included censorship intercepts of letters he had written to a friend at Tule Lake in which he criticized the US treatment of Japanese and Japanese Americans in the United States. In another, he wrote to his mother that he was applying for repatriation because he felt distrusted by his friends and country.[84]

In addition to Urata, at least 340 other internees from Hawai'i were transferred to Tule Lake during the war, from both Honouliuli and other camps in the continental United States, allegedly because "many of them became associated with trouble-making groups and were a disturbing influence."[85] At one point, Dillon Meyer, the director of the War Relocation Authority, asked that fewer internees be transferred from Hawai'i to the continental United States: "They have proved to be unwilling workers and about half of them have answered no to the loyalty question number 28 in the selective service registration form. They definitely are not the kind of people who should be scattered among the West Coast evacuees."[86] Meyer's statement builds upon the provost marshal's imperative to segregate the "loyal" from the "disloyal": after deciding that Japanese internees from Hawai'i were more likely to engage in disruptive behavior, Meyer decided that they should be interned separately from the more "well-behaved" internees in the continental United States. This technique of segregation reveals the US government's anxiety about the subversive power of those who they were imprisoning and the possibility of an uprising if these individuals were improperly organized and divided. Again, this is reminiscent of the earlier insinuation that the Japanese were "infected" or that disloyalty was a "disease" that could be spread to others. Yet at the same time, it reveals how this regime of racialized military detainment and the circulation of internees between these camps also created opportunities for internees to share strategies of resistance—as many did at Tule Lake and other camps in the continent.[87]

Between November 1942 and March 1943, 1,037 Japanese internees were transferred from camps in Hawai'i to WRA centers on the continent. Of these, 810 were sent to Jerome, 226 were sent to Central Utah, and one was sent to Minidoka. Between May 1943 and July 1945, 81 internees from Hawai'i entered WRA relocation centers. Additionally, between 1942 and 1944, 99 Japanese from Hawai'i were released or paroled from Department of Justice internment camps and transferred to WRA relocation centers.[88] The total number of Japanese from Hawai'i held in WRA centers throughout the war was 1,217.[89] Over the course of the war, the Department of Justice interned 897 Japanese from Hawai'i, along with 10 children who were born during the war in these camps, bringing the total to 907.[90]

The history of this movement of internees between camps in Hawai'i and the continent broadens our understanding of the wartime internment project. As discussed above, camps in Hawai'i were military projects administered by the Department of War, whereas the WRA and Department of Justice organized internment camps in the continental United States. Yet we can also see how these civilian and military institutions collaborated to create a network of camps that extended beyond the continental west coast and into the combat zone of the Pacific Theater. Furthermore, it is significant that the US government characterized relocation centers in the continental United States as "free" in contrast with the internment camps in Hawai'i. This resonates with Fujitani's analysis of the network of camps in the United States as a labyrinth of "(un)freedom" that disrupted the binary between "free" public space and the "unfree" camp. Fujitani argues that although the existence of relocation centers constituted the rest of America as "free," the range of internment methods within the larger system of camps, which included Tule Lake, the camp designated for "dangerous internees," rendered the primary relocation centers "free" by distinction. Thus, internees in primary camps such as Manzanar were simultaneously "free" in relation to prisoners at Tule Lake, and "unfree" in relation to the rest of the United States.[91]

This idea of the network of camps as a "labyrinth" in which one could be simultaneously "free" and "unfree" nuances our understanding of the reliance of liberal governance upon varying modes of racialized incarceration, and also highlights how this larger network of camps was constituted relationally. For example, camps in Hawai'i were depicted as "unfree" in relation to camps on the continent, and Hawai'i, a US territory under martial law, was designated as an "unfree" space in relation to the continental United States. It is precisely this variation in logics of racialized exclusion and liberal governance and the explicit collaboration between civilian camps and military camps that allowed this broader project of wartime racialized incarceration to rationalize itself across differing contexts in the US continent, Hawai'i, and Micronesia.

In addition to the movement of internees from Hawai'i to the continental United States, Hawai'i served as a hub for prisoners of war who were circulated between Asia, Micronesia, and the US continent. Because the Geneva Convention required that prisoners of war be moved from the combat zone to the interior as soon as possible, they could not be held in Hawai'i permanently.[92] For example, Japanese lieutenant Kazuo Sakamaki, the first prisoner of war captured by the United States in World War II, was captured at Waimanalo Beach on December 7, 1941, transferred to Sand Island in January 1942, and held there until February 1942. He was eventually transferred to Angel Island, San Francisco, and then finally to Camp McCoy, Wisconsin. Additionally, one male and one female Japanese civilian were captured in the Marshall Islands, transferred to Honouliuli, and then later sent to the continental United States. Another individual, Saburo Arakaki, was captured in the Battle of Saipan, held in a prisoner-of-war camp in the Mariana Islands, and then was sent to Hawai'i in 1945. Sadao Tazawa, who was Okinawan and born in O'ahu, returned to Okinawa with his family when he was twelve years old, was drafted into the Japanese Navy, and was captured during the Battle of Saipan. He was then sent to a camp in Hawai'i, where he continued to be held even into mid-1947.[93] As stated earlier, the US military government transferred at least twenty-one Japanese and Korean civilians and soldiers captured in the Marshall Islands to prisoner-of-war camps in Hawai'i.[94] Thousands of Japanese, Okinawan, and Korean prisoners of war and civilian noncombatants were transferred from Camp Susupe in the Northern Mariana Islands to Honouliuli Internment Camp in Hawai'i, but many would soon be returned to camps in the NMI in late 1945. Of those held at Honouliuli, all but 342 Japanese prisoners of war who were classified as soldiers were evacuated from Hawai'i to the continental United States by September 1945. Most were transferred to camps at McCoy, Wisconsin; Clarinda, Iowa; and Angel Island, California.[95] The Red Cross reported that some prisoners of war were held in Sand Island for longer than was desirable and blamed the wartime difficulties of transportation for this extended stay. This was true of Honouliuli as well: the majority of the Italian, Korean, Okinawan, Chinese, Formosan, Indo-Chinese, and Manchurian prisoners of war, many of whom were civilian noncombatants, still remained at Honouliuli in September 1945. We also know that the military governor preferred to keep Korean prisoners of war in Hawai'i as long as possible.[96]

After the war ended, all US internment and prisoner-of-war camps began to close and release those interned. Internees from Hawai'i who were transferred to the continental United States and interned in Department of Justice camps were permitted to return to the islands, except for those who were repatriated to Japan. Of the 907 internees held in Department of Justice camps, 671 returned to Hawai'i, 112 were sent to Japan, 8 were deceased, and 116 chose to remain in the continent. Of the 1,217 held in WRA relocation centers, 806 returned to Hawai'i, 125 remained in the continental United States, 136 were sent to Japan, and 10 were deceased.[97] Similarly, prisoners of war held in camps in the continent such as Camp McCoy immediately began to be released to their home country. However, those held in Hawai'i, Saipan, Guam, and other locations in the Pacific Islands continued to be held for up to one year or more because of concerns about security in the Pacific Islands as well as the need for labor.[98] Four hundred Japanese prisoners of war were transferred from Hawai'i to camps in Guam and Saipan in May 1946.[99] On December 3, 1946, the last Japanese prisoners of war departed from the Big Island, and camps at Kīlauea and Keaukaha both closed. The remaining 7,000 prisoners of war held in Hawai'i would be released to their home countries of Japan, Korea, and Okinawa later that year, but at that point there were at least 100,000 prisoners still held in camps in the Philippines, Okinawa, the Carolines, and the Mariana Islands.[100]

This circulation of internees and prisoners of war between camps and militarized sites in Asia, Micronesia, Hawai'i, and the US continent broadens our understanding of the role of these camps in the reproduction of US settler militarism and imperial war. The circulation of internees and prisoners of war across this differentiated yet linked network of camps exercised varying combinations of imprisonment and biopolitics upon those incarcerated across the Pacific Islands and the US continent, depending on colonial logics of race, indigeneity, and civilian/combatant status. Furthermore, this network of camps supported the primitive accumulation of labor for the construction of bases that were central to US military strategy in World War II and the Cold War. This network ostensibly attempted to move captured soldiers and civilians away from the combat zone, yet in many cases they were held in island outposts for the duration of the war and beyond as the US military continued to expropriate defense labor from prisoners of war. In this way, World War II camps were embedded in the expansion of US settler militarism and wartime capitalism across the Pacific Islands toward Asia.

Although the administration of these camps contributed to the making of US empire, the increased movement of peoples across these sites also created new opportunities for human connection and resistance. Earlier, I discussed how the director of the WRA, Dillon Meyer, was anxious about the fraternization between internees from the continental United States and those from Hawai'i because it had led to increased protest and unrest in the camps. Furthermore, at the Honouliuli and Sand Island internment camps in Hawai'i, the circulation of prisoners between camps in the Pacific Islands also reunited family members. Japanese settler migration across the Pacific Islands in the late nineteenth and early twentieth century had played a prominent role within Japanese colonial expansion—this was true in locations such as Hokkaido, Okinawa, Taiwan, Korea, Hawai'i, Micronesia, and the continental United States.[101] After this period of migration, Manichean wartime logics separated diasporic families who lived in territories that were controlled by the rival US and Japanese empires. As a result, almost all Okinawan prisoners of war, most of whom were civilians and by 1945 constituted approximately one-fourth of the more than ten thousand prisoners of war held in Hawai'i, had immediate family members or other relatives living in the islands whom they had not seen in years.[102] Thus, although these camps formed a carceral labyrinth of military detainment, the transfer of prisoners from Okinawa and Saipan to Hawai'i actually allowed many estranged family members to meet again. While Okinawan prisoners of war were doing forced labor such as the construction or cleaning of military facilities and parks, family and other community members would drive to these sites to offer material and emotional support in the form of candy, fruit, cigarettes, money, or other gifts. Others played music for those being forced to work, and some even dug holes under the fences so children could sneak rice balls into the camps.[103] As one prisoner wrote in a letter to their older sister, with whom they had just reunited, "Kindness that is deeper than the ocean and higher than the mountains; how shall I repay that kindness?"[104] However, these meetings were still constrained by camp regulations: in trying to reunite with family members when working on a job site, prisoners of war would risk the punishment of a two-thirds deduction of their pay and two weeks of confinement with only bread and water. Poignantly, one prisoner had endured this punishment seven times in order to visit with his family, and twenty-two others had been punished for this five times.[105] Although this type of occurrence surprised US military officials, it is indicative of how the US map of settler colonialism and military occupation mirrored and intersected with that of Japanese colonial expansion and migration. Moments of reunion and support between Okinawan family members on either side of the barbed wire in Hawai'i illustrate how community and kinship networks persisted in spite of this colonial and military history.

Much like Kaho'olawe and Mākua Valley—two places severely marked by the violence of settler militarism—were sites for Hawaiian activism and alternative placemaking, Sand Island and Camp Honouliuli likewise became spaces for commemoration and resistance. On June 4, 2017, more than two hundred people attended a memorial for twelve Okinawan prisoners of war who were held in Hawai'i and passed away in the camps. Those in attendance included two former prisoners, families of the twelve diseased, and community members from both Hawai'i and Okinawa. Despite reports that these individuals were buried at Schofield Barracks, there is also evidence that these graves were removed in 1946 during a military expansion project. Still, there is no record that the remains of these individuals were ever returned to Okinawa or Japan. Former prisoner of war Hikonobu Toguchi, who helped to organize the memorial, stated that "it is the role of the living to comfort the souls of those who must have been wandering in the sky of Hawaii. I hope many people come to know about this." This memorial was held at Jikoen Hongwanji Temple in Honolulu, but prior to the service, attendees traversed the sites of the former camps at Sand Island, Honouliuli, and Schofield Barracks, where these prisoners had been held and were perhaps even still buried.[106] Not only was the vast attendance of family and community members from both Okinawa and Hawai'i significant, but the attendees' conscious movement across these spaces of settler military confinement suggests both a remembrance and a critique of the violence that has affected these landscapes and those who lived—or were imprisoned—on these lands.

The larger landscape in and around Sand Island has long been affected by other forms of dispossession and resistance before, during, and after the World War II period. For example, adjacent to Sand Island is Mokauea, O'ahu's last Hawaiian fishing village. Mokauea was at one point completely self-sustaining through its community's repertoire of maritime knowledges, cultivation of medicinal and edible plants, and fishpond. It is also thought to once have been home to a master canoe builder. During World War II, this land was acquired by the US military and dredged for the construction of a seaplane runway, which runs directly between Sand Island and Mokauea.[107] Many Mokauea families lived there for generations until 1975, when the State of Hawaii attempted mass evictions in an effort to expand the Honolulu Airport and burned down at least five homes in the process. State of Hawaii transportation director E. Alvey Wright later admitted to hiring a private contractor to set these homes on fire.[108] Despite this colonial violence and displacement, residents fought back and, partially through the formation of the Mokauea Fishermen's Association, negotiated a sixty-five-year lease with the State of Hawai'i from 1978 through 2043. Today, the Mokauea Fishermen's Association and others continue to work to help Mokauea families restore their homes and make the village self-sustaining once again through educational and community-based work.[109] From the 1970s onward, Sand Island was also home to a community of more than one hundred families until the State of Hawaii Department of Land and Natural Resources demanded their eviction. Those living on Sand Island continually insisted on their right to remain through protest and negotiation with the state government, even as their homes were bulldozed and many were arrested. Although many of them were not able to return permanently, others, such as Puhipau Ahmad, who is renowned for his documentary films on Hawaiian sovereignty and culture, were motivated by this experience to enact change through other channels.[110] Overall, these narratives illustrate some of the many ways that Hawaiian and Asian diasporic communities have sought alternatives to settler militarism, and they also illustrate how lands affected by settler military violence can become meaningful spaces for this radical reimagining.

....

This chapter constructs a relational analysis of World War II camps across Hawai'i, the Marshall Islands, and the Northern Mariana Islands—three locations that have long been affected by histories of US and Japanese colonialism and war. Internment and prisoner-of-war camps in Hawai'i constituted a project of racialized military detainment that reinforced martial law's adjacent project of racial liberal biopower, which incorporated peoples of all races in its administration yet simultaneously intensified the boundaries for acceptable "loyal" behavior on the part of racialized groups. The histories of camps in the Marshall Islands and the Northern Mariana Islands illustrate how these complementary projects of racial inclusion and exclusion—which combined to intensify the primitive accumulation of land and labor—were reproduced across the Pacific Ocean in the service of US settler militarism. This heterogeneous project of wartime racialized incarceration created a geographic taxonomy that alternately organized, displaced, excluded, and assimilated racialized and Indigenous peoples in order to clear and secure land for US military projects. This network was further connected by the circulation of prisoners between these camps, which led to the sharing of experiences of containment and strategies for resistance, sometimes even reuniting familial relations. US military occupation throughout the Pacific Islands delineated a hierarchy of humanity through access to land and property that removed Indigenous communities from their own lands, imprisoned racialized peoples in militarized spaces, and expropriated defense labor from prisoners of war. These camps organized peoples, land, and labor along a military geography that stretched across the continental United States, Hawai'i, the Pacific Islands, and Asia in the service of US military security and territorial control during the Pacific War and beyond. Thus, World War II camps were not only complicit with the administration of state power and liberal governance, but they were also agents of US settler militarism and capitalist expansion, as the US racial state became a racial empire.

Conclusion

The Making of US Empire

During World War II in Hawai'i, militarized technologies of martial law, discourses of "military necessity," and the waging of imperial warfare articulated with settler colonial projects of occupation and Native land dispossession, racial liberal biopolitical logics of improvement and differentiation, and capitalist modes of primitive accumulation— including the racialized, gendered, and colonial expropriation of life, land, and labor. Together, these varying and contested regimes socially reproduced the contradictory relations of settler militarism, which is dependent upon the vitality of life and land in order to reproduce itself, yet also avariciously consumes those same lives and natural resources that it needs to subsist via violent and extractive projects. As this book traces, racial liberal biopolitical projects not only reproduced the worker in the service of total wartime mobilization, but they also sought to absolve and occlude the contradictions of settler militarism and capitalism while intensifying these structures' hierarchical conditions of emergence. Thus, although wartime settler militarism permeated everyday life in hyper-visible forms such as censorship, racialized incarceration, labor conscription, land occupation, and environmental destruction, it also operated through less ostensibly coercive though still insidious means— including health and hygiene regimes, nutritional and domestic campaigns, and education and language instruction.

Throughout this period the US military unilaterally conscripted and reorganized more than six hundred thousand acres of land in the islands to fortify racial liberal biopolitical projects in the service of imperial war. Despite the illusion of justice produced by eminent domain court cases, all exchange of land in Hawai'i is in fact primitive accumulation sustaining the reproduction of capitalist relations beneath the ruse of fair exchange. Further, the US military's supposed "improvement" of property according to the capitalist rendering of its "best and most profitable use" in eminent domain proceedings relied on a racial liberal biopolitical logic that rationalized its partition, organization, hierarchies of access, and desecration as in the service of public good, rather than as irrational and destructive. At the same time, this logic of improvement was always responding to Native sovereignty and assertions of the right to remain: Kanaka Maoli modes of resistance at Kahoʻolawe and Mākua Valley offer examples of social movements that refuse to be contained by these liberal capitalist logics.

Across these occupied spaces, settler militarism and racial liberal biopolitics operated together in the service of capitalism: martial law projects such as those concerning public health, domestic science, and education used logics of race, indigeneity, and gender as a means through which to differentiate and optimize the population for wartime production and reproduction. For example, the Honolulu Blood Bank allowed peoples of all races to donate, but the military government published statistics to artificially produce racialized and colonial notions of indebtedness that could be repaid via contributions to the blood bank. Racial liberal biopolitical projects such as mandatory immunization and blood donation programs, family health and nutrition campaigns, and Americanized education included peoples of all races out of wartime necessity, while also strengthening the code of gendered white patriotism as a regulatory power, intensifying racial differentiation, and precluding an analysis of indigeneity and colonialism. These settler military projects permeated all aspects of daily life, including the home and the classroom: martial law sharpened gendered roles and responsibilities, and it enlisted nurses, mothers, and teachers in the reproductive labor of raising healthy citizens and soldiers. "Home defense" projects constructed American mothering and nutritional practices as "healthy" and "secure" over and against those of Asian settler families, while seeking to suppress and mask the persistence of Kanaka Maoli land-based epistemologies of health. Not only did women's affective labor reproduce the racial and colonial dynamics of US settler militarism, but women of all races were also subject to military scrutiny in a way that was not the case in the continental United States.

Thus, martial law policies that sought to "improve" and reproduce a healthy population in Hawaiʻi also worked to regulate and differentiate it according to the racialized, gendered, and colonial desires of settler militarism, capitalism, and imperial war. As the subject of increased research and examination, wartime discourses of medicine, nutrition, and language exceeded the realm of bodily discipline and regulated at the level of the population by seeking to normalize standards for health, diet, speech, and comportment. Gendered and racialized biopolitical projects also nurtured the proper knowledges and sentiments within the community such that children and other civilians would grow to feel comfortable living and participating in a "home front" that was also located in the violent, militarized, and colonized space of the "war front." Domestic campaigns and wartime recipes combined rationing regulations with Americanized nutritional standards and the nostalgic comfort of family dining, thus bringing settler militarism into the domestic sphere. Hostesses planned themed dinner parties that made light of martial law conditions, domesticated the threat of the racialized enemy into consumable food and dress, and rendered settler colonial violence as benign fantasy. Teachers wielded wartime pedagogies to promote racial tolerance, US citizenship, and the supposed superiority of "American" speaking and writing skills to students and their families. Significantly, each of these racial liberal biopolitical projects sought to organize social life, affect, and biology such that racialized and colonial regimes of primitive accumulation would seem benevolent and life cultivating rather than predatory and life depleting. Yet Kanaka Maoli, Asian settlers, and others negotiated and resisted these violent projects at every turn during wartime and beyond: Hawaiian epistemologies envisioned health and sovereignty beyond and outside the realm of forced immunization and medical surveillance; Indigenous and immigrant foodways disrupted the Americanized and settler colonial logic of assimilationist nutrition campaigns; and Hawaiian, Pidgin, and Japanese language use continued despite the forced standardization of so-called American speech and writing in the classroom.

Capitalism has throughout history produced the conditions of its own demise, including the dynamics of scarcity and insufficiency that hinder its ability to reproduce itself without reiterating its violent regimes of primitive accumulation within and expanding them outward.[1] Settler militarism is one mode through which racial, gendered, and colonial means of expropriation recapitulated themselves in the service of capitalism via settler regimes of Indigenous land dispossession, racialized biopolitical projects of incorporation and differentiation, and military expansion toward additional markets, labor, land, and natural resources. During World War II and its aftermath, US empire continually rearticulated and elaborated its primitive accumulation of life, land, and labor as it expanded across the Pacific Islands toward Asia, while presenting its violent modes of expropriation as benevolent means toward modernization, democratization, or capitalist progress.

US internment and prisoner-of-war camps formed a crucial piece of this settler military occupation and expansion during World War II and beyond. Concurrent with racial liberal biopolitical projects that sought to "improve," surveil, and categorize according to the racialized and gendered requirements of settler militarism, the US military government interned Japanese settlers it deemed "disloyal" in military camps across the United States, Hawai'i, and the Pacific Islands. In this way, this supposedly "inclusionary" wartime biopolitical regime still relied upon spaces of racialized exclusion and internment, which not only strengthened the biopolitical optimization of the population for war but also facilitated the primitive accumulation of land and labor for US military expansion. That is, as the US military interned Japanese immigrants, Native peoples, and prisoners of war across camps in Hawai'i, the Marshall Islands, and the Northern Mariana Islands—and, further, governed the circulation of internees between these camps and the continental United States—these military occupations replicated and transformed the dynamic of settler militarism across the Pacific Ocean. As projects of land acquisition and Indigenous displacement, these camps contributed to US settler colonialism, yet as part of a broader US militarization project, they also contributed to US imperial expansion in Asia and the Pacific Islands. Yet significantly, even as this differentiated yet linked system of camps elaborated military mechanisms for incarceration, it also created new opportunities for resistance in the camps and produced circumstances for the reunification of families that had been separated by decades of US and Japanese colonialism.

As a "laboratory" for martial law, Hawai'i was a site of experiment in settler military culture that could be improvised and expanded elsewhere. The history of US military occupation and internment across Hawai'i and the Pacific Islands illustrates one way in which settler militarism reproduced itself across the Pacific Ocean. Beyond this, after the end of World War II these infrastructures continued in Hawai'i and across the Pacific Islands: settler militarism created the conditions of possibility for the ascension of the United States as a postwar global empire.[2] A key military outpost, Hawai'i formed a principal piece of a larger network of US military bases in the Pacific Islands and Asia that expanded dramatically during World War II, naturalized the power hierarchy between the United States and Japan's former empire during the Cold War period, and still continues to expand today. The extended period of martial law in Hawai'i created the conditions to refine, amplify, and elaborate biopolitical mechanisms to "'make' live and 'let' die" in the service of US settler militarism and capitalism. This expropriative repertoire of racialized and gendered differentiation, Indigenous displacement, land acquisition, and labor exploitation that proliferated in Hawai'i during World War II would continue to innovate means to manage life, lands, and peoples throughout the Pacific Islands and Asia.

That is, the wartime control of people and labor—through technologies such as land dispossession, public health, domestic science, education, and internment—constituted one period in a longer genealogy of settler militarism that continued to evolve and transform as it expanded to other sites in the Pacific Islands and Asia: from Guam and Okinawa, to the Korean War, to the Vietnam War. In addition to military occupations and internments in Hawai'i, the Marshall Islands, and the Northern Mariana Islands, the United States also evacuated and interned Unangax from the Aleutian and Pribilof Islands across six camps in Southeast Alaska from 1942 to 1945.[3] The US military had intentionally left Guam, an unincorporated territory since 1898, undefended when the Japanese military captured it on the same day as the bombing of Pearl Harbor, and then portrayed its subsequent recapturing in 1944 as a "liberation."[4] American forces evacuated and interned Okinawans and other Japanese nationals during the infamous March 1945 Battle of Okinawa, which led to more civilian casualties than any other battle in the Pacific Theater.[5] When World War II ended, in 1945, the United States began the early stages of the seven-year Allied occupation of Japan.[6] After acquiring the Marshall Islands as part of the Trust Territory of the Pacific Islands, the United States evacuated the Marshallese in order to conduct a series of military tests, including sixty-six nuclear-bomb trials between 1946 and 1958, then allowed them to return before the area was safe from radiation contamination, and subsequently conducted nonconsensual medical studies on them.[7] By the end of World War II and into the 1950s, the United States possessed the most expansive military base system in the world. Almost half of these units were located in the Southwest and Central Pacific circuits.[8] The United States would not end its official occupation of Okinawa until 1972, which made it a key military outpost for US wars and proxy interventions in Korea, Vietnam, Laos, and Cambodia.[9] US military bases still cover approximately 20 percent of Okinawa, where, as is the case across many US military outposts, there is an extensive history of militarized sexual violence.[10] The Pentagon currently plans to relocate five thousand marines from Okinawa to Guam and the Northern Mariana Islands: the US military already occupies a third of the land on Guam, and this expansion would take over two-thirds of the land on Tinian, as well as all of Pågan, for military exercises such as amphibious landings, bomb testing, and live-fire training.[11] Today, Hawai'i remains the headquarters of the United States Pacific Command.

Overall, World War II experiments in racial inclusivity in Hawai'i not only became hallmarks of racial liberalism in the postwar US continent; they also served as a model for a US racial liberal *empire* that expanded via its own obfuscation and combined logics of development and dispossession, care and regulation, inclusion and incarceration, and liberation and violence. Contemporary regimes of militarization, basing, and land acquisition in the so-called War on Terror demonstrate that the racial, colonial, capitalist, and carceral logics of settler militarism have only intensified within our current era of "permanent war."[12]

Yet, although the carceral realities of US martial law and military occupation, including its regime of forced patriotism and assimilation, suppressed many organized social movements during the World War II period, we can consider how these injustices were perpetrated in anticipation of an opposition that could have been, eventually would be, and continues to gain strength today: the multiracial labor unionization and activism that surged in postwar Hawai'i, the Protect Kaho'olawe 'Ohana movement, and the Hawaiian sovereignty movement that it emboldened are just a few examples of how opposition to settler militarism persists today across Hawai'i and the Pacific Islands. Hawai'i Youth for Democracy, an antifascist and pro-socialist movement spearheaded by radical Hawaiian and Asian women shortly after the war ended, wrote in its constitution, "Fascism does not end with the military defeat of Germany and Japan. Fascism does not end as long as we have anti-Negro practices, anti-Semitism, anti-Catholicism, labor-baiting, and red-baiting."[13] Today, anti-GMO activism in Hawai'i connects decolonization to environmental sustainability, and food sovereignty movements work to restore landscapes by centralizing Kanaka Maoli planting practices and food accessibility.[14] Likewise in Okinawa, farming and food production across militarized landscapes is one method for Okinawans to enact Indigenous resurgence and reciprocity to the land, community, and ancestors while foregrounding and envisioning a sustainable future that centralizes Okinawan practices and epistemologies.[15] Protests against the Thirty Meter Telescope (TMT) at Mauna Kea are a vital illustration of Hawaiian communities contesting the universality of settler military and capitalist logics.[16] Candace Fujikane articulates "mapping abundance" as a fundamentally decolonial act of refusal toward capitalism's destruction of life that "foreground[s] practices of ea—translated as life, breath, political sovereignty, and the rising of the people." In the case of Kanaka Maoli protests against the TMT, Fujikane argues that kia'i (protectors) refuse US settler representations of Mauna Kea as a "wasteland," instead insisting upon the laws of the akua that centralize the abundance of water forms, among other elemental relations, in this space.[17] In the Northern Mariana Islands, community opposition to current plans for US military expansion has taken many forms, including a 2010 lawsuit against the Department of Defense (DOD) over plans for firing ranges on ancestral lands on Guam, a 2015 lawsuit against the US Navy and the DOD for failing to produce an environmental impact statement concerning military buildup, and continuous actions by community organizers fighting for decolonization and demilitarization.[18]

To truly conceive of justice, one must start with decolonization. Kanaka Maoli and other racialized and Indigenous peoples have always sought alternatives to settler militarism, pushed against its prescribed limits, and refused to acquiesce to its projects, thus disrupting the social reproduction of settler militarism, its logics, and its modes of occupation. Settler militarism is an incomplete and flawed response to the continued vitality of Indigenous life and sovereignty and, as such, continually creates the conditions for its own demise. This book has endeavored to trace the historical contradictions at the heart of settler military and capitalist projects—which continue to structure our present—with the hope that this relational research can contribute to ongoing work that collectively envisions and moves toward their undoing.

Notes

ABBREVIATIONS

AR19: Japanese American Relocation and Internment—The Hawai'i Experience, JCCH

CM: Carey D. Miller Collection, HC

HC: Hawaiian Collection, Hamilton Library, University of Hawai'i at Mānoa, Honolulu, Hawai'i

HWRD: Hawaii War Records Depository, Hamilton Library, University of Hawai'i at Mānoa, Honolulu, Hawai'i

JCCH: Japanese Cultural Center of Hawai'i, Honolulu, Hawai'i

JIR: Japanese Internment and Relocation Files, Hamilton Library, University of Hawai'i at Mānoa, Honolulu, Hawai'i

NA: National Archives and Records Administration II, College Park, Maryland

NASF: National Archives at San Francisco, San Bruno, California

RG 21: RG 21, Records of District Courts of the United States, U.S. District Court, District of Hawaii, Honolulu, Civil Case Files, 1900–1984, NASF

RG 126: RG 126, Records of the Office of Territories, Classified Files, 1907–1951, NA

RG 181: RG 181, Records of Naval Districts and Shore Establishments, Naval Facilities Engineering Com. Western Division, Land Acquisitions, 1944–1961, NASF

RG 494: RG 494, Records of U.S. Army Forces in the Middle Pacific, 1942–1946, NA

INTRODUCTION. SETTLER MILITARISM, RACIAL LIBERAL BIOPOLITICS, AND SOCIAL REPRODUCTION

1   The *Honolulu Advertiser* and the *Honolulu Star-Bulletin* were two of the major newspapers in Hawai'i and still exist together in one entity as the *Honolulu Star-Advertiser*. Joseph Garner Anthony considered the two newspapers to be essentially an outlet for military government propaganda during this period. Anthony, *Hawaii under Army Rule*, 38.

2   Scheiber and Scheiber, *Bayonets in Paradise*, 80.

3   "Interview with Samuel K., Jr., Kamaka," in "An Era of Change: Oral Histories of Civilians in World War II Hawai'i," interview by Holly Yamada, 546, UH Center for Oral History, http://hdl.handle.net/10125/29869.

4   Throughout this book I use the terms *Kanaka Maoli*, *Native Hawaiian*, and *Hawaiian* to refer to the Indigenous people of Hawai'i. The term *Hawaiian*, in this sense, does not simply refer to an individual who was born or has lived in Hawai'i but rather denotes indigeneity to Hawaiian lands through genealogical ties. On logics of white possession, see Moreton-Robinson, *White Possessive*; and Arvin, *Possessing Polynesians*.

5   As Dean Itsuji Saranillio writes of Asian and Asian American settlers in Hawai'i, "These are the non-Indigenous and nonwhite groups who were exploited for their labor and have their own histories of subjugation by imperialism, yet occupying a kind of liminal space that traces racial difference and instances of cohesion with haole settlers and/or Native peoples. These processes consisted of a delicate arrangement of variously mediated struggles, which were orchestrated by U.S. designs for empire and global imperial politics, labor immigration and protest, economic depression and planter access to U.S. markets, racial tensions and alliances, and struggles for equality in tension with deoccupation." Saranillio, *Unsustainable Empire*, 74. Haunani-Kay Trask's work has been seminal to the study of Asian settler colonialism. See Trask, "Settlers of Color," as well as other essays in Fujikane and Okamura, *Asian Settler Colonialism*; and Saranillio, "Why Asian Settler Colonialism Matters." Keeping in mind this complex history of settler migration and racial formation, I use both *settler* and *immigrant* when referring to Asians in Hawai'i. This is because Asian immigrants and Asian Americans in Hawai'i were and are settlers.

6   Maui was also attacked on this date, as was Guam. Saranillio, *Unsustainable Empire*, 186; Camacho, *Cultures of Commemoration*, 41.

7   Walter Short had at that time occupied the position of Hawaiian Department commander lieutenant general. Okihiro, *Cane Fires*, 210.

8   "General Emmons Gives Views," *New York Times*, May 17, 1942; Okihiro, *Cane Fires*, 239.

9   The term *Nisei* is a Japanese-language term that refers to a Japanese American who is a second-generation immigrant. Accordingly, the term *Issei* refers to the first generation, and *Sansei* refers to the third generation. *Kibei* is a term used to refer to Japanese Americans (usually Nisei) who went to Japan to receive higher education and then returned to the United States. See Fujitani, *Race for Empire*.

10   Another principal example of US martial law is Military Governor General Arthur MacArthur Jr.'s declaration of martial law in the Philippines on December 10, 1900. In Hawai'i, at first, nightly curfews between 6:00 p.m. and 6:00 a.m. applied to every civilian, including citizens and "enemy aliens." On February 3, 1942, curfew was extended to 8:00 p.m. for all civilians except for "enemy aliens." This remained the same until September 1, 1942, when curfew was extended to 10:00 p.m. for US citizens. On December 10, 1943, "enemy aliens" were also

allowed to be out until 10:00 p.m. By General Orders No. 62 on July 19, 1944, all blackout restrictions were removed, but curfew remained from 10:00 p.m. to 5:30 a.m. "Part Four: Security Regulations Affecting Alien Enemies and Dual Citizens," folder 46, Box 4, AR19: Japanese American Relocation and Internment—The Hawai'i Experience (AR19), JCCH, 237–39.

11 Anthony, *Hawaii under Army Rule*.

12 For my previous work on settler militarism, see Nebolon, "'Life Given Straight'"; and Nebolon, "Settler-Military Camps."

13 Trask, *From a Native Daughter*; Fujikane and Okamura, *Asian Settler Colonialism*; Trask, "Settlers of Color," 45–65. Patrick Wolfe, though not the first to use the term "settler colonialism," authored influential work theorizing settler colonialism's structures and operation. See, for example, Wolfe, "Settler Colonialism." Other scholarship that has greatly influenced my understanding of how settler colonialism operates includes Deloria, *Playing Indian*; O'Brien, *Firsting and Lasting*; Kauanui, *Hawaiian Blood*; Byrd, *Transit of Empire*; Coulthard, *Red Skin, White Masks*; Saranillio, *Unsustainable Empire*; Estes, *Our History Is the Future*; Moreton-Robinson, *White Possessive*; and Arvin, *Possessing Polynesians*. On not letting settler colonial studies stand in for Native American and Indigenous studies, the role of Indigenous scholars in studies of settler colonialism, and the multiple genealogies of settler colonial studies, see Kauanui, "'Structure, Not an Event'"; and Kauanui, "False Dilemmas."

14 Woodward, "Military Landscapes." See also González, Gusterson, and Houtman, *Militarization*.

15 Manu Karuka analyzes this colonial dynamic as one of "countersovereignty." He states that "my invocation of 'countersovereignty' proceeds, first, from a sense that settler invocations of sovereignty require recognition of Indigenous modes of relationship, however muted or displaced, in order to maintain any semblance of stability or coherence." Karuka, *Empire's Tracks*, 2.

16 For example, Philip Deloria and Patrick Wolfe argue that claims of settler sovereignty paradoxically depend upon a symbolic idea of the "Native" as a necessary element of differentiating the settler colony from the mother country. Philip Deloria writes that a key contradiction of American identity is the simultaneity of its reliance on the so-called Indian Other in order to exist and its need to eliminate it in order to complete its individualization: "Here, then, lies a critical dilemma of American identity: in order to complete their rite of passage, Americans had to displace either the interior or the exterior Indian Other. As long as Indian Others represented not only us, but also them, Americans could not begin to resolve the questions swirling around their own identity vis-á-vis Indians and the British. Yet choosing one or the other would remove an ideological tool that was essential in propping up American identity without Indians. At the same time, there was no way to make a complete identity while they remained." Deloria, *Playing Indian*, 37. As Patrick Wolfe writes of settler colonialism, "On the one hand, settler society required the practical elimination of the natives

in order to establish itself on their territory. On the symbolic level, however, settler society subsequently sought to recuperate indigeneity in order to express its difference—and accordingly, its independence—from the mother country." Wolfe, "Settler Colonialism," 389.

17   Saranillio, *Unsustainable Empire*, 9.

18   For Lisa Yoneyama's insightful critique of this "good war" narrative, see Yoneyama, *Hiroshima Traces*; and Yoneyama, *Cold War Ruins*.

19   Kajihiro argues that the white oligarchy and the US military formed an alliance during the territorial period leading up to World War II. Furthermore, Saranillio analyzes how Hawai'i statehood continues to sustain and elaborate US settler, economic, and military investments in the islands. Trask, *From a Native Daughter*; Silva, *Aloha Betrayed*; Kajihiro, "Militarizing of Hawai'i," 172; Saranillio, "Colliding Histories," 283–309; Saranillio, *Unsustainable Empire*.

20   Trask, *From a Native Daughter*, 11, 12; Silva, *Aloha Betrayed*, 126; Gonzalez, "Wars of Memory."

21   Native Hawaiians continue to contest US possession of these 1.8 million acres today, which were never legally transferred by the Hawaiian Kingdom but were ceded in 1898 by the Republic of Hawaii, a de facto government created by white settlers in the aftermath of the overthrow. Kauanui, "Sorry State," 110–12.

22   Silva, *Aloha Betrayed*, 160.

23   Kauanui, *Hawaiian Blood*, 2, 28–29. See also Silva, *Aloha Betrayed*.

24   The Big Five included Castle and Cooke, Charles Brewer and Company, Alexander Baldwin, Theophilus H. Davis and Company, and Heinrich Hackfield and Company (eventually renamed the American Factors). On the Big Five, see Saranillio, *Unsustainable Empire*, 68–69, 70–71, 85, 97.

25   The allegation of rape was later proven to be falsified. The five men accused were Joseph Kahahawai, Ben Ahakuelo, Horace Ida, David Takai, and Henry Chang. Ida was severely beaten but survived his attack. The men responsible for these acts of violence were arrested but received a commuted sentence. Saranillio, *Unsustainable Empire*, 72–74. See also Stannard, *Honor Killing*; and Rosa, *Local Story*.

26   Anthony, *Hawaii under Army Rule*, 5.

27   United States Department of Defense, "Report on Study of Military Real Property, State of Hawaii," [Washington?], 1960, Hawaiian Collection, University of Hawai'i at Mānoa (HC), 5.

28   Gonzalez, *Securing Paradise*, 118–19.

29   Scholars such as T. Fujitani have critiqued the ideal of white military masculinity, particularly in regard to how it led to the problematic idealization of the "patriotic World War II Nisei soldier" as the model for the successful assimilation of Japanese American immigrants. Fujitani, *Race for Empire*. Scholars have analyzed the shifting racial triangulation between Native Hawaiians, Asian settlers, and white settlers throughout the twentieth century. J. Kēhaulani Kauanui argues that in the 1920s, Hawaiians were defined as "Native" over and against "alien" Asian immigrant laborers but were still considered subordinate to white

settlers, who prioritized Americanization as the path to success for the Hawaiian territory. My work on the World War II period contributes to this scholarship through its focus on how these racializations of Asians and Native Hawaiians changed so radically between the prewar and postwar periods. Fujikane and Okamura, *Asian Settler Colonialism*; Saranillio, "Colliding Histories"; Saranillio, *Unsustainable Empire*; Kauanui, "Colonialism in Equality," 636–37.

30   In her article "Asian American Studies and the 'Pacific Question,'" J. Kēhaulani Kauanui argues against the irresponsible inclusion of Pacific studies underneath the banner of Asian American studies, yet she also argues that because of the shared histories of Asia and the Pacific Islands, the comparative engagement of Pacific studies and Asian American studies is vital. The term *Asian/Pacific American* similarly erases this heterogeneity: work by Kauanui, Saranillio, Fujikane, and Okamura has illustrated how despite the fact that Asian American settlers have faced colonialism, oppression, and labor exploitation, they do not have the same relationship to the US state as do Native peoples in the Pacific Islands. Kauanui, "Asian American Studies." See also Diaz and Kauanui, "Native Pacific Cultural Studies on the Edge"; Diaz, "To 'P' or not to 'P'"; Kim and Sharma, "Center-To-Center Relationalities." Key volumes that place histories of US and Japanese colonialism and war in conversation include Fujitani, White, and Yoneyama, *Perilous Memories*; Shigematsu and Camacho, *Militarized Currents*; Chen, *Asia as Method*; Camacho, *Cultures of Commemoration*; Fujitani, *Race for Empire*; Yoneyama, *Hiroshima Traces*; and Yoneyama, *Cold War Ruins*.

31   On this call for "specificity," see, for example, Teaiwa, "bikinis and other s/pacific n/oceans." On the reorientation of the colonial gaze that perceives islands in Oceania through the lens of "smallness," see Hauʻofa, "Our Sea of Islands."

32   Byrd, *Transit of Empire*; Goldstein, *Formations of United States Colonialism*; Vimalassery, Hu Pegues, and Goldstein, "Introduction," quotation from 1; Vimalassery, Hu Pegues, and Goldstein, "Colonial Unknowing"; Leong and Carpio, "Carceral States"; Day, *Alien Capital*; Saranillio, *Unsustainable Empire*; Byrd, Goldstein, Melamed, and Reddy, "Predatory Value"; Karuka, *Empire's Tracks*; Singh, *Race and America's Long War*; Hernández, *City of Inmates*; Walia, *Border and Rule*; Hu Pegues, *Space-Time Colonialism*; Kim, *Settler Garrison*; Lê Espiritu Gandhi, *Archipelago of Resettlement*.

33   As Nick Estes writes, "Bloody wars of conquest defined the period following the United States' assertion of control over the river trade, lasting for nearly half of the nineteenth century," elaborating that these wars constituted a "total war on Indigenous life." Estes, *Our History Is the Future*, 90. See also Grenier, *First Way of War*. On the long history of militarization's impacts on and appropriation of Native communities and land, see LaDuke, *Militarization of Indian Country*.

34   Uenten, "Rising Up," 92. See also Ginoza, "R&R at the Intersection."

35   There is an extensive history of US biopolitical governance across colonial and racialized contexts. Among others, see Anderson, *Colonial Pathologies*; Polk, *Contagions of Empire*; Vora, *Life Support*; Moreton-Robinson, *White Possessive*;

Melamed, *Represent and Destroy*; and Reddy, *Freedom with Violence*. On biopower, see Foucault, *"Society Must Be Defended,"* quotation from 241; Foucault, *History of Sexuality*.

36 Federici argues that "Foucault's analysis of the power techniques and disciplines to which the body has been subjected has ignored the process of reproduction, has collapsed female and male histories into an undifferentiated whole." Further, Foucault's theories do not leave room to think about an individualized subject, a way "outside" of the regime, or resistance. Federici, *Caliban and the Witch*, 8. In this book I use Foucault alongside theorists of race and colonialism and Marxist theorists of social reproduction, whose dialectical approaches urge us to understand that any time power is exerted, there is inevitably resistance.

37 "Summary of Annual Report, Board of Health, Fiscal Year Ending, June 30, 1943," 942 Reports—Annual—Governor—1943, Box 561, RG 126, NA, 164. "Report of the Governor of Hawaii Honorable Joseph B. Poindexter to the Secretary of the Interior for the Fiscal Year Ended June 30, 1942," File No. 942 Reports—Annual—Governor—1942, Box 561, RG 126, NA, 12. See also Allen, *Hawaii's War Years*, 336, 366.

38 This was lower than the national average, in which women constituted 49.8 percent of the total population. Bailey and Farber, *First Strange Place*, 191–92. On World War II gender dynamics in the continental United States, see Escobedo, *From Coveralls to Zoot Suits*, 3. See also Milkman, *Gender at Work*; Yellin, *Our Mothers' War*; Anderson, *Wartime Women*; and Honey, *Creating Rosie the Riveter*.

39 By 1948, white residents made up 33.4 percent, Japanese made up 32.6 percent, and Hawaiians made up 15 percent. Statistics for 1940 draw from the US census, and those from 1948 were estimated by the Department of Health: T. H. Perry, F. Philipp, and Ralph Elliott, *Hawaii and Its People; Land Utilization*, Table 2 (Honolulu, 1949), HC.

40 After the passing of the Hawaiian Organic Act in 1900, all Native Hawaiians became US citizens. Kauanui, "Colonialism in Equality," 642; Kauanui, "Hawaiian Nationhood," 32–33; Polmar and Allen, *World War II*, 372.

41 Fujitani, *Race for Empire*.

42 On the shift from "vulgar" to "polite" racism, see Fujitani, *Race for Empire*; Dudziak, *Cold War Civil Rights*; Singh, *Black Is a Country*; Melamed, *Represent and Destroy*; and Man, *Soldiering Through Empire*. On Hawai'i statehood and liberal multiculturalism, see Saranillio, *Unsustainable Empire*; and Miller-Davenport, *Gateway State*.

43 Foucault, *Security, Territory, Population*, 6.

44 Brown, *Regulating Aversion*, 26, 28.

45 This is part of a larger historical trend in which colonial states have considered territories, particularly islands, as "laboratories." Edmond and Smith, *Islands in History and Representation*. Quotation from "Part I: Historical Overview of the Internal Security Program in Hawaii" (Part I), "Part I: Historical Overview of the

168   NOTES TO INTRODUCTION

Internal Security Program in (Copy #3)" (Part I: #3), Box 892, Military Government of the Territory of Hawaii (MGHI), RG 494, NA, 1; emphasis mine.

46 Melamed, *Represent and Destroy*, 5. See also Reddy, *Freedom with Violence*.

47 Kauanui, "Colonialism in Equality," 642; Kauanui, "Hawaiian Nationhood," 32–33.

48 On white possession, see Moreton-Robinson, *White Possessive*, 129. Further, as Maile Arvin argues, "In the logic of possession through whiteness, both Polynesia (the place) and Polynesians (the people) become exotic, feminized possessions of whiteness—possessions that never have the power to claim the property of whiteness for themselves. Instead, the Polynesian race is repeatedly positioned as almost white (even literally as descendants of the Aryan race), in a way that allows white settlers to claim indigeneity in Polynesia, since, according to this logic, whiteness itself is indigenous to Polynesia." Arvin, *Possessing Polynesians*, 3.

49 Part I, Part 1: #3, Box 892, Military Government of the Territory of Hawaii, RG 494, NA, 7.

50 Goodyear-Kaʻōpua, Hussey, and Wright, *Nation Rising*.

51 Moreton-Robinson, *White Possessive*, 47–61.

52 As Alyosha Goldstein writes of US colonialism, "United States colonialism is a continuously failing—or at least a perpetually incomplete—project that labors to find a workable means of resolution to sustain its logic of possession and inevitability by disavowing the ongoing contestation with which it is confronted and violent displacement that it demands." Goldstein, "Toward a Genealogy," in Goldstein, *Formations of United States Colonialism*, 3.

53 Robinson, *Black Marxism*; Johnson and Lubin, *Futures of Black Radicalism*; Day, *Alien Capital*; Goldstein, "'In the Constant Flux'"; Melamed, "Racial Capitalism"; Federici, *Caliban and the Witch*; Federici, "Silvia Federici"; Lowe, "Afterword"; Coulthard, *Red Skin, White Masks*; Byrd, Goldstein, Melamed, and Reddy, "Predatory Value"; Jenkins and Leroy, *Histories of Racial Capitalism*; Kosher, Cacho, Byrd, and Jefferson, *Colonial Racial Capitalism*; Nichols, *Theft Is Property!*; Bhandar, *Colonial Lives of Property*; Davis, "Women and Capitalism"; Weinbaum, *Afterlife of Reproductive Slavery*; Morgan, *Reckoning with Slavery*.

54 Marx conceives of primitive accumulation, or "so-called primitive accumulation," as the "original sin" of capitalism through which producers were forcefully divorced from their means of production and subsistence and transformed into "'unattached' proletarians" (Marx, *Capital*, 363–65). Although Marx considers the expropriation of the agrarian peasant and enclosure of the commons in England and Scotland as the paradigmatic case, he writes of primitive accumulation in the United States: "The discovery of gold and silver in America, the extirpation, enslavement, and entombment in mines of the aboriginal population, the beginning of the conquest and looting of the East Indies, the turning of Africa into a warren for the commercial hunting of black-skins, signalized the rosy dawn of the era of capitalist production. These idyllic proceedings are the chief

momenta of primitive accumulation" (Marx, *Capital*, 365–71, quotation from 376). Yet many scholars have since contested this fundamental understanding of primitive accumulation as a discrete "stage" in the progression from feudalism to capitalism, arguing that it is instead an ongoing dynamic central to the process by which capitalism reproduces itself. For example, Cedric Robinson argues that the dispossession of Black workers for the development of global capitalism did not end with the abolition of slavery: "As peasants, as tenant farmers, as migrant laborers, as day laborers, as domestic servants, and as wage labor, their expropriation extended into the present century" (Robinson, *Black Marxism*, 112). Silvia Federici argues that Marx was mistaken when he theorized that the violence of the earliest phase of capitalism would recede: "A return of the most violent aspects of primitive accumulation has accompanied every phase of capitalist globalization, including the present one" (Federici, *Caliban and the Witch*, 12–13). Glen Coulthard, Jodi Byrd, Alyosha Goldstein, Jodi Melamed, Chandan Reddy, Robert Nichols, and others write against Marx's and Marxist conceptions of colonial dispossession as an "originary," rather than continuing, structure of capitalist accumulation. These scholars argue that Marxist and other critiques that understand class as the central contradiction of capitalism (rather than dispossession in its settler colonial and racial forms) simply rehearse and perpetuate these violent logics and their accompanying structures. Coulthard, *Red Skin, White Masks*; Byrd, Goldstein, Melamed, and Reddy, "Predatory Value"; Nichols, *Theft Is Property!*; Bhandar, *Colonial Lives of Property*; Kosher, Cacho, Byrd, and Jefferson, *Colonial Racial Capitalism*; Goldstein, "'In the Constant Flux.'"

55 In *Capital* Marx writes on abstraction and the fetishism of commodities: "The equalization of the most different kinds of labor can be the result only of an abstraction from their inequalities, or of reducing them to their common denominator, viz. expenditure of human labor power or human labor in the abstract." He continues: "Whenever, by an exchange, we equate as values our different products, by that very act, we also equate, as human labor, the different kinds of labor expended upon them. . . . It is value, therefore, that converts every product into a social hieroglyphic." Marx, *Karl Marx*, 474.

56 Marx writes that "this abstraction of labour is only the result of a concrete aggregate of different kinds of labour. The indifference to the particular kind of labour corresponds to a form of society in which individuals pass with ease from one kind of work to another, which makes it immaterial to them what particular kind of work may fall to their share. Labour has become here, not only categorially but really, a means of creating wealth in general and has no longer coalesced with the individual in one particular manner. This state of affairs has found its highest development in the most modern of bourgeois societies, the United States. It is only here that the abstraction of the category 'labour,' 'labour in general,' labour *sans phrase*, the starting-point of modern political economy, becomes realized in practice. Thus the simplest abstraction which modern political economy sets up as its starting-point, and which expresses a relation dating back to antiquity and

prevalent under all forms of society, appears truly realized in this abstraction only as a category of the most modern society." Marx, *Karl Marx*, 389.

57 As Federici writes, "Primitive accumulation, then, was not simply an accumulation and concentration of exploitable workers and capital. It was also an accumulation of differences and division within the working class, whereby hierarchies built upon gender, as well as 'race,' and age, became constitutive of class rule and the formation of the modern proletariat." Federici, *Caliban and the Witch*, 63.

58 That is, as Saranillio argues, we must understand settler colonialism and capitalism as fundamentally unsustainable, always in contradiction, and tending toward crisis. Saranillio refers to this project as "unsustainable empire." Saranillio, *Unsustainable Empire*. This also resonates with Byrd, Goldstein, Melamed, and Reddy's conception of "economies of dispossession": "These are the rationalities that disavow racial and colonial violence by constituting people, land, and the relations of social life as translatable into value form, making incommensurate histories, experiences, and forms of social being commensurate by reducing them to their meaning and value within 'the capital relation,' placing them within the ontology of dis/possession." Byrd, Goldstein, Melamed, and Reddy, "Predatory Value," 7.

59 Scholars have theorized the relationship between capitalism and biopower, noting that capitalism's requirements for life and labor are insatiable and that this led to biopolitical projects that targeted life cultivation and population regulation in order to reproduce laborers. Furthermore, centering the racial and gendered context of slavery and colonialism—rather than that of the white male European metropole—reveals how death and life depletion have always formed the conditions for biopower's "make live" imperative, in the service of capitalist accumulation. In contrast to Foucault, Federici argues that techniques of biopower emerged prior to the eighteenth century: capitalism's consumption of life spurred the European demographic and economic crisis of the sixteenth and seventeenth centuries, and thus the need for labor that led to the rise of biopower and discipline of women's bodies and reproduction, including the persecution of so-called witches (Federici, *Caliban and the Witch*, 86). She writes that "we can also see that the promotion of population growth by the state can go hand in hand with a massive destruction of life; for in many historical circumstances—witness the history of the slave trade—one is a condition for the other" (16). Further, she argues that mercantilism, with its need for a large and disposable population of laborers, was the most "direct expression of requirements of primitive accumulation" (87). This resonates with Cedric Robinson's understanding of the relationship between transatlantic slavery and capitalism: in the English colonies, sugar production's desires for labor outpaced supply (with settler colonial genocide accentuating this labor shortage as well), thus requiring huge amounts of slave labor to the extent that from 1675 onward, English traders constituted the majority of the transatlantic slave trade. Robinson, *Black Marxism*, 117. As Nikhil Pal Singh observes, "Marx recognized that capital formed in contradiction not only to exploited labor, but to life itself. Capital accumulation

spurs population increase while voraciously depleting labor. The societal crisis that capitalism constantly faces is the ongoing violent dislocation of these two processes." Singh, "On Race, Violence," 58. This dynamic reverberates in various ways into our present. Writing in the context of global capitalism and the outsourcing of reproductive labors and biological resources, Kalindi Vora argues that contemporary capitalism's extraction of life is inherently asymmetrical and builds upon colonial legacies: "This form of accumulation and production can be seen in its historical context of colonialism and its antecedents as a system of continuing the transmission of what I call vital energy—the substance of activity that produces life (though often deemed reproductive)—from areas of life depletion to areas of life enrichment." Vora, *Life Support*, 3. Furthermore, capitalism's devouring of life is not confined to labor. Writing specifically about capitalism's depletion of the natural environment in Hawai'i, Candace Fujikane states that "capital expands its domain through the evisceration of the living earth into the inanimacies of non-life, depicting abundant lands as wastelands to condemn them." Fujikane, *Mapping Abundance*, 3.

60 "*As much Land* as a Man Tills, Plants, *Improves*, Cultivates, and can use the Product of, so much is his *Property*. He by his Labour does, as it were, enclose it from the Common." Locke, *Two Treatises of Government*, 291.

61 Federici understands capitalism to be perpetually incomplete and precarious: "If capitalism has been able to reproduce itself it is only because of the web of inequalities that it has built into the body of the world proletariat, and because of its capacity to globalize exploitation." Federici, *Caliban and the Witch*, 17. David Harvey posits the dynamic "accumulation by dispossession" as one that interrogates "the continuous role and persistence of the predatory practices of 'primitive' or 'original' accumulation within the long historical geography of capital accumulation," exploring how capitalism requires a preexisting or manufactured "other" or "outside" in order to stabilize itself. Harvey, *New Imperialism*, 141–44. However, although Harvey acknowledges the "original" and continuing roles of colonialism and slavery within the history of capitalist accumulation, his analysis primarily focuses on neoliberalism, financialization, and privatization in the 1970s onward—within both the so-called core and periphery—as the "cutting edge" example of accumulation by dispossession. Harvey, *New Imperialism*, 152–61. This characterization overlooks how racialized, gendered, and colonial forms of primitive accumulation have never ceased to undergird capitalist state building and empire building. For example, whereas Giovanni Arrighi differentiates between "territorialist" and "capitalist" logics of power, he argues that within settler colonial contexts like that of the United States, capitalism and territorialism are "indistinguishable from one other" and, further, form the conditions of possibility for the existence of the settler state. Thus, throughout history the continental and overseas territorial expansion of the United States has been an expression of *both* capitalist accumulation and settler colonial state and empire building. Arrighi, *Long Twentieth Century*, 59–60. As Alyosha Goldstein

notes, "Colonialism in this context is not or not only a process of expansion and incorporation, but is a primary social, economic, and political feature of the United States itself." Goldstein, "'In the Constant Flux,'" 67. See also Nichols, *Theft Is Property!*, 67–68; and Kosher, Cacho, Byrd, and Jefferson, "Introduction." Writing specifically about Hawai'i, Saranillio analyzes "unsustainable empire" in Hawai'i through the dynamic of "settler accumulation by Native dispossession," which figures as continual the process by which capitalism "fails forward" toward an aspirational settler future via the continuation of primitive accumulation and its appropriation of Indigenous lands and means of subsistence. Saranillio, *Unsustainable Empire*, 22. On how we cannot separate neoliberal financialization from the ongoing and historical process of colonialism, see Byrd, Goldstein, Melamed, and Reddy, "Predatory Value," 7. Nikhil Pal Singh analyzes the reiterative nature of primitive accumulation and its role in territorial expansion through the dynamic of war capitalism, which creates "exceptional zones of armed appropriation," which are "not only domains for enacting 'plunder'— that is, primitive accumulation (or accumulation by dispossession)—but also for developing cutting-edge procedures, calculations, and fungible systems of commercial and military infrastructure . . . that are able to proceed insofar as they are unfettered by legally protected human beings, thus advancing new prejudices that build upon the old." Singh, "On Race, Violence," 55.

62   Fujitani discusses the US state's biopolitical impulse during World War II amid labor scarcity in Fujitani, "Right to Kill." On the extreme labor requirements for the US military empire, see Bender and Lipman, *Making the Empire Work*; and Friedman, "US Empire."

63   Scheiber and Scheiber, *Bayonets in Paradise*, 80, 81–83, 84.

64   "The HSPA reported at the war's end that, from December 1941 to the end of 1944, Hawaii's sugar and pineapple plantations had loaned out 514,130 person-days of labor to the military." Jung, *Reworking Race*, 134.

65   Scheiber and Scheiber, *Bayonets in Paradise*, 82.

66   Scheiber and Scheiber, *Bayonets in Paradise*, 87, 84.

67   Evelyn Nakano Glenn defines reproductive labor as "activities that recreate the labor force: the physical and emotional maintenance of current workers and the nurturing and socializing of future workers. In other words, people as well as things have to be produced." Nakano Glenn, "Racial Ethnic Women's Labor," 104. Both Nakano Glenn and Rhacel Salazar Parreñas further analyze an international and racialized division of reproductive labor in which "class-privileged women free themselves of the 'mental, emotional, and manual labor' needed for the 'creation and recreation of people as cultural and social, as well as physical beings' by hiring low-paid women of color," and immigrant women's domestic labor "connects systems of gender inequality in both sending and receiving nations to global capitalism." Parreñas, "Migrant Filipina," 562. Here, Parreñas draws from Nakano Glenn, "From Servitude to Service Work." Following Michael Hardt, we might also consider affective labor—e.g., care labor, health care, teaching,

mothering—as the labor of biopower. He writes that "its products are intangible: a feeling of ease, well-being, satisfaction, excitement, passion—even a sense of connectedness or community." Hardt, "Affective Labor," 96. Yet as Silvia Federici reminds us, affective and reproductive labor should be considered both immaterial *and* material in order to avoid making an artificial distinction that privileges the waged productive laborer as revolutionary subject and reproduces the sexual and colonial division of labor that devalues racialized and gendered work. Federici, "Silvia Federici," 157. Kalindi Vora analyzes how this dynamic has continued to structure the context of contemporary global capitalism: "In transmitting vital energy to US residents, they enter into a history of US capitalist accumulation in relation to conquest, racial slavery, and immigration, where the reproductive labor of working-class women of color continues to support the value of whiteness and class privilege that does not include them." Vora, "Limits of 'Labor,'" 698. Recent Marxist feminist work has contributed understandings of "social reproduction theory": Bhattacharya theorizes that social reproduction encompasses the "'production of goods and services and the production of life [as] part of one integrated process.'" Bhattacharya, *Social Reproduction Theory*, 3.

68   Oren E. Long, "War Records Project," Department of Public Instruction, Territory of Hawaii, December 1944, 24.01 Department of Public Instruction, HWRD, 4, emphasis in original.

69   Federici argues that "state control over every aspect of [social] reproduction, became the cornerstones of primitive accumulation." Federici, *Caliban and the Witch*, 22.

70   We can consider this a part of the longer history in which certain bodies and lands—in this case, multiracial plantation workers and Indigenous lives and landscapes—have historically been more available and disposable, and in which race and colonialism make primitive accumulation invisible. As Vora states, "the legacies of imperialism continue to affect the hyperavailability of racialized and gendered bodies" (694). Vora, "Limits of 'Labor,'" 694–97.

71   As Vora writes of contemporary regimes of biocapital and labor outsourcing, "Labor, like human vital organs, can be understood as a specific portion of a person's body and life that can be made free to travel." Vora, *Life Support*, 2.

CHAPTER 1. "NATIONAL DEFENSE IS BASED ON LAND":
LANDSCAPES OF SETTLER MILITARISM IN HAWAI'I

Epigraph: Norman Littell, quoted in "U.S. Acquires 757 Tracts in Year," August 14, 1941, *Honolulu Star-Bulletin*, microfilm, Newspapers in Hawai'i, Hamilton Library, University of Hawai'i at Mānoa (HNM).

1   "U.S. Acquires 757 Tracts in Year."

2   In these cases the United States transferred lands from territorial to federal possession via presidential executive order. McKinley, "Proclamation

427—Reserving for Naval Purposes Certain Lands in Honolulu, Hawaii," November 2, 1898. For example, the US military acquired 1,510 acres of land via President Woodrow Wilson's Executive Order 2565 on March 28, 1917, for the Waimanalo Military Reservation, now known as Bellows Air Force Station. That same day, Executive Order 2566 transferred 274.07 acres of land in Aiea from the territorial government to the federal government for military purposes. This information was provided by unpublished research by Gwen Sinclair in the Government Documents department of the Hamilton Library, University of Hawai'i at Mānoa (hereafter referred to as Sinclair).

3   "Defendant Trustees' Instruction No. 11," Instructions: Campbell Estate, Trial, United States District Court for the District of Hawaii, *United States of America v. 537.2931 Acres of Land*, Civil 466 et al, Civil 466 *USA v 537.2931 Acres of Land*, etc., Appeal pleadings [4 of 5], Box 96, RG 21, NASF. "The Government must pay to the person whose property is condemned *just compensation* therefor." "Defendant Trustees' Instruction No. 9," Instructions: Campbell Estate, Trial, United States District Court for the District of Hawaii, *United States of America v. 537.2931 Acres of Land*, Civil 466 et al, Civil 466 *USA vs 537.2931 Acres of Land*, etc., Appeal pleadings [4 of 5], Box 96, RG 21, NASF, emphasis mine.

4   "You may take into consideration any evidence which indicates the *best and most profitable use* to which the land is adapted and can probably be put in the reasonably near future." "Defendant Trustees' Instruction No. 11," emphasis mine.

5   Park argues that property law is structurally reliant upon colonial and racial hierarchies embedded in the Discovery Doctrine and subsequent court cases such as *Johnson v. M'Intosh*. Park, "History Wars"; Park, "Money, Mortgages."

6   On the legacy of slavery within property law, Harris writes that "because whites could not be enslaved or held as slaves, the racial line between white and black was extremely critical; it became a line of protection and demarcation from the potential threat of commodification, and it determined the allocation of the benefits and burdens of this form of property. White identity and whiteness were sources of privilege and protection; their absence meant being the object of property" (Harris, "Whiteness as Property," 279). On the colonial origins of property, she notes that "Indian custom was obliterated by force and replaced with the regimes of common law which embodied the customs of the conquerors. . . . The founders, for instance, so thoroughly embraced Lockean labor theory as the basis for a right of acquisition because it affirmed the right of the New World settlers to settle on and acquire the frontier. It confirmed and ratified their experience" (280).

7   Bhandar, *Colonial Lives of Property*, 25, emphasis mine.

8   Park, "Money, Mortgages," 3; Coulthard, *Red Skin, White Masks*.

9   As Saranillio writes, "In the death of these nonhuman relations is the continual birth and rebirth of capitalism." Saranillio, *Unsustainable Empire*, 22.

10   On the "abstract legal subject who was defined by his capacity for self-ownership," see Bhandar, *Colonial Lives of Property*, 99.

11 Harris, "Whiteness as Property"; Bhandar, *Colonial Lives of Property*; Park, "History Wars"; Federici, *Caliban and the Witch*; Robinson, *Black Marxism*. On white possession, see Moreton-Robinson, *White Possessive*; and Arvin, *Possessing Polynesians*.

12 Bhandar, *Colonial Lives of Property*, 99. This logic also resonates with what Jodi Byrd, Alyosha Goldstein, Jodi Melamed, and Chandan Reddy call *economies of dispossession* or "those multiple and intertwined genealogies of racialized property, subjection and expropriation through which capitalism and colonialism take shape historically and change over time." Byrd, Goldstein, Melamed, and Reddy, "Predatory Value," 2.

13 "Defendant Trustees' Instruction No. 11."

14 Kauanui, *Paradoxes of Hawaiian Sovereignty*, 85; Kameʻeleihiwa, *Native Land and Foreign Desires*, 27.

15 Kauanui, *Paradoxes of Hawaiian Sovereignty*, 87, quoted from Lâm, "Kuleana Act Revisited," 261.

16 Kauanui, *Paradoxes of Hawaiian Sovereignty*, 83; Osorio, *Dismembering Lāhui*, 32, 11.

17 Osorio, *Dismembering Lāhui*, 55. See also Oliveira, *Ancestral Places*, 44–45. Referenced and quoted by Kauanui, *Paradoxes of Hawaiian Sovereignty*, 89–90.

18 "As several scholars have noted, only 8,421 claims were awarded out of 14,195 applications made for kuleana awards in 1848 (among approximately 80,000 Hawaiians at the time)." Kauanui, *Paradoxes of Hawaiian Sovereignty*, 88.

19 Kauanui, *Paradoxes of Hawaiian Sovereignty*, 81.

20 Trask, *From a Native Daughter*; Silva, *Aloha Betrayed*; Kajihiro, "Militarizing of Hawaiʻi," 172; Saranillio, "Colliding Histories."

21 Although federal, territorial, and state governments refer to these lands as "ceded," this descriptor is misleading because these lands were never actually "ceded" by treaty but were taken by force. Kauanui, "Sorry State," 110–12.

22 "Brief of the Dowsett Company, Limited, Defendant," June 6, 1947, United States District Court for the District of Hawaii, April Term 1947, Civil 466 *USA v. 537.2931 Acres of Land*, etc., [West Loch] File III Memorandums [3 of 5], Box 96, RG 21, NASF, 1–2.

23 United States Department of Defense, "Report on Study of Military Real Property, State of Hawaii," [Washington?], 1960, HC, 5.

24 "The Armed Forces required more land for airfields, camps, training grounds, storage areas, communication facilities, gun emplacements, searchlight positions, and many other installations." Erich Otto Kraemer, "Recent Developments in Hawaiian Land Utilization, a Paper Prepared for the Seventh Pacific Science Congress, New Zealand, February 1949," Honolulu, 1949, HC, 6.

25 Kraemer, "Recent Developments," 9.

26 Kraemer, "Recent Developments," 9.

27 The US Army acquired up to 210,000 acres, and the US Navy acquired up to 118,694 acres of this total. Kraemer, "Recent Developments," 9.

28 Kraemer, "Recent Developments," 3, 9.

29   Sugar cane land decreased from 235,110 acres to 204,111 acres. The peak of sugar plantation lands in Hawaiʻi was in 1917, with 276,813 acres, and these landholdings declined by 26.1% between 1917 and 1948. Kraemer, "Recent Developments," 10–11.

30   "The relative importance of the military to the economy of Hawaii is apparent from the above statistics and has been confirmed by numerous economic studies. . . . A recent survey by leading economists predicts that the normal anticipated expansion of the economy will not be impeded by current military land holdings for the foreseeable future." United States Department of Defense, "Report on Study of Military," 5–6.

31   Harland Bartholomew and Associates, "A Summary Report upon the Concentration of Military and Civilian Activities on Oahu, Territory of Hawaii, Prepared for the Territorial Planning Director, Honolulu, Hawaii," Honolulu, 1958, HC, 3.

32   "With such high values for urbanized uses, it follows that adjacent agricultural uses would be significantly affected. Agricultural land values on the island of Oahu are almost unbelievable as compared to agricultural values on the mainland and on the other Islands of the Hawaiian group." Harland Bartholomew and Associates, "Summary Report," 5.

33   Hirsch, *Making the Second Ghetto*; Connolly, *World More Concrete*.

34   Ammon, *Bulldozer*, 6–7.

35   "Hawaiians Lose Lease Rights in 'Land Grabs,'" *Honolulu Advertiser*, August 19, 1946, HNM.

36   This was notably faster than the previous average of six days and five hours. It was indicative of the attorney general's effort to streamline this process leading up to the war. "U.S. Acquires 757 Tracts in Year."

37   "Jury Sets $70,000 on Land Taken by Navy," *Honolulu Advertiser*, June 22, 1948, HNM.

38   US interest in building this base began as early as January 3, 1939, when the navy informed Congress that it urgently required thirty additional air, submarine, destroyer, and mine bases in both the US continent and its "outlying possessions." "Condemnation Suit Jury Chosen," *Honolulu Advertiser*, March 16, 1948, HNM.

39   The US Navy declared that the naval air base at Kāneʻohe Bay was one of its most important projects and that the expansion of facilities at Pearl Harbor should also be a priority. Other important projects included naval air bases at Midway, Wake Island, Guam, Johnston, Palmyra, Kodiak Island, Sitka Islands, and San Juan, Puerto Rico. Other locations chosen for "early completion" included Ford Island and Canton and Rose Islands. "Navy Asks for Thirty New Bases," *Honolulu Star-Bulletin*, January 3, 1939, Civil 441, Box 5, RG 21, NASF.

40   "Report on Need of Additional Naval Bases to Defend the Coasts of the United States, Its Territories, and Possessions," 76th Congress, 1st Session, House of Representatives, January 3, 1949, Civil 441, Box 5, RG 21, NASF, 24, 36; "Navy Carrying on Surveys at Kaneohe," *Honolulu Advertiser*, January 23, 1939, Civil 441, Box 5, RG 21, NASF; "Navy Asks for Thirty New Bases"; "Report on Need of Additional Naval Bases," 34.

41 The House Naval Affairs Committee considered a $65,000,000 naval air base program that extended across US-occupied locations including Alaska, the Pacific Islands, the Caribbean, and the continental United States. "Kaneohe Navy Base Project Details Given," *Honolulu Star-Bulletin*, January 31, 1939, Civil 441, Box 5, RG 21, NASF.

42 It was not immediately clear whether the US military would use all or just a portion of the Heleloa tract for this naval base. "Approve Site for Mokapu Air Base," *Honolulu Star-Bulletin*, April 12, 1939, Civil 441, Box 5, RG 21, NASF. "Kaneohe Bay Navy Air Base Site Is Approved," *Honolulu Advertiser*, April 13, 1939, Civil 441, Box 5, RG 21, NASF.

43 Locke, *Two Treatises of Government*, 297, emphasis mine.

44 Park argues that the Discovery Doctrine initiated these racial and colonial dynamics of the labor theory and conceptions of property value. Park, "History Wars," 1102–10. See also Saranillio, *Unsustainable Empire*, 22.

45 Accordingly, Locke elaborates: "*As much Land* as a Man Tills, Plants, Improves, Cultivates, and can use the Product of, so much is his *Property*. He by his Labour does, as it were, enclose it from the Common." Locke, *Two Treatises of Government*, 291.

46 Locke, *Two Treatises of Government*, 290–91. See also Bhandar, *Colonial Lives of Property*, 30, 36.

47 In April 1939 the Naval Affairs Committee approved a bill seeking $65,000,000 for naval bases, including that which was planned at Kāneʻohe Bay. "Approve Site for Mokapu Air Base"; "Kaneohe Bay Navy Air Base Site."

48 "Authorizing the Secretary of the Navy to Proceed with the Construction of Certain Public Works," 76th Congress, 1st Session, Senate, April 13, 1939, Civil 441, Box 5, RG 21, NASF, 17–18; "Kaneohe Bay Navy Air Base Site." Another source says the budget was $5,820,500. "Funds Are on Hand to Begin Construction," *Honolulu Star-Bulletin*, July 15, 1939, Civil 441, Box 5, RG 21, NASF.

49 "Funds Are on Hand to Begin Construction."

50 Fujikane, *Mapping Abundance*, 3.

51 The proceedings began on August 10, 1939, and were settled on December 8, 1942. "Navy Acts to Take Kaneohe Land as Base," *Honolulu Star-Bulletin*, August 3, 1939, Civil 441, Box 5, RG 21, NASF; "Navy 'Niggardly' in Setting Property Values, Owners Say," *Honolulu Advertiser*, August 1946, Sinclair; "Navy Acts to Take Kaneohe Bay Property," *Honolulu Star-Bulletin*, August 10, 1939, Civil 441, Box 5, RG 21, NASF.

52 "Navy Acts to Take Kaneohe Land."

53 The Navy originally deposited $115,000. The court's stipulated judgment was for $300,000, or $185,000 more than the original deposit. The proceedings started on August 10, 1939, and were settled on December 8, 1942. "Navy 'Niggardly' in Setting Property Values"; "Navy Acts to Take Kaneohe Bay Property."

54 "US Attorney Files Condemnation Suit," *Honolulu Advertiser*, January 28, 1941, HNM; "Navy Takes Over 34 More Acres in Kaneohe Bay Area," *Honolulu Star-Bulletin*, September 8, 1939, Civil 441, Box 5, RG 21, NASF.

55 Interestingly, home economist Marjorie Abel was one of the claimants in Civil 441. Civil 441 *USA v. 464.66 Acres of Land*, etc., Box 87, RG 21, NASF; "US Attorney Files Condemnation Suit."

56   "US Attorney Files Condemnation Suit."

57   The Second War Powers Act was passed as Public Law 507 in the 77th Congress. "To United States Attorneys and Field Attorneys of the Lands Division Engaged in the Acquisition of Land, Re: Supplemental Instructions for the Acquisition of Land for the War Department under the Second War Powers Act of March 27, 1942 (56 Stat. 176, 177; 50 U. S. C., Supp. App. 632)," June 17, 1944, RE-284.0 Beckoning Point John Ii Est., Oahu Sugar Co. Civil 516, Box 10, RG 181, NASF.

58   The Secretary of War then quickly forwarded the executed Declaration of Taking to the Department of Justice. See "To United States Attorneys and Field Attorneys."

59   "Hawaiians Lose Lease Rights in 'Land Grabs,'" *Honolulu Advertiser*, August 19, 1946, HNM. Frank C. Churchill, a veteran, leased 40,000 square feet of land at Iroquois Point to the navy in 1942 for a landing area, only to have the navy condemn it in 1944. As Churchill stated, "I have given up my home for the ridiculous price of $2.50 a square foot. It would cost me $10 a square foot to replace it today." J. J. Arsenault, a retired army warrant officer who owned land in Pearl City, argued that he lost 20,000 to 30,000 dollars when the US Navy condemned his land for $9,374. "Two War Veterans Suffer: Forced to Sell Ocean Frontage at Big Sacrifice," *Honolulu Advertiser*, August 1946, Sinclair; "Land 'Grabs' Hit by Home Owners," *Honolulu Advertiser*, August 1946, Sinclair.

60   In Civil Case 729, the federal government officially condemned a tract of land in October 1944 to construct the Ewa Marine Corps Air Station, yet it was later revealed in court that the military had actually occupied this land since 1942. The owners argued that the US Navy had initially informed them that they would be reimbursed for rent and taxes from the date of occupation but never followed through on this promise. Lawyers in the case stated that "this of course has not been done, since title has not been taken. It now appears likely that the Government will not consummate its former intention to buy at all." In this case, the federal government evaded the promise of compensation by simply occupying the land rather than going through with the condemnation proceedings. DPWO to OinC, J. B. Musser, RE-14.1 Marine Corps Air Station-Civil 729, Expansion of fee-233.741 #1, To: Dec 1945—C12-28-0A, Box 3, RG 181, NASF.

61   "Navy Land Condemning Tactics Hit by Owners," *Honolulu Advertiser*, August 1946, Sinclair.

62   "Owners Say Navy Tried Intimidation to Get Land," *Honolulu Advertiser*, August 1946, Sinclair.

63   "Navy Land Condemning Tactics."

64   On March 10, 1943, known as Restoration Day, the US government restored to the territorial governor, Ingram Stainback, many of the functions that the Office of the Military Governor had previously controlled. Yet at this point Hawai'i would still be technically under martial law until October 24, 1944. Although many news outlets celebrated this transition as the restoration of civil governance, this change merely shifted control from the US military government back to the

US territorial government, a settler colonial institution established by the 1900 Hawaiian Organic Act in the aftermath of the overthrow. Furthermore, Stainback quickly reinstated many of the military general orders that had just been lifted in the form of Hawaii Defense Act Rules, such as those that required the registration of hospitals, laboratories, and nurses with the OCD, and those that required immunization against smallpox, typhoid, paratyphoid, and diphtheria. "Departmental War Records Project, Board of Health, Territory of Hawaii," August 1944, 30.02 Board of Health, Box 18, HWRD, 18. "Part III: Security Controls for the Public Good, or Civilian Defense," "Civilian Defense or Security Controls for the Public Good (original copy) Final Draft," Folder 1, Box 892, Military Government of the Territory of Hawaii, RG 494, NA, 3–35.

65   On critiques of liberal violence and liberal multiculturalism, see Reddy, *Freedom with Violence*; and Morgensen, *Spaces between Us*.

66   "Defendant Trustees' Instruction No. 11," emphasis mine.

67   As Locke writes, "'Tis *Labour* then which *puts the greatest part of Value upon Land*, without which it would scarcely be worth any thing: 'tis to that we owe the greatest part of all its useful Products: for all that the Straw, Bran, Bread, of that Acre of Wheat, is more worth than the Produce of an Acre of as good Land, which lies wast [waste], is all the Effect of Labour." Locke, *Two Treatises of Government*, 298.

68   "Ewa Plantation Company Instruction No. 3," Request for Instructions, Trial, United States District Court for the District of Hawaii, *United States of America v. 537.2931 Acres of Land*, Civil 466 et al., Civil 466 USA v. *537.2931 Acres of Land*, etc., Appeal pleadings [4 of 5], Box 96, RG 21, NASF; "Judgment," *United States of America, Petitioner, v. 537.2931 Acres of Land, More or Less*, at West Loch, District of Ewa, Oahu, Territory of Hawaii, Albert N. Campbell, et al., Defendants, October Term 1941, Civil 466 USA v. *537.2931 Acres of Land*, etc., [West Loch] File III Memorandums [3 of 5], Box 96, NASF.

69   "The evidence shows that Ewa Plantation Company had certain crops on part of the land condemned at the date of taking. Since the growing crops in this case are not the subject of sale and purchase in the open market just compensation for this item is arrived at by taking the estimated yield of the crop and deducting costs and expenses to bring the crop to maturity, harvest, and market the same." "Ewa Plantation Company Instruction No. 3"; "Judgment."

70   Saranillio, *Unsustainable Empire*, 11, 22.

71   "Navy Condemns Family's Land Twice in 4 Years," *Honolulu Advertiser*, August 27, 1946, Sinclair.

72   In Civil Case 487, USA v. *1033.594 Acres of Land* alone, the Campbell estate received a payment of $78,788.48, which included a deficiency of $58,758.37 plus interest of $19,030.11. In Civil Case 466, USA v. *537.2931 Acres of Land*, the Campbell estate gained $80,958.65, which included a deficiency of $59,043.10 and interest of $21,915.55. "Civil 487 U.S. v. 1033.594 acres of land, etc.," Civil 487 File No. II Motion and Order for Immediate Possession and Certificate, Box 101,

RG 21, NASF; "Civil 466 *USA v. 537.2931 Acres of Land*," Civil 466 *USA v. 537.2931 Acres of Land*, etc., [West Loch] "Certif." and "Order" File II [2 of 5], Box 96, RG 21, NASF.

73 "Armed Services 'Land Grabs' Hit by Homeowners," *Honolulu Advertiser*, August 1946, Sinclair.

74 "Hawaiians Lose Lease Rights."

75 The Waites decided to take the loss of money and were able to move their house to a different lot. Mrs. Cridad D. Avecilla of Honolulu, whose house was also moved to a new lot in Honolulu by the US Navy, was paid $2,100 for her lot, which she argued was an unfair price. Yet despite this, she stated that she did not want to "fight the United States government in court." The US Navy took over Waipio peninsula, which was owned by the 'Ii estate, for security reasons. However, George and Kenneth Brown and Senator Francis H. Brown, who administered the estate, did not fight this condemnation in court. "Family Loses $6500 on Navy Land Condemnation," *Honolulu Advertiser*, August 1946, Sinclair. "Land Owners Charge Lack of Responsibility to Navy Aides," *Honolulu Advertiser*, August 1946, Sinclair.

76 Frank E. Midkiff to Vice Admiral Robert L. Ghormley, June 3, 1944, 41.8 Civil 507 #1 NAS Honolulu To: Dec. 1944. Box 5, RG 181, NASF; John J. Courtney to Commandant, Fourteenth Naval District, March 30, 1944, 41.8 Civil 507 #1 NAS Honolulu To: Dec. 1944. Box 5, RG 181, NASF. "In view of anticipated local reluctance to immediate possession due to hardship resulting to tenants (277) recommend condemnation under 2nd War Powers." The same case stated, "Recommendation for condemnation of lease under 2nd War Powers Act." BUDOCKS to COM15, 29 December 1943, 41.8 Civil 507 #1 NAS Honolulu To: Dec. 1944. Box 5, RG 181, NASF. Real estate division progress report, 41.8 Civil 507 #1 NAS Honolulu To: Dec. 1944. Box 5, RG 181, NASF.

77 J. L. Noel, Jr. to Hon. Robert S. Tarnay, December 29, 1944, RE-336.0 Damon Estate #2 6/44 to 6/45 12.973 Acs WAVES Qtrs NAS CIVIL 559, Box 1, RG 181, NASF; memorandum from F. H. Johnston to Chief Lee Ward, November 3, 1944, RE-336.0 Damon Estate #2 6/44 to 6/45 12.973 Acs WAVES Qtrs NAS CIVIL 559, Box 1, RG 181, NASF; H. H. Good by Direction, Authenticated by L. H. Stout to BuDocks, November 27, 1944, RE-336.0 Damon Estate #2 6/44 to 6/45 12.973 Acs WAVES Qtrs NAS CIVIL 559, Box 1, RG 181, NASF.

78 "Navy Land Condemning Tactics."

79 John J. Courtney to Commandant, Fourteenth Naval District, December 7, 1944, RE-336.0 Damon Estate #2 6/44 to 6/45 12.973 Acs WAVES Qtrs NAS CIVIL 559, Box 1, RG 181, NASF; Memorandum to Officer-in-Charge, Appraisal Section, Real Estate Division, DPWO, J. L. Noel, Jr., December 16, 1944, RE-336.0 Damon Estate #2 6/44 to 6/45 12.973 Acs WAVES Qtrs NAS CIVIL 559, Box 1, RG 181, NASF.

80 John J. Courtney to Commander H. F. Bruns, May 5, 1941, RE-89.0 Civil 452 Halawa—North Aiea Naval Hospital (1), Box 3, RG 181, NASF; C. C. Bloch to J. J. Kiefer, September 8, 1941, RE-89.0 Civil 452 Halawa—North Aiea Naval Hospital (1), Box 3, RG 181, NASF; Kama Yonashiro to John J. Courtney, Esq., June 7, 1941,

RE-89.0 Civil 452 Halawa—North Aiea Naval Hospital (1), Box 3, RG 181, NASF; Ka-mato Tokuhara to John J. Courtney, Esq., June 7, 1941, RE-89.0 Civil 452 Halawa—North Aiea Naval Hospital (1), Box 3, RG 181, NASF. On June 9, John J. Courtney wrote to H. Oliver O'Farrell that it did not seem that the navy had use for these buildings and asked whether it would be acceptable to allow these individuals to salvage them. John. J. Courtney to H. Oliver O'Farrell, June 9, 1941, RE-89.0 Civil 452 Halawa—North Aiea Naval Hospital (1), Box 3, RG 181, NASF; C. C. Bloch to K. Yonashiro, August 18, 1941, re-89.0 Civil 452 Halawa—North Aiea Naval Hospital (1), Box 3, RG 181, NASF.

81 As Saranillio argues, "Understanding that power does not simply target historically oppressed communities but also operates through their practices, ambitions, narratives, and silences offers a way to examine other dynamics of power—labor exploitation, anti-immigrant laws and sentiment, and imperialist wars—that have historically shaped Asian groups, without misrecognizing the context for framing an Asian diaspora on Native lands seized by the U.S. settler state." Saranillio, *Unsustainable Empire*, 24.

82 "Hawaiians Lose Lease Rights." "In 1983, a Federal-State Task Force concluded that 13,580 acres of Hawai'ian [sic] Home Lands were improperly withdrawn from the trust through presidential executive orders during World War II." Kaji-hiro, "Resisting Militarization in Hawai'i," 303.

83 "Navy Land Condemning Tactics." For more on annual rent, see Kauanui, *Hawaiian Blood*, 4.

84 The early stages of the Hawaiian Homes Commission Act initiative involved the Hawaiian Protective Association and the Hawaiian Civic Club, two organizations made up mostly of Native Hawaiian elites. Kauanui, *Hawaiian Blood*, 80–81, quotation from 113.

85 Kauanui, *Hawaiian Blood*, 126.

86 "Civilians, Military Fight for Territory of Hawaii Land Nears Climax," *Honolulu Star-Bulletin*, HNM, November 3, 1949.

87 United States Department of Defense, "Report on Study of Military Real Prop-erty," 2.

88 A report in 1958 claimed that of O'ahu's total 386,560 acres, only 164,000 of these acres (43 percent) were less than 10 percent slope, which is what the territorial planning director deemed a requirement for land that could be most economically developed for "urban and other intensive uses." Of this land that was less than 10 percent slope, 34,800 acres (21 percent) were urbanized areas, 21,800 (13 percent) were military and federal lands, and 107,400 (66 percent) were used for agriculture and grazing. United States Department of Defense, "Report on Study of Military Real Property," 4–5; Harland Bartholomew and Associates, "Summary Report," 2.

89 United States Department of Defense, "Report on Study of Military Real Prop-erty," Exhibit VIII, 1.

90 United States Department of Defense, "Report on Study of Military Real Prop-erty," 15, emphasis mine.

91 Kelly and Aleck, "Mākua Means Parents," 2, 4, 6.

92 "Beginning in the northwest corner of the Island there is the Makua training area under Army control. Makua totals 7,119 acres, of which 6,497 is on permit from the State of Hawaii. 170 acres was acquired in fee to avoid small 'islands' in the training area. Finally, a 436 acre lease is included which lease expires June 30, 1962. This is a negotiated leasehold cancellable by the Government on 30 days' notice or by the lessor on 180 days' notice." United States Department of Defense, "Report on Study of Military Real Property," Exhibit VIII, 2; "Layout Showing Location of Land Commission Awards Makua Valley, Waianae, Oahu, November 5, 1943, US DC / Hono Civ, #485 / U.S. vs. 165.847 acres of land, etc. Exhibits / Hearing on L.L. McCandless / Estate / December 1949, Box 4, RG 21, NASF.

93 Quotations from United States Department of Defense, "Report on Study of Military Real Property," Exhibit VII, 2. Mei-Singh, "Carceral Conservationalism," 696, 709.

94 "Sixteen kuleana were awarded in Mākua Valley in the 1850s. The rest remained Government Land that was leased out by the government to non-Kānaka Maoli for ranching. . . . Most of the Japanese who lived in Mākua Valley in the early 1900s came as railroad workers and stayed at the Section Camp. For a dollar a day pay they built and maintained the track." Kelly and Aleck, "Mākua Means Parents," 2, 4, 6.

95 Kelly and Aleck, "Mākua Means Parents," 9, 8.

96 On Hawai'i training grounds during the Vietnam War, see Simeon Man, "Aloha, Vietnam."

97 United States Department of Defense, "Report on Study of Military Real Property," Exhibit VIII, 2, and Exhibit VII, 2; Davis, Empires' Edge, 72, 76.

98 "Makua: Wildfires and Military Toxins," DMZ Hawai'i Aloha 'Āina, www.dmzhawaii.org.

99 Mei-Singh, "Carceral Conservationalism," 696, 709; Davis, Empires' Edge, 72, 76.

100 Mākua Valley is also a site with much cultural meaning for Native Hawaiians. As Kelly and Aleck write, "The mo'olelo (oral histories) of Wai'anae claim the entire coastline from Kea'au around Ka'ena to Kawaihāpai as a wahi pana (sacred place). It was here that the Kānaka Maoli were formed from the 'āina (land). It is here that our spirits return to Pō (the spirit realm) at Leina a Ka'uhane (soul's leap). Mākua means parents: it is the site where Papa (the earth-mother) and Wākea (the sky-father) meet." Kelly and Aleck, "Mākua Means Parents," 2; Mei-Singh, "Carceral Conservationalism," 709, 710.

101 Kajihiro, "Resisting Militarization in Hawai'i," 317–20; Mei-Singh, "Carceral Conservationalism," 696, 709; Davis, Empires' Edge, 72, 76.

102 Mei-Singh, "Carceral Conservationalism," 703–5.

103 Commander Third Fleet, US Navy, "A Report on the Island of Kahoolawe," March 1976, HC, 8.

104 Commander Third Fleet, US Navy, "A Report on the Island of Kahoolawe," 9, 17; Inez MacPhee Ashdown, Recollections of Kaho'olawe (Honolulu: Topgallant, 1979), HC, 66.

105   "History," Protect Kahoʻolawe ʻOhana. Accessed April 15, 2024. www
      .protectkahoolaweohana.org/history.html.

106   Commander Third Fleet, US Navy, "A Report on the Island of Kahoolawe," 9–10.

107   United States Department of Defense, "A Report on Study of Military Real Prop-
      erty," Exhibit VIII, 1.

108   Commander Third Fleet, US Navy, "Report on the Island of Kahoolawe," HC, 10.
      Mei-Singh's work illustrates how this rationalization of environmental steward-
      ship continues to be a technique of military occupation in the present. Mei-
      Singh, "Carceral Conservationism," 695–721.

109   "Called in ancient times, 'Kanaloa' or 'Kohemalamalama,' the island was a place
      where kahuna and navigators were trained and played an important role in early
      Pacific migrations. Named for the god of the ocean and the foundations of the
      earth, Kahoʻolawe is a sacred island that in modern times has served as the foun-
      dation for the revitalization of Hawaiian cultural practices." "Moʻolelo ʻĀina,"
      Protect Kahoʻolawe ʻOhana, http://www.protectkahoolaweohana.org/mo699olelo
      -699256ina.html.

110   "Moʻolelo ʻĀina."

111   Osorio, "Hawaiian Souls," 139, 143.

112   Osorio, "Hawaiian Souls," 143–49.

113   Osorio, "Hawaiian Souls," 137.

114   Osorio, "Hawaiian Souls," 138, 157.

115   Kraemer, "Recent Developments," 10.

116   Areas that the territorial government hoped would be returned also included
      6 acres on the waterfront at Richards Street in Honolulu, 142 acres of shore land
      at Fort Kamehameha, 131 acres of additional area for the extension of Honolulu
      Airport, Nanakuli Reservation and Lualualei Beach at Waianae, and Aiea Military
      Reservation. Areas that the territorial government believed should stay under
      military control included Sand Island, Fort Shafter, Kapiʻolani, Fort Weaver,
      Hickam Air Force Base, Fort Barrett, and Camp Malakole in Ewa. "Territory
      of Hawaii Asks Return of Military Acreages on Oahu," *Honolulu Star-Bulletin*,
      September 26, 1949, HNM.

117   "That efforts be continued to develop ways and means to enable replacement of
      essential facilities located on land of such value that the present military use is
      not consistent with the highest and best use of the land." United States Depart-
      ment of Defense, "Report on Study of Military," 7, 9.

118   "Civilian Land Use Halfed, Army Reveals," *Honolulu Advertiser*, August 1946,
      Sinclair.

119   "Bates Plan Ends Pearl Harbor Land Seizure," *Honolulu Advertiser*, July 6, 1947, HNM.

120   Training areas at Halamanu, Barber's Point, and Kahana Bay in Oʻahu had been
      returned to their prior ownership. General Lyman and Morse Fields on the island
      of Hawaiʻi and Homestead Field on Molokaʻi were also in the process of being
      returned. "Territory of Hawaii Asks Transfer of Military Lands," *Honolulu Adver-
      tiser*, September 25, 1949, HNM.

NOTES TO CHAPTER ONE

121 "Civilians, Military Fight for Territory of Hawaii Land Nears Climax," *Honolulu Star-Bulletin*, November 4, 1949, NHM; Kraemer, "Recent Developments," 9.

122 "Civilians, Military Fight."

123 Kraemer, "Recent Developments," 9.

124 United States Department of Defense, "Report on Study of Military," 15.

CHAPTER 2. "LIFE GIVEN STRAIGHT FROM THE HEART": SECURING BODY, BASE, AND NATION UNDER MARTIAL LAW

An early version of chapter 2 appeared as "'Life Given Straight from the Heart': Settler Militarism, Biopolitics, and Public Health in Hawai'i during World War II," in *American Quarterly* 69, no. 1 (2017): 23–45.

Epigraph: News release, April 2, 1942, Office of the Territorial Commissioner of Public Health, Immunizations, Box 878, MGHI, RG 494, NA, 2.

1 "'I'm Happy—I've Given My Blood,'" *Honolulu Star-Bulletin*, September 3, 1942, Blood Banks, Box 882, Military Government of the Territory of Hawaii, RG 494, NA.

2 "Giving Life via Blood Bank," *Honolulu Star-Bulletin*, October 14, 1944, Box 37, Folder 2, HWRD.

3 Swanson, *Banking on the Body*, 80.

4 "Public Urged to Get 'Shots,' Injections for Typhoid Required by June 15," *Honolulu Advertiser*, March 17, 1944; "Group Arranging for 'Booster' Shots," *Honolulu Star-Bulletin*, March 29, 1944; "Free Clinics Will Open Tomorrow," *Honolulu Advertiser*, May 21, 1944; "Booster Shot Deadline June 15," *Honolulu Advertiser*, May 18, 1944; "Health Officials Urge 'Booster Shots' Now," *Honolulu Advertiser*, May 17, 1944; "'Booster' Shots Due by June 15, Health Official Says," *Honolulu Star-Bulletin*, March 18, 1944; "Booster Shots 'Must' before Next June 15," *Honolulu Star-Bulletin*, March 3, 1944; "Booster Shots Must Be Obtained prior to June 15," *Honolulu Advertiser*, March 7, 1944; "'Booster' Shots Are Mandatory," *Honolulu Star-Bulletin*, March 7, 1944, Miscellaneous, Box 889, MGHI, RG 494, NA.

5 Kim TallBear questions the universality of scientific knowledge and illustrates how science has historically been part of the social construction of race and indigeneity. TallBear, *Native American DNA*.

6 For example, Dr. M. F. Haralson held powerful influence in both the territorial and the military governments. He was both the territorial commissioner of Public Health and the administrator of Emergency Medical and Related Services of OCD. He held this post in OCD from January 1, 1942, until he resigned on May 18, 1942, because of the pressure of his duties and was replaced by Dr. Harry L. Arnold. He was also a senior surgeon of the US Public Health Service. Haralson is pictured in the photograph of Susan Kang receiving a vaccination. "Departmental War Records Project, Board of Health, Territory of Hawaii," August 1944, 30.02 Board of Health, Box 18, HWRD, 6–7.

7 "Departmental War Records Project," 3.

8   Germain LaBerge, "The Mother of Blood Banking: Irwin Memorial Blood Bank and the American Association of Blood Banks, 1944–1994" (Regional Oral History Office, 1998), 20–29, Bancroft Library, University of California, Berkeley.

9   "Report of the Governor of Hawaii Honorable Joseph B. Poindexter to the Secretary of the Interior for the Fiscal Year Ended June 30, 1942," File No. 9 4 2 Reports—Annual—Governor—1942, Box 561, RG 126: Office of Territories, Classified Files, 1907–1951 (RG 126), NA, 5–6.

10   Guy Swope, director of Division of Territories and Island Possessions of the DOI, visited the islands in January 1942, as did Benjamin Thoron of the DOI on February 16, 1942. Allen, *Hawaii's War Years*, 395–97. "Report of the Governor of Hawaii," 5–6.

11   The emergency ambulance service had 52 ambulances on hand and 250 volunteer ambulances for use in emergency, with 301 volunteer drivers. "Departmental War Records Project," 9–13.

12   "Report of the Governor of Hawaii," 1942, 9; "Report of the Governor of Hawaii to the Secretary of the Interior for the Fiscal Year Ended June 30, 1944," File No. 9 4 2 Reports—Annual—Governor—1944, Box 561, RG 126, NA, 6.

13   "Departmental War Records Project," 4.

14   Others, such as those hired to control the dengue fever outbreak, remained employed by the US Public Health Service. "Report of the Governor of Hawaii," 1942, 9–12.

15   "United States Public Health Service and Its Relationship to the Board of Health," Charles L. Wilbar Jr., *Board of Health Radio Talks*, Station KGU, Honolulu, T. H., February 20, 1944, HC; "Departmental War Records Project," 13.

16   "Report of the Governor of Hawaii," 1942, 9–12.

17   This included the Sacred Hearts Convent (500 beds) and emergency units at Shriners Hospital (90 beds), Mānoa (113 beds and cots), and Wahiawā (resources for 250 patients). These measures took place on all of the neighbor islands as well. "Departmental War Records Project," 6.

18   Sturken, *Tangled Memories*, 224.

19   This included General Orders No. 71 (February 7, 1942), 80 (February 27, 1942), 86 (March 17, 1942), 97 (April 17, 1942), and 107 (May 21, 1942). "Departmental War Records Project," 19.

20   "Health Officials Urge 'Booster Shots' Now."

21   "Summary of Annual Report, Board of Health, Fiscal Year Ending, June 30, 1943," 9 4 2 Reports—Annual—Governor—1943, Box 561, RG 126, NA, 164; "Report of the Governor of Hawaii," 1942, 12. See also Allen, *Hawaii's War Years*, 336, 366.

22   Transcript, "An Era of Change: Oral Histories of Civilians in World War II Hawai'i," interview by Joe Rossi, 328–330, UH Center for Oral History, http://hdl .handle.net/10125/29873.

23   Dengue fever, which was spread by mosquitoes and allegedly began in Saipan, developed into an epidemic in 1943. "Part III: Security Controls for the Public Good, or Civilian Defense," "Civilian Defense or Security Controls for the Public

Good (original copy) Final Draft," Folder 1, Box 892, Military Government of the Territory of Hawaii, RG 494, NA, 35, 50, 54. See also "Dengue Mosquito Breeding Increases," *Honolulu Star-Bulletin*, March 9, 1944; "Dengue Fever Cases Doubled in February," *Honolulu Advertiser*, March 9, 1944, Miscellaneous, Box 889, MGHI, RG 494, NA; and Allen, *Hawaii's War Years*, 336–37.

24 "Part III," "Civilian Defense," Folder 1, Box 892, MGHI, RG 494, NA, 35–63; News release, April 25, 1942, BOH, Immunization, Box 878, MGHI, RG 494, NA.

25 The racial logics of these health projects in Hawai'i resonate with those discussed in Nayan Shah's work on disease control in San Francisco's Chinatown. Shah argues that public health discourse, which in the nineteenth century excluded racialized populations, shifted at the beginning of the twentieth century to more assimilationist rhetoric that accommodated racial difference by prescribing norms of behavior. On the "controlled burning" of Honolulu's Chinatown, see Shah, *Contagious Divides*, 127–28. See also Inglis, *Ma'i Lepera*; Moran, *Colonizing Leprosy*; and Mohr, *Plague and Fire*.

26 Inglis, *Ma'i Lepera*, 90, 96–100; Moran, *Colonizing Leprosy*, 107, 111.

27 "Part III," "Civilian Defense," 63–64.

28 Some of this registration process was conducted in temporarily closed-down schools, with the teachers conducting the work. "Report of the Governor of Hawaii," 1942, 12.

29 "Hawaii Health Messenger vol. I, no. 10, April, 1942," Immunizations, Box 878, MGHI, RG 494, NA, 2; "Part III," "Civilian Defense," 35–36.

30 "Hawaii Health Messenger," Immunizations, Box 878, MGHI, RG 494, NA, 1–2; "Press release: 10 March 1942," "Office of the Military Governor: 6 Apr. 42," Immunizations, Box 878, MGHI, RG 494, NA.

31 "War Records BH," August 1944, 30.02, Box 18, HWRD, 12–13, 18.

32 Allen, *Hawaii's War Years*, 120.

33 Transcript, "An Era of Change," interview by Michiko Kodama-Nishimoto, 1602, UH Center for Oral History, http://hdl.handle.net/10125/29861.

34 Allen, *Hawaii's War Years*, 120; "Part III," "Civilian Defense," 36; "Hawaii Health Messenger," 3.

35 Foucault, *"Society Must Be Defended,"* 252.

36 Foucault, *Discipline and Punish*.

37 Kauanui, "Colonialism in Equality," 637, 641; Moreton-Robinson, *White Possessive*.

38 In 1940 there were fifty-six cases, including ten deaths, of typhoid fever, and ninety-five cases, including six deaths, because of diphtheria. By 1944, there were only seven cases and one death caused by typhoid fever, and twenty-four cases of diphtheria, with no deaths. Because there had not been a case of smallpox in Hawai'i for thirty years, this statistic went unchanged. "Army Activities Resulting in Benefits to the Territory of Hawaii: Series B, Disease Prevention," Hawaiian Sugar Planters' Association (HSPA), Honolulu, 1945, HC; Allen, *Hawaii's War Years*, 336.

39 "Part III," "Civilian Defense," 63.

40 Osorio, *Dismembering Lāhui*, 44–47.

41   Goodyear-Kaʻōpua, "Introduction," 4.

42   McGregor, *Nā Kuaʻāina*, 132, 76, 31, 108. See also Blaisdell, "Historical and Cultural Aspects," 6–7, 13, 15; and Blaisdell, "Historical and Philosophical Aspects."

43   "In the cultural kīpuka, traditional Native Hawaiian custom, belief, and practices
continue to be a practical part of everyday life." McGregor, *Nā Kuaʻāina*, 15.

44   "Giving from the Heart," *Hawaii Herald*, January 7, 1943, Blood Banks, Box 882,
Military Government of the Territory of Hawaii, RG 494, NA; "The Bank of Life,"
Honolulu Star-Bulletin, February 21, 1942, Box 37, Folder 1, HWRD.

45   "Honolulu Blood Plasma Bank" (For Archives of Hawaii Committee — War Records Depository, University of Hawaii), 41.01 Blood Plasma Bank, Box 24, HWRD,
1–2; Bill Cogswell, "Man of the Hour," December 9, 1944, 41.01 Blood Plasma
Bank, Box 24, HWRD, 2–3; Allen, *Hawaii's War Years*, 68–69.

46   "Honolulu Blood Plasma Bank," 1–2; Allen, *Hawaii's War Years*, 30; "Need of Blood
Donors Urgent," *Honolulu Star-Bulletin*, December 12, 1941; "More Blood Donors
Sought," *Honolulu Star-Bulletin*, December 13, 1941; "2,000 Donors Answer Urgent
Call for Blood," *Honolulu Advertiser*, December 13, 1941; "Life and Time Can Be
Saved by Blood Bank," *Honolulu Advertiser*, December 17, 1941, Box 37 (uncata-
logued), HWRD.

47   Pinkerton, "Honolulu Blood Plasma Bank," December 8, 1942, Folder 2, Box 17,
Andrew Lind papers, HWRD, 4; "Help Your Blood Bank! Call 67771," *Honolulu
Star-Bulletin*, March 15, 1946, Box 37 (uncatalogued), HWRD; "Lend-Lease Plan
Important Part of Blood Bank's Work," *Honolulu Star-Bulletin*, July 20, 1943, Blood
Banks, Box 882, Military Government of the Territory of Hawaii, RG 494, NA.

48   "Pinkerton Says Blood Bank Here Second to None," *Honolulu Star-Bulletin*,
June 22, 1943, Blood Banks, Box 882, Military Government of the Territory of
Hawaii, RG 494, NA.

49   Pinkerton, "Honolulu Blood Plasma Bank," 5; "Honolulu Blood Bank Operates on
a 3-Fold Basis," *Hawaii Times*, February 24, 1943, Blood Banks, Box 882, Military
Government of the Territory of Hawaii, RG 494, NA; "Blood Bank Here One of the
Few in U.S. with Complete Setup," *Hawaii Herald*, February 24, 1943, Blood Banks,
Box 882, Military Government of the Territory of Hawaii, RG 494, NA. During this
time this bank had one of the lowest transfusion-reaction rates in the United
States. "Facts about the Honolulu Blood Bank," *Honolulu Star-Bulletin*, October 9,
1945, Box 37 (uncatalogued), HWRD.

50   Swanson, *Banking on the Body*.

51   Waldby and Mitchell, *Tissue Economies*, 6–14.

52   "Islanders Urged by Dr. Pinkerton to Continue Blood Bank," *Honolulu Star-
Bulletin*, September 22, 1945, Box 37 (uncatalogued), HWRD; "Blood Bank Needs
Your Support," *Honolulu Star-Bulletin*, October 17, 1945; "Help Your Blood Bank!"

53   The cost of plasma was eventually reduced to a service charge of $5 and an out-
right price of $20 per dose. "Honolulu Blood Plasma Bank," 10–12; F. J. Pinkerton
to All Members of the Honolulu County Medical Society and All Civilian Staffs,
October 1, 1944, 41.01 Blood Plasma Bank, Box 24, HWRD; F. J Pinkerton to Whom

It May Concern, January 20, 1945, 41.01 Blood Plasma Bank, Box 24, HWRD; "Help
Your Blood Bank!"

54 Waldby, *Visible Human Project*, 19, 33–34, 52.

55 *Statistical and Narrative Report, Territorial Nutrition Committee, 1938–1945*, 33.03
Territorial Nutrition Committee, HWRD, 8.

56 "Blood Donors and the Technique of Collection of Blood."

57 Frannie Lee to Parents, February 1, 1945, Box 9 (uncatalogued), HWRD.

58 "Tattoo Tip Puts Blood Type on the Bottom of Foot," *Honolulu Star-Bulletin*, Janu-
ary 8, 1943, Blood Banks, Box 882, Military Government of the Territory of Hawaii,
RG 494, NA; "Identification Tags," *Honolulu Advertiser*, January 22, 1943, Blood
Banks, Box 882, Military Government of the Territory of Hawaii, RG 494, NA.

59 Transcript, "An Era of Change," interview by Joe Rossi, 328–30, UH Center for
Oral History, http://hdl.handle.net/10125/29873; "36 Defendants Offer Blood to
Lift Sentences," *Honolulu Advertiser*, December 28, 1941, File 1, Box 37 (uncata-
logued), HWRD; "More Blood Given," *Honolulu Star-Bulletin*, December 30, 1941,
File 1, Box 37 (uncatalogued), HWRD; Allen, *Hawaii's War Years*, 173–74. This also
occurred in Atlanta at one point in 1947. "Convicts Pay Banks with Blood," *Hilo
Tribune-Herald*, September 20, 1947, Box 37 (uncatalogued), HWRD.

60 Allen, *Hawaii's War Years*, 174; Anthony, *Hawaii under Army Rule*, 55.

61 Anthony, *Hawaii under Army Rule*, 55.

62 Allen, *Hawaii's War Years*, 173–74.

63 "36 Defendants Offer Blood to Lift Sentences"; "More Blood Given"; Anthony,
Hawaii under Army Rule, 56.

64 Kalindi Vora observes this dynamic through the example of transnational gesta-
tional surrogacy, writing that these practices operated by "initiating them into
property relations to their bodies. . . ." Vora, *Life Support*, 11.

65 This was a calculation of the percentage donated by each race in relation to total
number of blood donors for that month.

66 Pinkerton, "Honolulu Blood Plasma Bank."

67 "872 Persons Gave Blood in April," *Hawaii Herald*, June 5, 1943; "589 Donate
Blood in July," *Honolulu Advertiser*, August 13, 1943; "'Lend-Lease' at Blood Bank
Is Reorganized," *Honolulu Advertiser*, September 23, 1943, "Peacetime Blood Bank
Established," *Honolulu Advertiser*, October 26, 1943, Blood Banks, Box 882, MGHI,
RG 494, NA.

68 This racial liberal logic continued at the blood bank after World War II ended.
For example, a Honolulu Blood Bank membership card from 1947 bears the
message "BLOOD FROM ALL RACES IS EQUALLY GOOD!" Blood Bank Membership
Card, 1947, Hawaii Medical Library, Queen's Medical Center, Honolulu, Hawai'i.
Monographs that contribute to this liberal narrative of Hawai'i as a multiracial
paradise include Adams, *Interracial Marriage in Hawaii*; Takaki, *Pau Hana*; and
Beechert, *Working in Hawaii*.

69 This gendered pattern of blood donation continued throughout the war. For
example, in June 1943, 564 men donated blood, and 66 women donated blood.

In July 1943, 533 men donated blood, and 56 women donated blood. Pinkerton, "Honolulu Blood Plasma Bank"; "531 Blood Donors Reported during June," *Honolulu Star-Bulletin*, July 26, 1943, RG 494, Box 882, NA; "589 Donate Blood in July"; Swanson, *Banking on the Body*, 80.

70   Quoted in Swanson, *Banking on the Body*, 80.

71   For an example of this colonial taxonomy at work in academic scholarship, see Adams, *Interracial Marriage in Hawaii*.

72   Moreton-Robinson, *White Possessive*.

73   "AJA Donors Aided OCD Blood Bank Program in March," *Hawaii Herald*, April 12, 1943, Blood Banks, Box 882, MGHI, RG 494, NA.

74   On the consolidation of the "Caucasian subject," see Jacobson, *Whiteness of a Different Color*.

75   See Adams, *Interracial Marriage in Hawaii*.

76   Kauanui, *Hawaiian Blood*, 2, 124–35.

77   Arvin, "Still in the Blood," 686–88. See also Arvin, *Possessing Polynesians*, 135–67.

78   Wolfe, "Settler Colonialism," 393, 402.

79   Guglielmo, "'Red Cross, Double Cross.'"

80   For example, Guglielmo cites Red Cross workers who admitted to not always sticking to blood-segregation procedures, and an interview with Daniel Inouye, in which he claimed that he received African American blood on a battlefield during the war. Guglielmo, "'Red Cross, Double Cross,'" 89.

81   Swanson, *Banking on the Body*, 65.

82   As Guglielmo writes, "In November 1944, the *Chicago Herald American* ran a feature story about a local war worker, Kazuo Saito, who was 'first in line' at the Red Cross blood donor center after hearing the news that both his brothers had died fighting overseas for the U.S. Army. An accompanying photo showed Saito donating blood while looking at a picture of his brothers" (75). This evidence complements Fujitani's argument that during World War II, racializations of Japanese and Japanese Americans transitioned from "vulgar" to more "polite" forms because of the need for the United States to present itself as an antiracist global power and also because of the growing needs for manpower in the US military. Fujitani, *Race for Empire*; Guglielmo, "'Red Cross, Double Cross,'" 73–75.

83   Ngai, *Impossible Subjects*.

84   Beth Bailey and David Farber argue that although African American soldiers faced less racism in Hawai'i, racist views of soldiers and defense workers from North America permeated discourse in O'ahu. Bailey and Farber, *First Strange Place*, 133–38.

85   Pinkerton, "Rh Blood Types in Hawaii," August 11, 1945, 41.01, Box 24, HWRD.

86   As Arvin argues, the black/white binary has throughout history informed how Indigenous peoples are racialized: "It is important to see how central both antiblack (most obvious in relation to explicitly disparaging race discourses about Melanesians) and anti-Indigenous logic (most obvious in relation to the exoticization and conditional white identification with Polynesians to undermine the

power of Polynesians in their own lands) are to the settler colonial ideologies about the Polynesian race." Here, we can see this logic operating as part of a wartime regime of racial liberalism. Arvin, *Possessing Polynesians*, 39.

87 Waldby and Mitchell, *Tissue Economies*, 24.

88 "Percentage of Blood Donors by Races," *Honolulu Star-Bulletin*, March 5, 1943, Blood Banks, Box 882, Military Government of the Territory of Hawaii, RG 494, NA. For another letter to the editor, by a member of the US Air Force, defending Japanese Americans on this issue, see "Japanese as Blood Donors," *Honolulu Star-Bulletin*, February 11, 1943, Folder 1, Box 37 (uncatalogued), HWRD.

89 "Pinkerton Questions Licenses of Doctors Enemy to Nation," *Honolulu Advertiser*, August 16, 1944, Box 55 (uncatalogued), HWRD; "Revocation of Licenses of Alien Doctors Deported to Japan Urged," *Honolulu Star-Bulletin*, August 16, 1942, Box 55 (uncatalogued), HWRD; "Japanese Asked to Help," *Hawaii Hochi*, August 14, 1942, Blood Banks, Box 882, Military Government of the Territory of Hawaii, RG 494, NA.

90 "How about That Blood Donation?," *Hawaii Herald*, January 23, 1943, Blood Banks, Box 882, Military Government of the Territory of Hawaii, RG 494, NA.

91 Chinn, *Technology and the Logic*, 106; "It's Easy to Donate Blood," *Honolulu Advertiser*, December 18, 1941, Folder 1, Box 37 (uncatalogued), HWRD; "Blood Donations as Evidence of Patriotic Willingness," *Honolulu Star-Bulletin*, February 15, 1943, Folder 1, Box 37 (uncatalogued), HWRD.

92 "'I'm Happy—I've Given My Blood.'"

93 "Blood on Deposit," *Honolulu Advertiser*, January 19, 1943, Blood Banks, Box 882, MGHI, RG 494, NA.

94 Takaki, *Different Mirror*, 385.

95 Kelli Nakamura, "Emergency Service Committee," *Densho Encyclopedia*, accessed June 22, 2016, http://encyclopedia.densho.org/Emergency%20Service%20Committee; Masaji Marumoto, "Emergency Service Committee, Report of Activities, February 10, 1942 to June 30, 1942," Chinese (Morale, WWII), Box 1, War Research Lab (A1979:042a), HWRD; Yutaka Kakahata and Ralph Toyota, "Varsity Victory Volunteers: A Social Movement," in *Social Process in Hawai'i*, vol. 8, ed. Dora Seu (Honolulu: Department of Sociology, University of Hawai'i, 1943), HC, 29.

96 Hungwai Ching, "Progress Report, First Six Months," Chinese Research and Education Committee, June 15, 1944, Chinese (Morale, WWII), Box 1, War Research Lab (A1979:042a), HWRD, 2.

97 Homer F. Barnes to Parents or Guardians of Kamehameha Schools, March 19, 1942, 24.02 Private Schools Oahu—Kamehameha Schools (24.02), HWRD; "K.S.G. Students Do Volunteer Work at Red Cross Centers," *Ka Moi*, January 23, 1942, HWRD; "Queen's Hospital Receives Blood of K.S.B. Instructors; Fred Young Donates to a Baby," *Ka Moi*, January 23, 1942, HWRD.

98 "A Student Letter from Honolulu," *Weekly News Review*, March 29, 1943, 24.02, HWRD.

99 *Ka Palapala*, University of Hawai'i, 1942, http://hdl.handle.net/10125/34283, 109; *Ka Palapala*, University of Hawai'i, 1943, http://hdl.handle.net/10125/34459, 87.

100 "Report of Proceedings of a Board of Officers and Civilians," October 14, 1942, 421. S-31 Shigeo (Robert) Muroda Case File, Japanese Internment and Relocation Files: The Hawai'i Experience, 1942–1982, Japanese American Veterans Collection, University of Hawai'i at Mānoa, 1–3.

101 "Blood Donors," *Honolulu Advertiser*, June 22, 1943, Folder 1, Box 37 (uncatalogued), HWRD. See also the Editor's Note printed below "Japanese as Blood Donors," *Honolulu Star-Bulletin*, February 11, 1943, Folder 1, Box 37 (uncatalogued), HWRD.

102 Quoted in LaBerge, "Mother of Blood Banking," 42.

103 "Human Blood Values Here Are Same as in the Rest of the World," *Honolulu Star-Bulletin*, March 21, 1941, Folder 1, Box 37 (uncatalogued), HWRD; "No Such Thing as 'Tropical Anemia,' Doctor Here Assures," *Honolulu Advertiser*, September 21, 1945, Folder 1, Box 37 (uncatalogued), HWRD; "The Tropical Anemia Bugaboo," *Honolulu Advertiser*, December 17, 1945, Folder 1, Box 37 (uncatalogued), HWRD.

104 Wailoo, *Drawing Blood*, 163.

105 "Postwar Public Health," Charles L. Wilbar, *How to Keep Well*, Station KGU, August 27, 1944, HC.

106 "Army Activities"; "War Records BH," August 1944, 30.02, Box 18, HWRD; "Report of the Governor of Hawaii," 1944.

107 Joseph Palma, *A Guide to Mothers in Hawaii* (Honolulu: Advertiser Publishing Company, 1952), 57, HC.

108 Much like the immunization program, the Honolulu Blood Bank continued to operate even after Restoration Day on March 10, 1943. The management of the blood bank transferred from the Office of Civilian Defense to the territorial government and a board of trustees, which was again headed by Pinkerton. "Honolulu's Peacetime Blood Bank Now Nationally Famous," *Honolulu Advertiser*, July 22, 1945, Box 37 (uncatalogued), HWRD.

CHAPTER 3. "THE FIRST LINE OF DEFENSE IS OUR HOME": SETTLER MILITARY DOMESTICITY IN WORLD WAR II–ERA HAWAI'I

Epigraph: Biennial Report of the Department of Public Instruction of the Territory of Hawaii, 1941–1942, 24.01 Department of Public Instruction—Division of Health Education, HWRD, 2.

1 *Bulletin to Parents*, vol. 1, no. 1, November 1942, 24.01 Department of Public Instruction—Division of Health Education, HWRD.

2 Kaplan, *Anarchy of Empire*, 34. On the colonial politics of ice and cooling as a means of bolstering settler notions of comfort and structures of dispossession and extraction in Hawai'i, see Hobart, *Cooling the Tropics*.

3 As Federici argues, "The counterpart of the market, the instrument for the privatization of social relations and, above all, for the propagation of capitalist discipline and patriarchal rule, the family emerges in the period of primitive

accumulation also as the most important institution for the appropriation and concealment of women's labor" (*Caliban and the Witch*, 97). Evelyn Nakano Glenn critiques the universalization of this construction, arguing that the family is also a site of solidarity for women and families of color. Nakano Glenn, "Racial Ethnic Women's Labor," 101–5.

4 Dower, *War Without Mercy*, 4–5. On the shift from "vulgar" to "polite" racism during the Pacific War, see Fujitani, *Race for Empire*. See also Melamed, *Represent and Destroy*; and Dudziak, *Cold War Civil Rights*.

5 Evelyn Nakano Glenn and Rhacel Salazar Parreñas refer to this dynamic as the racial or international division of reproductive labor. See Nakano Glenn, "Racial Ethnic Women's Labor"; Nakano Glenn, "From Servitude to Service Work"; and Parreñas, "Migrant Filipina."

6 Escobedo, *From Coveralls to Zoot Suits*, 3. See also Milkman, *Gender at Work*; Yellin, *Our Mothers' War*; Anderson, *Wartime Women*; and Honey, *Creating Rosie the Riveter*.

7 Allen, *Hawaii's War Years*, 306, 398.

8 *Maternal and Child Health Services of the Territory of Hawaii*, Postwar Planning Committee, hc, 43.

9 The Department of Public Instruction's Division of Health Education and Parent-Teacher Association organized this newsletter. *Biennial Report of the Department of Public Instruction*, 21–22.

10 *Bulletin to Parents*, vol. 1, no. 4, May–June 1943, 24.01 Department of Public Instruction—Division of Health Education, HWRD.

11 As early as the 1920s, sugar plantations in Hawai'i had used nutrition and public health as methods to boost labor productivity. It is not clear when Larsen ma de this statement, but it would have been between 1920 and 1946. Clark Blake, "Nils Larsen, Pioneer in Plantation Health," *Hygeia*, vol. 24, no. 11, November 1946, HC.

12 On capital's contradictory relation to life, see note 59 of this book's introduction.

13 *Statistical and Narrative Report*, Territorial Nutrition Committee, 1938–1945, 33.03 Territorial Nutrition Committee, HWRD, 2.

14 The College of Hawaii would eventually become the University of Hawai'i. Hawaii Home Economic Association, Box 3, CM; Agnes Hunt Cade, "Beginnings of the Home Ec Dept," "The Home Economics Department, University of Hawaii," UH Home Ec History Bazore Gruelle, Box 7, CM.

15 "Home Economics Department," 2.

16 Bazore, *Hawaiian and Pacific Foods*, HC, xii; "Home Economics Department," 2.

17 UH Hist Home Ec WWII, Box 7, CM; "Home Economics Department," 3.

18 UH Hist Home Ec WWII.

19 *Statistical and Narrative Report*, 1; *A Program and Plan for the Territorial Nutrition Committee*, March 20, 1942, 33.03 Territorial Nutrition Committee, HWRD, 13; "Health Means Victory: Eat Right to Work and Win," March 31, 1943, 33.01 Home Defense Committee, HWRD.

20 UH Hist Home Ec WWII, Box 7, cm; *Program and Plan*, 2–3.

21 This was also true in the continental United States. *Program and Plan*, 9; Bentley, *Eating for Victory*, 24.

22 "Home Defense Group Is One Year Old Today," *Honolulu Advertiser*, December 15, 1942, 33.01 Home Defense Committee, HWRD; Miriam J. Emery to T. G. S. Walker, January 18, 1943, 33.01 Home Defense Committee, HWRD; "Home Defense Committee Meeting," Saturday, May 23, 1942, Miriam J. Emery, 33.01 Home Defense Committee, HWRD.

23 "Home Defense Committee," Membership Report, Dec. 15, 1941 to Dec. 31, 1942; and 1943, 33.01 Home Defense Committee, HWRD; "Mrs. Helen McGill Joins Home Defense Group for Radio," 1943 Report, 33.01 Home Defense Committee, HWRD; Home Defense Committee, January 13 meeting, 1945, 33.01 Home Defense Committee, HWRD.

24 "Home Defense Committee Celebrates 1st Birthday," *Honolulu Star-Bulletin*, December 15, 1942, 33.01 Home Defense Committee, HWRD.

25 Brigadier General Thomas H. Green to Miriam Jackson Emery, February 6, 1943, 33.01 Home Defense Committee, HWRD; "Home Defense Committee Has Made a Fine Record," *Honolulu Star-Bulletin*, n.d, Riley H. Allen to Miriam Jackson Emery, December 14, 1942, 33.01 Home Defense Committee, HWRD.

26 Miriam J. Emery to Colonel W. R. White, February 3, 1942, 33.01 Home Defense Committee, HWRD; W. R. White to Miriam J. Emery, February 6, 1942, 33.01 Home Defense Committee, HWRD.

27 "Hints for Homemakers," *1943 Report*, 33.01 Home Defense Committee, HWRD; *Statistical and Narrative Report*, 5.

28 "Hints for Homemakers: Homemakers Can Help to Win the War," *Honolulu Star-Bulletin*, June 20, 1942, 33.01 Home Defense Committee, HWRD.

29 "Helpful Hints on Foods and Nutrition for Home Makers," *Hawaii Hochi*, July 16, 1942, 33.01 Home Defense Committee, HWRD.

30 "Welfare News in Wartime," March 15, 1943, 33.01 Home Defense Committee, HWRD, 15.

31 Mary Musgrove to Mrs. Emery, Hawaiian Electric Co., January 19, 1943, 33.01 Home Defense Committee, HWRD; "10 Demonstrations in Homemaking to Be Held at Schools," *Honolulu Star-Bulletin*, April 10, 1942, 33.01 Home Defense Committee, HWRD; "Mothers Learn Wartime Economy," *Honolulu Star-Bulletin*, May 21, 1942, 33.01 Home Defense Committee, HWRD; "Summary of Demonstrations for Mothers of the Free Kindergarten and Child Aid Association," Kindergarten Demonstrations, 33.01 Home Defense Committee, HWRD; *Statistical and Narrative Report*, 5–6.

32 "Suggestions for the Instructors," Kindergarten Demonstrations, 33.01 Home Defense Committee, HWRD; "Health-Giving Desserts," Kindergarten Demonstrations, 33.01 Home Defense Committee, HWRD; "Mothers Learn Wartime Economy," *Honolulu Star-Bulletin*, May 21, 1942, Kindergarten Demonstrations, 33.01 Home Defense Committee, HWRD; Home Demonstration Agents, 1942–1951,

Record Group: Hawaii Cooperative Extension Service Annual Plans of Work, Box 13, University Archives, University of Hawai'i.

33 Alexa Ames to Miriam Jackson Emery, January 16, 1943, 33.01 Home Defense Committee, HWRD; M. A. Mulrony to Miriam J. Emery, January 21, 1943, 33.01 Home Defense Committee, HWRD; Home Defense Radio Schedule, January-July, 1945, 33.01 Home Defense Committee, HWRD; M. A. Mulrony to Miriam J. Emery, January 12, 1942, 33.01 Home Defense Committee, HWRD; Miriam J. Emery to M. A. Mulrony, January 13, 1942, 33.01 Home Defense Committee, HWRD; M. A. Mulrony to Miriam J. Emery, January 14, 1942, 33.01 Home Defense Committee, HWRD; "A Diet to Promote Good Health Should Include Each Day," Kindergarten Demonstrations, 33.01 Home Defense Committee, HWRD; Erma Meeks to Allen Cunningham, July 11, 1945, 33.01 Home Defense Committee, HWRD; Erma Meeks to Peter Simmons, July 11, 1945, 33.01 Home Defense Committee, HWRD.

34 *Statistical and Narrative Report*, 5; "Summary of Newspaper Contribution of the Home Defense Committee," Newspaper Work, 33.01 Home Defense Committee, HWRD; Miriam Jackson Emery to Mr. Marion A. Mulrony, January 9, 1942, 33.01 Home Defense Committee, HWRD.

35 For more on how food and eating are located at the intersection of the social and the biological, see Tompkins, *Racial Indigestion*, 3–6.

36 Home Ec History 1922+ Nutrition Lab 3, Box 7, CM.

37 Biography—Lind, Helen Yonge, "Talk on Carey D. Miller," May 17, 1986, Box 7, CM.

38 Biography—Lind, Helen Yonge, "Talk on Carey D. Miller," May 17, 1986, Box 7, CM.

39 Home Ec History 1922+.

40 Kim TallBear critiques the colonial history of scientific research on Native peoples in *Native American DNA*.

41 Arvin, "Still in the Blood," 686–88; Kauanui, *Hawaiian Blood*.

42 Home Ec History 1922+, 3.

43 *Japanese Foods Commonly Used in Hawaii*, Carey D. Miller, Hawaii Agricultural Experiment Station, Honolulu, Hawaii, Bulletin No. 68, November, 1933, Box 4, CM, 1.

44 *Japanese Foods Commonly Used in Hawaii*, 2–9, 15–25.

45 *Foods Used by Filipinos in Hawaii*, Carey D. Miller, Lucille Louis, Kisako Yanazawa, Hawaii Agricultural Experiment Station, Honolulu, Hawaii, Bulletin No. 98, 1946, Box 4, CM, 14–15.

46 *Foods Used by Filipinos in Hawaii*, 18, 55–56.

47 "Nutrition Posters," exh. 7a, page 8, 33.03 Territorial Nutrition Committee, HWRD; Marian R. Weaver to Erma Meeks, January 18, 1943, Japanese and Filipino, 33.01 Home Defense Committee, HWRD; "Nutrition and Health Notes; Yardstick of Food Values," *Hawaii Hochi*, July 24, 1942, 33.01 Home Defense Committee, HWRD.

48 This experience was not limited to Hawai'i: Asian immigrant families living in San Francisco also had to eat more Western-style foods once imports became scarce. In both Hawai'i and the continental United States, immigrant families'

use of American foods rather than the "impractical" imported food was portrayed as evidence of assimilation and loyalty. *Program and Plan*, 10; *Statistical and Narrative Report*, 10; Yung, *Unbound Feet*, 273.

49 "Good Americans Eat Good Food," children's posters, undated, Oversized Materials, HWRD; Carey Miller, *A Study of the Dietary and Value of Living of 44 Japanese Families in Hawaii*, Hawaii University Res. Pub. 18, 1938; M. Potgeiter, "The Adequacy of Diets of 38 Honolulu Families on Relief," Bulletin No. 94, University of Hawaii Agricultural Experiment Station, 1994; Winifred R. Vinacke, Eva Hartzler, and Yoshinori Tanada, *Processed Rice in Hawaii: Nutritive Value, Susceptibility to Insect Infestation and Consumer Acceptance as Compared with White and Brown Rice*, Technical Bulletin No. 10, University of Hawaii Agricultural Experiment Station, March 1950, 62–66.

50 Miller, *Study of the Dietary*, 15; "Good Americans Eat Good Food."

51 "Warfare News in Wartime," March 24, 1943, 15, 33.01 Home Defense Committee, HWRD.

52 Marian R. Weaver to Erma Meeks, January 18, 1943, Japanese and Filipino, 33.01 Home Defense Committee, HWRD.

53 Marian R. Weaver to Erma Meeks; "Helpful Hints on Foods and Nutrition for Homemakers—Meal Planning for Health," *Hawaii Hochi*, August 20, 1942, 33.01 Home Defense Committee, HWRD; "Helpful Hints on Foods and Nutrition for Homemakers—Article I," *Hawaii Hochi*, July 17, 1942, 33.01 Home Defense Committee, HWRD.

54 "Milk Each Day," Marian R. Weaver, for Filipino program, August 17, 1942 [marked "translated into Filipino"], 33.01 Home Defense Committee, HWRD.

55 Gupta, "Dairy's Decline," 495.

56 *Foods Used by Filipinos in Hawaii*, 55–56.

57 Charlotte Wakugawa, "Nutritional Report," UH—Nutritional History, Student Papers, Box 7, CM.

58 "Haole" refers to white settlers in Hawai'i. For more on the term and the racialization of whiteness in Hawai'i, see Rohrer, *Haoles in Hawai'i*. Eleanor M. Maeda, "My Nutritional History," UH—Nutritional History, Student Papers, Box 7, CM, February 24, 1958; Setsuko Matsubara, "My Personal and Nutritional History," UH—Nutritional History, Student Papers, Box 7, CM, February 25, 1952; and Pauline Apuna, "Nutrition History," UH—Nutritional History, Student Papers, Box 7, CM.

59 "New Ways of Old," Marjorie Abel, KGMB, Nov 11, 1942, 33.01 Home Defense Committee, HWRD; "Food for Flight," Mary Bartow, KGU, date not specified, 33.01 Home Defense Committee, HWRD.

60 "Thanksgiving Left-Overs," Esther Corbaley, KGMB, November 25, 1942, 33.01 Home Defense Committee, HWRD, 1.

61 "Hawaii's Soups and Stews," Katherine Bazore, KGMB, April 22, 1942, 33.01, HWRD.

62 Else, "Breakdown of the Kapu System."

63　"Life Histories of Native Hawaiians," interview by June Gutmanis, UH Center for Oral History, November 1978, 224.

64　Blaisdell, "Historical and Cultural Aspects"; Richard Kekuni Blaisdell, "Comparison: Pre-Western Hawaiian, Prudent Adapted, and Typical American-Island Diets," 1985, accessed July 12, 2016, www.papaolalokahi.org/comparison-of-diets -in-hawaii-chart-developed-by-r-kekuni-blaisdell-md-phd-1985; Aluli, "Prevalence of Obesity."

65　The condemnation of fisheries began as early as 1900. "By 1953, the territorial government had condemned 37 konohiki fisheries on Maui and Oʻahu (including multiple fisheries purchased to facilitate construction of Pearl Harbor) and the Attorney General had initiated condemnation of nine more on Maui and Kauaʻi." Vaughan and Ayers, "Customary Access," 523. See also Winter et al., "*Moku* System," 15.

66　Else, "Breakdown of the Kapu System," 241–55.

67　Blaisdell, "Historical and Cultural Aspects"; Else, "Breakdown of the Kapu System," 241–55.

68　Aikau and Camvel, "Cultural Traditions and Food," 545; Gupta, "Return to Freedom."

69　Vaughan and Ayers, "Customary Access."

70　Winter et al., "*Moku* System," 16.

71　Blake, "Nils Larsen."

72　Letters to friends—1942 December, Box 1, CM.

73　Sybil Smith—US Dept of US Dept of Agriculture to Carey Miller, Box 3, CM; Stanley, Louise—US Dept of Agriculture to Carey Miller, Box 3, CM.

74　*Fruits of Hawaii: Description, Nutritive Value, and Use,* Carey Miller and Katherine Bazore, 1936, Box 3, CM; *Ways to Use Vegetables in Hawaii,* by Helen Yonge Lind, Mary L. Bartow, Carey D. Miller, 1946, Box 3, CM, 82–83.

75　"Onion Fiasco Endangers Maui Farmers' Livelihood," *Honolulu Star-Bulletin,* August 5, 1943, Newspaper articles by Home Defense Committee to promote sale of surplus onions and cabbage, 33.01 Home Defense Committee, HWRD.

76　"To help us plan better programs for you, please give us the following information," 1943–1944 Kindergarten, 33.01 Home Defense Committee, HWRD; M. Chow, "Our Own Nutritional Problems," UH—Nutritional History, Student papers, Box 7, CM; Annie Chun, "Nutritional History," February 13, 1953, UH—Nutritional History, Student papers, Box 7, CM.

77　Carey D. Miller, Letter to Friends, December 1942, CM; "Guavas: Let None Go to Waste," Home Defense Committee, 33.01 Home Defense Committee, HWRD. "Isle Guava Preservation Is Discussed," *Honolulu Advertiser,* September 11, 1942, 33.01 Home Defense Committee, HWRD; "Guava Has 'War Vitamin,'" *Honolulu Advertiser,* August 29, 1942, 33.01 Home Defense Committee, HWRD; "Guavas: Let None Go to Waste," 33.03 Territorial Nutrition Committee, 6, exhibit 4; "'Save the Guava' Campaign," *Honolulu Star-Bulletin,* September 27, 1942; "Guava Preserving

Here Being Urged," *Honolulu Star-Bulletin*, August 9, 1942; photo of guava demonstration, "Learning to Use Local Fruits." This was also supported by the Board of Health. "Make Guava Jelly Housewives Urged," *Honolulu Advertiser*, August 9, 1942, 33.01 Home Defense Committee, HWRD.

78 "Guava Has 'War Vitamin'"; "Guava Display at Gas Company," *Honolulu Star-Bulletin*, November 12, 1942, 33.01 Home Defense Committee, HWRD.

79 "My Favorite Onion Recipe," *Honolulu Star-Bulletin*, July 21, 1942; "My Favorite Onion Recipe," *Honolulu Star-Bulletin*, July 22, 1942; "My Favorite Onion Recipe," *Honolulu Star-Bulletin*, July 23, 1942, 33.01 Home Defense Committee, HWRD.

80 Significantly, many of these fruits are not actually indigenous to Hawai'i, such as pineapples and figs. "Suggestions for the Instructors"; "Health-Giving Desserts"; "Mothers Learn Wartime Economy."

81 "Get Your Money's Worth of Food," Marian R. Weaver, KGMB, June 12, 1942, 33.01 Home Defense Committee, HWRD; "Emergency Uses of Coconut," Alice P. Trimble, Radio KGMB, January 8, 1942, 33.01 Home Defense Committee, HWRD; "Recipes," Kindergarten Demonstrations, 33.01 Home Defense Committee, HWRD; "Recipes," 1943 Report, 33.01 Home Defense Committee, HWRD. The recipe for pineapple upside-down cake actually originated in the 1920s as a result of the canned-pineapple trade between the United States and Hawai'i. "Recipes," 1943–1944 Kindergarten, 33.01 Home Defense Committee, HWRD; Okihiro, *Pineapple Culture*, 144; *Ways to Use Vegetables in Hawaii*, 84–85, 88, 131; *Fruits of Hawaii*, 48, 63, 93, 96.

82 Hobart, *Cooling the Tropics*.

83 Chiko Abe, "My Nutritional History," UH—Nutritional History, Student Papers, Box 7, CM; Clara Arakaki, UH—Nutritional History, Student Papers, Box 7, CM; Ruth Okahara, "My Nutritional History," UH—Nutritional History, Student Papers, Box 7, CM.

84 Brigadier General Thomas H. Green to Miriam Jackson Emery, February 6, 1943, 33.01 Home Defense Committee, HWRD; "Home Defense Committee Has Made a Fine Record," *Honolulu Star-Bulletin*, n.d.; Riley H. Allen to Miriam Jackson Emery, December 14, 1942, 33.01 Home Defense Committee, HWRD.

85 "Hawaii's Soups and Stews," Katherine Bazore, KGMB, April 22, 1942. 33.01 Home Defense Committee, HWRD.

86 Marian R. Weaver to Erma Meeks, January 19, 1943, Japanese and Filipinos, 33.01 Home Defense Committee, HWRD.

87 George Armitage, *Hawaiian Hospitality*, ed. Helen Berkey (Honolulu: Advertiser Publishing, 1943), HC; Jean Hobbs, *Here's How in Hawaiian Hospitality*, Honolulu, 1943, HC; *Cooking for a Crowd*, Honolulu: Hawaii Dietetic Association, 1944, HC.

88 Bazore, *Hawaiian and Pacific Foods*, xxvii.

89 It is telling that there is a "Portuguese Foods and Food Customs" section, which implies that at this point Portuguese immigrants were not considered a "Caucasian" race. This is consistent with contemporary racializations in Hawai'i, in which Portuguese immigrants worked on the plantations under the "Caucasian

field boss." As discussed in chapter 2, Portuguese were categorized separately from Caucasians in blood-donation statistics. Takaki, *Pau Hana*, 77; Bazore, *Hawaiian and Pacific Foods*, 35–41.

90　*Hawaiian and Pacific Foods* was also published and circulated in the continental United States and provided optional substitutions for hostesses in the US continent who could not access certain ingredients. It continued to be updated and reprinted into the 1960s. Bazore, *Hawaiian and Pacific Foods*, HC, xii.

91　Bazore, *Hawaiian and Pacific Foods*, xii.

92　Bazore, *Hawaiian and Pacific Foods*, 90. A "substitutions" page has Western ingredients that can replace ones from Asia and the Pacific Islands. Bazore, *Hawaiian and Pacific Foods*, 90, 127–28.

93　Bazore, *Hawaiian and Pacific Foods*, 92, 105.

94　On "scriptive things," see Bernstein, *Racial Innocence*.

95　Nakano Glenn and Parreñas refer to this dynamic as the racial or international division of reproductive labor. See Nakano Glenn, "Racial Ethnic Women's Labor"; Nakano Glenn, "From Servitude to Service Work"; and Parreñas, "Migrant Filipina."

96　UH Home Ec History Bazore Gruelle, Box 7, CM, 1–7; "Miller Hall—Carey D. Miller," July 31, 2015, http://hdl.handle.net/10125/36628.

97　Biography—Lind, Helen Yonge, "Talk on Carey D. Miller," 4; Cheryl Ernst, "Carey D. Miller Remembered," September 2005, www.hawaii.edu/malamalama/2005/09/f6_miller.html.

98　UH Home Ec. History 1958 Retirement, Box 7, CM.

99　Hawaii Home Economic Association, Box 3, CM; Laudan, *Food of Paradise*, 101.

100　"Ada B Erwin in the 1940 Census," Ancestry, www.ancestry.com/1940-census/usa/Hawaii/Ada-B-Erwin_2r8xyy; Katherine Bazore to Carey Miller, August 8, 1945, Lehman, Katherine Bazore 1929, Box 2, CM; Louise Stanley to Carey Miller, July 3, 1946, Stanley, Louise—US Dept of Agriculture, Box 3, CM; Letters to friends—1944 December (2 copies), Box 1, CM; Letters to friends—1946, 1948, 1949 December, Box 1, CM; W Folder, Box 3, CM.

101　Faderman, *Odd Girls and Twilight Lovers*, 23, 31.

102　Biography—Lind, Helen Yonge, "Talk on Carey D. Miller," 1, 3; Biography—Lind, Helen Yonge, "Cary D. Miller," Pacific Orchid Society 1985, Box 1, CM; Miller Bio-Carey Dunlap Miller by Lind HI Dietetic Ass. 2005, Box 1, CM; Carey D. Miller to C. A. Gregory, January 17, 1956, Bio—Power of Attorney Lind, CM; "Know All Men by These Presents," No. 4920, Oahu Cemetery Association, Biography—Will and related documents, CM; "These Are My Wishes," Carey D. Miller, July 9, 1964, Biography—Will and related documents, CM; "These Are My Wishes," Ada B. Erwin, July 13, 1964, Biography—Will and related documents, CM.

103　For example, Miller's 1946 description of holiday travel plans in a letter to friends—"Ada Erwin, my housemate in Honolulu, has been visiting family and relatives in the middle west. If we can find a place to live in New York City, she expects to join me there the last of January when we hope to have a gay time for three weeks" — could include a hint about plans to explore "gay" life in New York, or it could not. During World War II the word *gay* did not exclusively denote homosexuality and usually meant "carefree" or "frivolous." Yet George Chauncey argues that the word had become a coded term for queer life in New York by this time. Chauncey, *Gay New York*, 19; Letters to friends — 1946, 1948, 1949 December, Box 1, CM.

104 Letters to friends — 1940 December, Box 1, CM.

105 Letters to friends — 1944 December, Box 1, CM.

106 Carey D. Miller to Miss Nagareda, August 18, 1943, Home — Maid 1943, CM.

107 Carey Miller to Mrs. H. A. Rogers, May 31, 1943, Home — Maid 1943, CM; Letters to friends — 1942 December, Box 1, CM; Letters to friends — 1944 December.

108 Letters to friends — 1942 December, Box 1, CM; Letters to friends — 1944 December.

109 Carey Miller to Asako, May 23, 1943, Home — Maid 1943, CM; "Ada B Erwin in the 1940 Census."

110 Carey D. Miller to Miss Shizue Oka, July 24, 1943, Home — Maid 1943, CM.

111 Allen, *Hawaii's War Years*, 307; Nakano Glenn, *Issei, Nisei, War Bride*, 95; Nakano Glenn, "From Servitude to Service Work," 9; Escobedo, *From Coveralls to Zoot Suits*.

112 Nakano Glenn, "Racial Ethnic Women's Labor"; Nakano Glenn, "From Servitude to Service Work," 9; "Ada B Erwin in the 1940 Census."

113 Joseph Palma, *A Guide to Mothers in Hawaii* (Honolulu: Advertiser Publishing Company, 1952), 39, HC.

CHAPTER 4. "A CITIZENSHIP LABORATORY": EDUCATION AND LANGUAGE REFORM IN THE WARTIME CLASSROOM

1 *Hawaiian Schools, A Curriculum Survey, 1944-45*, American Council on Education, Washington, DC, 1946, HC, 34.

2 As Frantz Fanon observed of the importance of language education to colonial governance, "To speak means to be in a position to use a certain syntax, to grasp the morphology of this or that language, but it means above all to assume a culture, to support the weight of a civilization." Fanon, *Black Skin, White Masks*, 17–18.

3 Okihiro, *Cane Fires*, 235; Report of the Joint Legislative Holdover Investigating Committee to the Twenty-Second Legislature of the Territory of Hawaii, Foreign Language Schools and Other Matters, March 29, 1943, HC, 4.

4 *Biennial Report 1941-1942*, Department of Public Instruction, Territory of Hawaii, Honolulu, 24.01 Department of Public Instruction, HWRD, 9.

5 Oren E. Long, "A Letter to Teachers," Department of Public Instruction, Territory of Hawaii, Honolulu, January 10, 1942, 24.01 Department of Public Instruction, HWRD, emphasis mine.

6 A total of 2,604 taught at public schools, and 503 taught at private schools. These data are from December 31, 1942. *Biennial Report 1941-1942*, 57.

7   A total of 82,548 students were enrolled in public schools. There were 86 private schools and 186 public schools during this time. Of the 86 private schools, 63 were in Oʻahu. These data are from December 31, 1942. *Biennial Report 1941–1942*, 57, 62.

8   Of the 82,548 public school students, 82,277 were US citizens, and 17,077 of 17,225 private school students were citizens. *Biennial Report 1941–1942*, 5, 59; Polmar and Allen, *World War II*, 372.

9   "Few communities offer such a challenge to education leadership as the Hawaiian Islands because nowhere else will be found an amalgamation of so many diverse races, living, working, playing together—and, most important, going to school together." *Hawaiian Schools, A Curriculum Survey, 1944–45*, American Council on Education, Washington, DC, 1946, HC, v; "Morale Committee of Educational Institutions," minutes of a meeting held January 23, 1942, 24.01 Department of Public Instruction, HWRD.

10 Oren E. Long, "War Records Project," Department of Public Instruction, Territory of Hawaii, December 1944, 24.01 Department of Public Instruction, HWRD, 1.

11 A. L. Dean to All Principals and Teachers, January 12, 1942, 24.01 Department of Public Instruction, HWRD; Long, "War Records Project," 4, emphasis in original.

12 Despite these calls for racial tolerance, the Morale Committee of Education Institutions found that discrimination against Japanese settlers continued in the islands and discussed ways that the schools could mitigate this issue. *Hawaiian Schools*, v; "Morale Committee of Educational Institutions"; Long, "War Records Project," 4.

13 *Hawaiian Schools*, 25.

14 "Personal Experiences of the Faculty of Kaiulani School Re the Dec. 7th Attack and Their Experiences up to March, 1942," 24.01 Department of Public Instruction Oahu—Kaiulani School, HWRD, 5.

15 Long, "War Records Project," 5–6; *Hawaiian Schools*, 25.

16 Long, "War Records Project," 5–6; *Hawaiian Schools*, 25.

17 These schools included Farrington High School, Wahiawā Elementary School, Kalāheo Elementary School, Huleia Elementary School, Makawao Elementary School, Mountain View Elementary School, and Waimea Elementary School. Long, "War Records Project," 5–6.

18 *Biennial Report 1941–1942*, 6; Long, "War Records Project," 5–6.

19 "Personal Experiences of the Faculty of Kaiulani School."

20 Nayan Shah argues that the US Public Health Service's association of the bubonic plague, its spreading by rats, and Chinatowns racialized these spaces as filthy, overcrowded, breeding grounds for the plague, and racialized Chinese immigrants as particularly susceptible to the disease. John Dower argues that metaphors connoting the extermination of vermin were used to "soften" the wartime killing of Japanese soldiers during the Pacific War. Shah, *Contagious Divides*, 127, 151; Dower, *War Without Mercy*, 98–93.

21 "Personal Experiences of the Faculty of Kaiulani School."

22 "Personal Experiences of the Faculty of Kaiulani School," emphasis in original.

23 *Hawaiian Schools*, 3. Quoted from *Postwar Needs of Education in Hawaii*, for the Editing Committee of the Hawaii Committee on Education in Postwar Reconstruction, an unpublished report, December 1944.

24 *Hawaiian Schools*, 12.

25 "Morale Committee of Educational Institutions."

26 *Biennial Report 1941-1942*, 3, 9, emphasis in original; Long, "War Records Project," 9.

27 Between December 1941 and 1943, the number of public school teachers dropped from 3,346 to 2,645. *Hawaiian Schools*, 25–26, 27.

28 The student population dropped from 91,121 in June 1941 to 80,320 in June 1942. After an effort to increase school enrollment, the number of students rose to 81,794 in the 1943–44 academic year. By June 1944, there were 82,104 students enrolled in school. Long, "War Records Project," 7.

29 Long, "War Records Project," 5–6; Long, "Letter to Teachers"; *Hawaiian Schools*, 28–29.

30 Long, "Letter to Teachers," 1.

31 "We Americans in Hawaii: A study of citizenship problems, particularly as they pertain to the people of Hawaii," published as a supplement to the *Daily Pinion*, McKinley High School, Honolulu, May 1941, HC.

32 A 1937 US Congress committee of twenty-six senators and representatives for a study of Hawai'i's "social, political and economical life" stated that "the public schools of Hawaii are the foundation of good citizenship. . . . As a part of their curriculum, they inculcate the basic principles of American democracy in the youth who pass through them. With so many children of alien parentage among them, a definite program of Americanization is necessary. . . . Through the schools, more than by any other means, the people of Hawaii are being molded together into the American pattern and philosophy of life. . . ." Long, "War Records Project," 2–3.

33 "Morale Committee of Educational Institutions."

34 Long, "War Records Project," 10; *Hawaiian Schools*, 30.

35 *Biennial Report 1941-1942*, 12; *Hawaiian Schools*, 30, 31; Long, "War Records Project," 5; "Personal experiences of the faculty of Kaiulani School," 16; "The Public Schools of Hawaii, a series of articles sponsored by the Joint Public Relations Committee of the P.T.A., H.E.A., O.E.A., Principals' clubs and the central office, D.P.I.," *Honolulu Star-Bulletin*, 1945, HC, 10.

36 *Hawaiian Schools*, 33.

37 "Combined impressions of Miss Curtis and Ann Frances Ellison, written by Miss Caroline Curtis, an Account of the Reaction of a Japanese Student," 24.02 Private Schools Oahu—Hanahauoli, HWRD.

38 "Calendar for 1944—printed from linoleum blocks made by students, from Mr. Fred R. Giddings, Honolulu," 24.01 Department of Public Instruction Oahu—Robert Louis Stevenson School, HWRD; Hanahaouli School Calendar, "'Hawaii in War Time,' printed from linoleum blocks by students, for year 1942," 24.02 Private Schools Oahu—Hanahaouli, HWRD.

39 "Donate your blood" and "'Imfomation' Please," Children's posters, undated, Oversized Materials, HWRD.

40 "Childhood in performance enabled divergent political positions each to appear natural, inevitable, and therefore justified. I call this dynamic 'racial innocence.'" Bernstein, *Racial Innocence*, 4.

41 Long, "War Records Project," 11.

42 *Biennial Report 1941–1942*, 13.

43 Oliveira, "E Ola Mau ka ʻŌlelo Hawaiʻi," 79–80, 81.

44 Silva, *Aloha Betrayed*, 144; Oliveira, "E Ola Mau ka ʻŌlelo Hawaiʻi." On how Native Hawaiians negotiated and resisted Americanized education in the prewar period, see Taira, "Embracing Education."

45 Significantly, the goal of this second study was to determine whether the use of a language other than English in the home would affect the success of this student at the university level, and it found that whereas Caucasian students scored highest on their entrance exams, Japanese students had the highest grade point average of all racial groups once attending university. Madorah E. Smith, "The English of Hawaiian Children," 1942, HC, 16; Madorah E. Smith, "The Effect of Bilingual Background on College Aptitude Scores and Grade Point Ratios Earned by Students at the University of Hawaii," 1942, HC, 357, 363–64.

46 Bruce White, "A Summary of the Testing Program in Grades 3 and 6 of the Honolulu Public Schools," Department of Public Instruction, Honolulu, 1945, HC, 1–4.

47 Foucault, *Security, Territory, Population*, 63.

48 "Community Survey of Education in Hawaiʻi: Supplementary Statement," Honolulu, 1945, HC, 19, 120; O. Robinson, "Procedures in the Field of English," Department of Public Instruction, Territory of Hawaii, Honolulu, November 18, 1943, 24.01 Department of Public Instruction, HWRD.

49 The 1943 Oral English program was planned to help this. "Community Survey of Education in Hawaiʻi," 201. English standard schools, a system established in Hawaiʻi in 1920, required students to pass an English language test in order to be admitted. This system came to an end after the World War II period due to political pressure from Japanese American settlers in the Democratic Party and changing public opinion after the *Brown v. Board of Education* decision in 1954. Hughes, "Demise of the English Standard School," 70, 84–85.

50 William Norwood Brigance, "Report on Speech Education in the University of Hawaii, with Special Reference to the Progress Made since 1938," Crawfordsville, Indiana, 1947, HC, 6–7; "Community Survey of Education in Hawaiʻi," 201.

51 O. Robinson, "Suggestions That May Help Students to *Practice* the Use of *English*," Department of Public Instruction, Territory of Hawaii, Honolulu, November 19, 1942, 24.01 Department of Public Instruction, HWRD.

52 O. Robinson, "Procedures in the Field of English," Department of Public Instruction, Territory of Hawaii, Honolulu, November 18, 1943, 24.01 Department of Public Instruction, HWRD, emphasis in original.

53 *Biennial Report 1941–1942*, 28.

54 Letters to friends — 1942 December, Box 1, CM.

55 *Maikai* is a Hawaiian word meaning "good," "fine," or "I agree." It is a common word in Hawaiian Creole English (Pidgin) as well. "Personal experiences of the faculty of Kaiulani School," 3.

56 *Hawaiian Schools*, 11.

57 "Pidgin represents a linguistic and cultural collective, invested with an established historical perspective that observes, perpetuates, and ceremonialises the values of 'our own culture' and sometimes celebrates a *de*marginalising resistance to the formal linguistic demands of a colonial economic system." Marlow and Giles, "Who You Tink You, Talkin Propah?," 62.

58 The department claimed that "our best and most serious students have, in the past, been the ones who had to work against the dominant attitude, which was that of apathy, indifference, and complete unwillingness to practice outside of school hours." O. Robinson, "Procedures in the Field of English."

59 Takaki, *Pau Hana*, 115–26.

60 Jung, *Reworking Race*.

61 Lee, *At America's Gates*; Ngai, *Impossible Subjects*; Takaki, *Pau Hana*.

62 Romaine, "Hawaiian Creole English," 227–28; Romaine, "Hawai'i Creole English."

63 A "Report on Speech Education" in the University of Hawai'i argued in 1947 that the public education system had improved the English speech of children in Hawai'i dramatically during the war years and described this as a community-wide transformation. It reported that graduates of the Teachers College of the University of Hawai'i had begun to teach English in primary and secondary schools, that the 1943 expansion of kindergartens had "distinctly" improved the speech of those entering the first grade, and that more families were speaking English regularly in their homes. William Norwood Brigance, "Report on Speech Education," 1, 4.

64 Scheiber and Scheiber, *Bayonets in Paradise*, 20.

65 *Hawaiian Schools*, 10. See also Okihiro, *Cane Fires*, 235; Report of the Joint Legislative Holdover Investigating Committee," 4; and Long, "War Records Project," 11.

66 "Please Get the Facts," *Honolulu Star-Bulletin*, August 11, 1941, 34A Japanese Language Schools, RASRL Clippings File Sub. 2, Box 2, HWRD.

67 "Not a Valid Issue," *Hawaii Hochi*, September 4, 1941, 34A Japanese Language Schools, RASRL Clippings File Sub. 2, Box 2, HWRD.

68 "What Is the Core of Japanese Language School Problem," *Nippu Jiji*, May 27, 1941, 34A Japanese Language Schools, RASRL Clippings File Sub. 2, Box 2, HWRD; "Language School Problems," *Hawaii Hochi*, May 14, 1941, 34A Japanese Language Schools, RASRL Clippings File Sub. 2, Box 2, HWRD.

69 "Language Schools Blamed for Sickness in Kindergartens," *Nippu Jiji*, January 18, 1941, 34A Japanese Language Schools, RASRL Clippings File Sub. 2, Box 2, HWRD.

70 Okihiro, *Cane Fires*, 234; Office of the Military Governor, Morale Section, *Final Report of the Emergency Service Committee*, Honolulu, 1946, HC, 2, 21.

71 Office of the Military Governor, Morale Section, *Final Report*, HC, 21.

72 Scheiber and Scheiber, *Bayonets in Paradise*, 67.

73 "Speak American, the one language for all of us loyal Americans," Speak American Campaign, Folder 9, Box 52, HWRD; "Pidgin is better than nothing," Speak American Campaign, Folder 9, Box 52, HWRD; "Don't speak the enemy's language!," Speak American Campaign, Folder 9, Box 52, HWRD.

74 "Save Countless Allied Lives: 3,500 Minnesota-Trained Nisei Act as 'Eyes, Ears,'" October 22, 1945, *Minnesota Star-Journal*, 44.09 Interpreters, HWRD. In Hawai'i, many of those who were recruited to the MIS language school were students at the University of Hawai'i. "Army Japanese Linguists in Training," 44.09 Interpreters, HWRD, 2; Gregg M. Sinclair, "Important Notice to Faculty Regarding A.J.A. Students," November 1943, 44.09 Interpreters, HWRD.

75 "243 Inducted Here into Interpreter Unit," *Honolulu Advertiser*, June 14, 1943, 12 Scrapbooks, Clippings, Margaret Makino Scrapbook on US Army Interpreters, Book 1, 1942–1945, Box 55 (uncatalogued), HWRD.

76 "Morale Group to Assist in Drive for Volunteers," *Hawaii Times*, November 12, 1943, 12 Scrapbooks, Clippings, Margaret Makino Scrapbook on US Army Interpreters, Book 1, 1942–1945, Box 55 (uncatalogued), HWRD.

77 "Sgt. Kubo Talks Three Enemy Japanese into Surrendering," *Pacific Citizen*, September 2, 1944, 12 Scrapbooks, Clippings, Margaret Makino Scrapbook on US Army Interpreters, Book 1, 1942–1945, Box 55 (uncatalogued), HWRD.

78 "Nisei Heroes of World War II: What about Those in Pacific and Far East?," *Honolulu Star-Bulletin*, October 9, 1944, 12 Scrapbooks, Clippings, Margaret Makino Scrapbook on US Army Interpreters, Book 1, 1942–1945, Box 55 (uncatalogued), HWRD.

79 "Save Countless Allied Lives."

80 *Hawaiian Schools*, 3, quoting from *Postwar Needs of Education in Hawaii*.

CHAPTER 5. SETTLER MILITARY CAMPS: INTERNMENT AND PRISONER-OF-WAR CAMPS ACROSS THE PACIFIC ISLANDS

A previous version of chapter 5 appeared as "Settler-Military Camps: Internment and Prisoner of War Camps across the Pacific Islands during World War II" in *Journal of Asian American Studies* 24, no. 2 (2021): 299–335.

1 On internment in Hawai'i and the Pacific Islands, see Okihiro, *Cane Fires*; Scheiber and Scheiber, *Bayonets in Paradise*; Nakamura, "'Into the Dark Cold I Go'"; and Camacho, *Cultures of Commemoration*. On the internment of Japanese Latin Americans and the "global reach of U.S. practices of internment," see Paik, *Rightlessness*, 47–50. See also Gardiner, *Pawns in a Triangle of Hate*; and Higashide, *Adios to Tears*.

2 Camacho, *Cultures of Commemoration*; Hein and Selden, *Islands of Discontent*; Shigematsu and Camacho, *Militarized Currents*.

3 Blaker, *United States Overseas Basing*, 19.

4   I analyze internment and prisoner-of-war camps as two different but intercon-
    nected and collaborating technologies of wartime racialized incarceration,
    which were governed by either civilian or military administrations. For example,
    in the continental United States, internment camps were administrated by the
    Department of Justice or the War Relocation Authority, and prisoners of war
    were held in US military camps. In Hawai'i and the NMI, both internment and
    prisoner-of-war camps were military projects, and internees and prisoners of
    war were imprisoned in the same camps in separate compounds. Prisoners of
    war were transferred between camps in the Pacific Islands and the US continent
    throughout the war, and there were even some, such as Japanese Americans who
    were transferred from internment camps in Hawai'i to those in the US continent,
    who were held in both civilian and military camps during this period.

5   Key volumes that place histories of US and Japanese colonialism and war in
    conversation include Fujitani, White, and Yoneyama, *Perilous Memories*; and
    Shigematsu and Camacho, *Militarized Currents*.

6   The League of Nations transferred the former German territories in Micronesia
    to Japan as a class C mandate. As Mark R. Peattie argues, "For all practical pur-
    poses, the islands were now to be administered as Japanese possessions not as
    territories under quite temporary guardianship by the international community."
    Peattie, *Nan'yō*, 56–57.

7   In 1938 there were up to 45,000 Japanese citizens and nationals living in Saipan,
    NMI, most of whom were tenant farmers or laborers working in the sugar
    plantation industry. Although agricultural production did not take place in the
    Marshall Islands, there was a small community, growing from around 250 to
    under 1,000, of Okinawan fishermen in Jaluit in the Marshall Islands during the
    1930s. Peattie, *Nan'yō*, 155–61, 186.

8   Peattie, *Nan'yō*, 251–52.

9   Kauanui, "Sorry State," 110–12; Kauanui, *Hawaiian Blood*, 2, 28–29. See also Silva,
    Aloha Betrayed.

10 Jung, *Reworking Race*; Takaki, *Pau Hana*.

11 Trask, *From a Native Daughter*, 11, 12; Silva, *Aloha Betrayed*, 126; Gonzalez, "Wars
    of Memory at Pu'uloa/Pearl Harbor"; McKinley, "Proclamation 427 — Reserving
    for Naval Purposes Certain Lands in Honolulu, Hawaii," November 2, 1898, www
    .presidency.ucsb.edu/ws/?pid=69248, Sinclair.

12 Peattie, *Nan'yō*, 155–61, 251–52; Azuma, *Between Two Empires*, 18–31.

13 For detailed statistics on these demographics, see Camacho, *Cultures of Commemo-
    ration*, 70; and Peattie, *Nan'yō*, 161. See also Perry F. Philipp and Ralph Elliott,
    "Hawaii and Its People"; Land Utilization, Table 2 (1949), HC. On Asian settler co-
    lonialism in Hawai'i, see Trask, "Settlers of Color and 'Immigrant' Hegemony," as
    well as other essays in Fujikane and Okamura, *Asian Settler Colonialism*; Saranillio,
    Unsustainable Empire, 74; and Saranillio, "Why Asian Settler Colonialism Matters."

14 After World War II, the United Nations entrusted the previously Japanese Micro-
    nesian territories — currently known as the Republic of the Marshall Islands, the

Federated States of Micronesia (F.S.M.), the NMI, and the Republic of Palau—to the United States as part of the Trust Territory of the Pacific Islands (T.T.P.I.). The peoples of the Marshall Islands, the F.S.M., and Palau eventually opted to become freely associated states (F.A.S.), but the Northern Marianas sought to negotiate their status separately with the United States, and the citizens almost unanimously elected to become the Commonwealth of the Northern Mariana Islands (CNMI) in 1976, "in political union with and under the sovereignty of the United States of America." Statham, *Colonial Constitutionalism*, 106. See "Covenant to Establish the U.S. Commonwealth of the Northern Mariana Islands" in Willens and Siemer, *Honorable Accord*, 378.

15   Although Roosevelt delegated the control of "alien enemies" in the continental United States, Puerto Rico, and the Virgin Islands to the attorney general, he assigned these responsibilities within US territories in the combat zone—including the Canal Zone, the Hawaiian Islands, Alaska, and the Philippines—to the secretary of war. President Roosevelt shifted control over Alaska to the secretary of war via Proclamation 2533 on December 29, 1941. "Part Four: Security Regulations Affecting Alien Enemies and Dual Citizens," Folder 46, Box 4, AR19, JCCH, 15.

16   Franklin D. Roosevelt, Memorandum for the Secretary of the Navy, February 26, 1942, 244. Japse Removal, JIR; "Part Four: Security Regulations Affecting Alien Enemies and Dual Citizens," Folder 46, Box 4, AR19, WWII, 19–20.

17   "Chapter IX, Prisoners of War and Internees," 224. History of the Provost Marshal's Office pt. 2, JIR, 115, 186.

18   "Chapter IX, Prisoners of War and Internees," 184.

19   418. S-29 Statistics of Internees and POWs Held in Central Pacific Area, JIR; "Report on the Prisoner of War Camps in the Territory of Hawaii Visited by Mr. Alfred Cardinaux during December 1944," Folder 24, Box 9, AR19, JCCH, 3–4; "Vital Statistics—POW Compounds, Prisoners of War and Internees—In Hawaiian Islands," Folder 30, Box 9, AR19, JCCH; "United States Army Forces Middle Pacific, Prisoners of War in Army Custody, Hawaiian Area, Week Ending 16 February 1946," 36 Internment, Relocation Camps, HWRD; "Recapitulation of PW Strength Data Report—Base Camp—AP 950," July 28, 1945, 36 Internment, Relocation Camps, HWRD. See also Kramer, "Japanese Prisoners of War in America," 79.

20   At the beginning of World War II, Japan was the colonial power in Okinawa and Korea. "Report on the Prisoner of War Camps in the Territory of Hawaii Visited by Mr. Alfred Cardinaux" 3–4; Richardson COMGENPOA to CG CPBC, August 26, 1944, Folder 24, Box 9, AR19, JCCH.

21   223. History of Provost Marshal's Office, pt. 1, JIR, 20–28, 38, 10–11. Nisei born in Hawai'i or the United States prior to 1924 were automatically granted dual citizenship with Japan and the United States. "Dual Citizenship," *Densho Encyclopedia*, accessed October 15, 2020, http://encyclopedia.densho.org/Dual_citizenship.

22   On December 18, General Orders No. 32 superseded this order by expanding its reach to include "enemy aliens" from any country. One of Military Governor

Walter Short's first acts was General Orders No. 5 on December 8, 1941, which specified that noncitizen Japanese age fourteen and older could not publish any attack on the United States, make a threat against the government or a military official, or give information to an enemy country. "Part Four: Security Regulations Affecting Alien Enemies and Dual Citizens," Folder 46, Box 4, AR19, JCCH, 16–20, 25, 26, 28–34.

23 Even if Emmons was including US citizens of Japanese descent in this figure, it is likely an exaggerated one. Yet it still speaks to the extent to which Emmons considered the labor of Japanese and Japanese Americans as central to the wartime mobilization effort. Secret radiogram, Emmons to Adjutant General, February 11, 1942, 356. A-8 Recommendation to Use Japse Labor, JIR.

24 Appendix A: "Factors to Be Considered in Investigations of Japanese Subjects," 224. History of the Provost Marshal's Office pt. 2, JIR, 818; "Part Four: Security Regulations," 50.

25 "Chapter V. Collection and Custody of Enemy Aliens," 224. History of the Provost Marshal's Office pt. 2, JIR, 114; "Part Four: Security Regulations," 146–47.

26 224. History of the Provost Marshal's Office pt. 2, JIR, 112, 200–201.

27 Kibei are American-born US citizens of Japanese ancestry who lived for part of their adolescence in Japan, then returned to the United States. "Part Four: Security Regulations," 88; 224. History of the Provost Marshal's Office pt. 2, JIR, 200.

28 "Part Four: Security Regulations," 91.

29 On the contradictory logics of questions 27 and 28, see Fujitani, *Race for Empire*, 163–205.

30 "Part Four: Security Regulations," 56–57.

31 Harry Urata lived in both Japan and Korea from 1924 to 1937. On Urata, see Odo, *Voices from the Canefields*, 143–48. "Record of the Hearings of a Board of Officers and Civilians Convened Pursuant to Paragraph 24, Special Orders No. 32, Headquarters, Hawaiian Department, Dated at Fort Shafter, T. H., 1 February, 1943, in the Case of Harry Minoru Urata," 420. Harry Minoru Urata, ISN-HUS-855-CI, JIR, 14–15.

32 Slattery to Colonel Morrison, November 18, 1943, 421. Shigeo R. Muroda (Robert), ISN-HUS-666-CI, JIR.

33 "Record of the Hearings of a Board of Officers and Civilians," 17; "Record of the Hearings of a Board of Officers and Civilians Convened Pursuant to Paragraph 32, Special Orders No. 130, Headquarters, Hawaiian Department, Dated at Fort Shafter, T. H., 14 May, 1942, in the Case of Shigeo Muroda, alias Shigeo Robert Muroda," 421. Shigeo R. Muroda (Robert), ISN-HUS-666-CI, JIR, 3.

34 "Part Four: Security Regulations," 146–47; Appendix A, "Factors to Be Considered in Investigations of Japanese Subjects," 227. History of Provost Marshal's Office, pt. 5, JIR, 813.

35 "Part Four: Security Regulations," 81; 224. History of the Provost Marshal's Office, pt. 2, JIR, 196.

36　W. G. Strench to CGHD, July 1, 1941, 349. A-1 Acquiring Immigration Station, JIR; Francois Biddle to Henry L. Stimson, July 10, 1941, 349. A-1 Acquiring Immigration Station, JIR; Walter C. Short to the Adjutant General, Washington, DC, July 3, 1941, 350. A-2 Construction of Internment Facilities, JIR.

37　224. History of the Provost Marshal's Office pt. 2, JIR; 192. "Vital Statistics — POW Compounds, Prisoners of War and Internees."

38　348. US Immigration Map, JIR; 350. Walter C. Short to the Adjutant General; "Chapter IX, Prisoners of War and Internees," 224. History of the Provost Marshal's Office pt. 2, JIR, 187.

39　Walter C. Short to the Adjutant General.

40　"Part Four: Security Regulations," 47–48.

41　"Chapter IX, Prisoners of War and Internees," 224. History of the Provost Marshal's Office pt. 2, JIR, 187.

42　Fujitani, *Race for Empire*; Paik, *Rightlessness*, 41; Paik, *Bans, Wall, Raids, Sanctuary*; Hernández, *City of Inmates*.

43　"Chapter IX, Prisoners of War and Internees," 224. History of the Provost Marshal's Office pt. 2, JIR, 187–88; "Chapter V. Collection and Custody of Enemy Aliens," 224. History of the Provost Marshal's Office pt. 2, JIR, 113.

44　"Chapter IX, Prisoners of War and Internees," 188.

45　Paul Hedrick to Stephen Early, October 29, 1942, 1; Hedrick to FDR Sec Reviews of Japs Subversion, JIR.

46　412. S-23 Red Cross Report, JIR.

47　"Chapter IX, Prisoners of War and Internees," 224. History of the Provost Marshal's Office pt. 2, JIR, 188, 190–91. Olsen did express uncertainty about his role with American citizens of Japanese descent, mostly Kibei, who were not technically his responsibility yet were also held in the camp: "I have wondered whether the same protective interest and solicitude which I exercise on behalf of the alien Japanese should be extended to these American citizens whose loyalty has been questioned." "Chapter IX Prisoners of War — Appendix 9-A," 224. History of the Provost Marshal's Office, pt. 4, JIR, 652–53; Gustaf W. Olsen to Colonel Erik de Laval, January 4, 1943, 411. S-22 Olsen's Sand Island Reports, JIR.

48　412. S-22 Red Cross Reports, JIR.

49　The source refers to this as the "Swiss legation." It is possible that this was a different person or that Nishikawa mistook the nationality of Olsen. "Dan Toru Nishikawa memoir #2," AR06 Don Toru Nishikawa Collection, JCCH, 1.

50　From context, I believe that here Nishikawa meant "no regard for human rights." "Dan Toru Nishikawa memoir #2," 2–7.

51　"Chapter V. Collection and Custody of Enemy Aliens," 224. History of the Provost Marshal's Office pt. 2, JIR, 191; "Part Four: Security Regulations," 77; 418. S-29 Statistics of Internees and POWs Held in Central Pacific Area, JIR, 1.

52　Fujitani, *Race for Empire*.

53　Weglyn, *Years of Infamy*; Fujitani, *Race for Empire*; Drinnon, *Keeper of Concentration Camps*.

54 T. Fujitani argues that internment projects in the US continent "reflect rather than contradict the positive methods of liberal governmentality in managing rather than simply restricting freedom." In a similar but slightly different framing, Naomi Paik argues that the technology of the camp is a paradigm through which we can understand how the extension of rights via liberal governance relies upon the definition, exclusion, and detention of the "rightless." You can see both these frameworks at work in various ways across camps in this chapter. Fujitani, *Race for Empire*, 127; Paik, *Rightlessness*, 4.

55 Eugene V. Slattery, "Requests for Family Internment on the Mainland of the United States," December 1, 1943, Folder 19, Box 9, AR19, JCCH.

56 "Chapter IX, Prisoners of War and Internees," 224. History of the Provost Marshal's Office pt. 2, JIR, 186; Military Government Section, Staff, Commander Marshalls—Gilberts Area, "A Report on the U.S. Navy Military Government of the Marshall Islands, for the Year 31 January 1944 (Date of Invasion by U.S. Forces) to 31 January 1945," Box 42 (uncatalogued), HWRD, 6–7; *Camp Susupe: A Photographic Record of the Operation of Military Government on Saipan, 1944–1945.* Compiled from available sources by military government: Navy number 3245 (San Francisco), Northern Mariana Islands Museum of History and Culture, Saipan, CNMI. See also Camacho, *Cultures of Commemoration.*

57 Military Government Section, Staff, Commander Marshalls—Gilberts Area, "Report"; "Chapter IX, Prisoners of War and Internees," 224. History of the Provost Marshal's Office pt. 2, JIR, 192–93.

58 Carolinians had lived in the NMI since a tsunami ravaged the Caroline Islands in the 1800s. Chamorros are the Native people of the Mariana Islands. Camacho, *Cultures of Commemoration.*

59 On discourses of "liberation" in internment projects in the Northern Mariana Islands, see Camacho, *Cultures of Commemoration*, 68–77. For an example of rhetoric of rehabilitation in the Marshall Islands, see Military Government Section, Staff, Commander Marshalls—Gilberts Area, "Report," 16–17. On the role of postwar narratives of "rehabilitation" for US occupation projects across the former Japanese empire, see Fujitani, White, and Yoneyama, *Perilous Memories.*

60 Military Government Section, Staff, Commander Marshalls—Gilberts Area, "Report," 1.

61 *Camp Susupe*, 1.

62 *Camp Susupe*, 61; Camacho, *Cultures of Commemoration*, 71.

63 *Camp Susupe*, 1, 18, 21, 22, 69, 146.

64 Camacho, *Cultures of Commemoration*, 72; *Camp Susupe*, 1, 18, 21, 22.

65 Military Government Section, Staff, Commander Marshalls—Gilberts Area, "Report," 4–5, 7, 12.

66 Military Government Section, Staff, Commander Marshalls—Gilberts Area, "Report," 4–5, 7, 12, 20–23.

67 Ordinance No. 2, Annex C, "An Ordinance to Provide Regulations for Marshallese Affairs and the Administration Thereof," United States Navy Military

Government of the Marshall Islands, Box 42 (uncatalogued), HWRD, 7, 13–14. 16–17.

68 *Camp Susupe*, 55, 50.

69 There were many casualties during the invasions of the Marshall Islands and the NMI, and even those who survived lost family members or were dispossessed of their houses, their land, and their crops.

70 *Camp Susupe*, 69, 146.

71 On this history of land acquisition, see chapter 1. United States Department of Defense, "Report on Study of Military Real Property, State of Hawaii," [Washington?], 1960, HC, 5.

72 On ri-pālle and imōn aje as Indigenous strategies to retain land, social status, and epistemological frameworks, see Labriola, "Planting Islands." See also Military Government Section, Staff, Commander Marshalls—Gilberts Area, "Report," HWRD, Annex A; "Proclamation No. 3," Military Government Section, Staff, Commander Marshalls—Gilberts Area, "Report," HWRD.

73 Military Government Section, Staff, Commander Marshalls—Gilberts Area, "Report," 31–32.

74 Camacho, *Cultures of Commemoration*, 79–81.

75 Smith-Norris, *Domination and Resistance*, 6. Johnston, "Nuclear Landscapes," 182. For more on the environmental contamination in the Marshall Islands and the radiation poisoning that the Marshallese people were exposed to after these tests, see Teaiwa, "bikinis and other s/pacific n/oceans"; Aguon, *What We Bury at Night*; and Dvorak, *Coral and Concrete*.

76 "We Drank Our Tears," 172.

77 Smith-Norris, *Domination and Resistance*, 6. Johnston, "Nuclear Landscapes," 182–84. On "nuclear normalizing," the colonial process by which the United States "undermine[s] Indigenous narratives of illness," see Hogue, "Nuclear Normalizing and Kathy Jetñil-Kijiner's 'Dome Poem,'" quotation from 209.

78 "Dan Toru Nishikawa memoirs #1," AR06 Don Toru Nishikawa Collection, JCCH, 3; E. J. King and G. C. Marshall, Memorandum to the President, July 15, 1942, 246. Japse Evacuation, JIR.

79 224. History of the Provost Marshal's Office pt. 2, JIR, 203.

80 War Relocation Authority, "Summaries of the activities of persons of Japanese Ancestry [*sic*], since arriving on the mainland after evacuation from Hawaii; who are not residing at Tule Lake Center, Newell, California," April 24, 1945, Folder 41, Box 2, AR19, JCCH.

81 Nishimura, Samuel Masao, "Diary of Sam Nishimura, 1943–1945, Honolulu: Nishimura, ca. 2004," JCCH, 3.

82 Paul A. Taylor to Dillon S. Meyer, February 28, 1943, Attached: "Hawaiian Evacuees," Folder 7, Box 9, AR19, JCCH.

83 It is interesting that both Urata and the military government use the term *repatriation* throughout these exchanges, for Urata was born in the United States and was a dual citizen of the United States and Japan. This process would then

perhaps be more accurately be described as "expatriation," yet the continual use of "repatriation" here is a World War II–era example of racial discourse that portrayed Americans of Asian descent as "perpetual foreigners." Harry M. Urata to Major Luis F. Springer, August 17, 1944, 420. Harry Minoru Urata, ISN-HUS-855-CI, JIR; Wm. R. C. Morrison to Harry M. Urata, August 29, 1944, 420. Harry Minoru Urata, ISN-HUS-855-CI, JIR.

84   Urata's brother was drafted into the US Army, and his sister planned to move away from home after her marriage, which would leave his mother at home alone. Harry M. Urata to Maj. L. F. Springer, October 6, 1944, 420. Harry Minoru Urata, ISN-HUS-855-CI, JIR; "Individual Pay Data Record," 420. Harry Minoru Urata, ISN-HUS-855-CI, JIR; Commanding General's Internee Review Board, Office of Internal Security, "Review of Internee Case," October 1944, 420. Harry Minoru Urata, ISN-HUS-855-CI, JIR.

85   "Part Four: Security Regulations," 192.

86   Dillon S. Meyer to John J. McCloy, February 27, 1943, 372. A-24 Myers Recommendation to Stop Evacuation, JIR.

87   Konrad Aderer, *Resistance at Tule Lake* (Third World Newsreel, 2017).

88   This number also included 140 individuals who were transferred to Department of Justice camps during the war (25 voluntarily and 115 involuntarily).

89   J. A. Krug and D. S. Meyer, "The Evacuated People—A Quantitative Description," United States Department of the Interior, War Relocation Authority, 1946, 191–92.

90   Morris Rieger to Joseph R. Farrington, February 8, 1949, 36 Internment, Relocation Camps, HWRD.

91   Fujitani, *Race for Empire*, 127.

92   Hawai'i was technically part of the combat zone until April 1944. "Part Four: Security Regulations," 149, 154.

93   "Chapter IX, Prisoners of War and Internees," 224. History of the Provost Marshal's Office pt. 2, 182–83; "Part Four: Security Regulations," 150; Mōri, *Rainbow over Hell*; "War Still Going on for Japanese Prisoners of War Held on Oahu," *Honolulu Star-Bulletin*, August 26, 1946, 36 Internment, Relocation Camps, HWRD; "Japanese Didn't Like Iwo Either, Talk with Correspondent Reveals," *Honolulu Star-Bulletin*, August 29, 1946, 36 Internment, Relocation Camps, HWRD.

94   Military Government Section, Staff, Commander Marshalls—Gilberts Area, "Report," 4–5, 7, 12.

95   418. S-29 Statistics of Internees and POWs Held in Central Pacific Area, JIR; "Report on the Prisoner of War Camps in the Territory of Hawaii Visited by Mr. Alfred Cardinaux," 3–4; "Vital Statistics—POW Compounds, Prisoners of War and Internees"; "United States Army Forces Middle Pacific, Prisoners of War in Army Custody"; "Recapitulation of PW Strength Data Report"; Kramer, "Japanese Prisoners of War," 76.

96   412. Red Cross Report, JIR; 418. S-29 Statistics of Internees and POWs Held in Central Pacific Area, JIR; "Report on the Prisoner of War Camps in the Territory

of Hawaii Visited by Mr. Alfred Cardinaux," 3–4; "Vital Statistics—POW Compounds, Prisoners of War and Internees"; "United States Army Forces Middle Pacific, Prisoners of War in Army Custody; "Recapitulation of PW Strength Data Report"; Richardson COMGENPOA to CG CPBC.

97   Morris Rieger to Joseph R. Farrington, February 8, 1949, 36 Internment, Relocation Camps, HWRD; J. A. Krug and D. S. Meyer, "Evacuated People," 192.

98   Kramer, "Japanese Prisoners of War in America," 89.

99   "400 Japanese Prisoners to Be Moved from Hawaii," *Honolulu Star-Bulletin*, May 2, 1942, 36 Internment, Relocation Camps, HWRD.

100 "POWS to Leave," *Honolulu Star-Bulletin*, November 26, 1946, 36 Internment, Relocation Camps, HWRD; "Liberty Ship Carries Last of Japanese POWs in Hawaii Home," *Honolulu Star-Bulletin*, December 13, 1946, 36 Internment, Relocation Camps, HWRD.

101 Azuma, *Between Two Empires*, 18–31. See also Azuma, *In Search of our Frontier.*

102 At this time 10,619 prisoners of war were held at Honouliuli. "WWII Hawaii: Japanese P.O.W. and Local Fraternization Problem, 9/26, 28/45," Folder 22, Box 12, AR19, JCCH.

103 "WWII Hawaii"; "With First Memorial Service for Okinawan POWs in Hawaii, Japan Is Obligated to Collect Remains of Fallen," *Ryukyu Shimpo*, June 6, 2017. Many thanks to Megumi Chibana for pointing me to articles in *Ryukyu Shimpo* regarding these events.

104 "Hawaii POW Letters Written between 1945 and 1946 Discovered," *Ryukyu Shimpo*, August 24, 2018.

105 During this time, many Okinawan prisoners of war hoped to remain in Hawaiʻi after the war. Yet because of US immigration restrictions, this was not possible. "WWII Hawaii."

106 "First Memorial Service Held for 12 Okinawan POWs Who Died in Hawaii," *Ryukyu Shimpo*, June 5, 2017; "Committee to Hold Memorial Service for Okinawa-Born War Dead in Hawaii," *Ryukyu Shimpo*, January 20, 2017.

107 Many thanks to Dean Saranillio for suggesting that I consider the history of Mokauea in the discussion of Sand Island. "Map 16" and "Appendix E: History of Ownership of the Mokauea Fishery," in Nathan Napoka, *Mokauea Island: A Historical Study*, Historic Preservation Office, Division of State Parks, Outdoor Recreation and Historic Sites, Department of Land and Natural Resources, 1976, accessed October 20, 2020, www.ahamoku.org/docs/Doc%20 Napoka.pdf.

108 "Kai Makana: Ocean Education through Action," www.kaimakana.org/mirp.htm; "About Mokauea Fishermen's Association," www.mokauea.org/about; "Tiny Mokauea Island Has Eventful History," *Hawaii News Now*, 2011; Puhipau, "Puhipau," 136.

109 "Kai Makana"; "About Mokauea Fishermen's Association"; "Tiny Mokauea Island."

110 Puhipau, "Puhipau," 131–35.

1   On the rearticulation of primitive accumulation, see Federici, *Caliban and the Witch*; Harvey, *New Imperialism*; Nichols, *Theft Is Property!*; Saranillio, *Unsustainable Empire*; Byrd, Goldstein, Melamed, and Reddy, "Predatory Value"; Singh, "On Race, Violence"; Kosher, Cacho, Byrd, and Jefferson, "Introduction"; and Goldstein, "'In the Constant Flux.'" On the relationship between capitalism and territorial acquisition, see Arrighi, *Long Twentieth Century*.

2   As Camacho and Shigematsu argue, "Colonial histories constituted the conditions of possibility for ongoing forms of militarization." Shigematsu and Camacho, *Militarized Currents*, xv.

3   Unangax have also been referred to by the colonial term "Aleut." On their history of internment in Alaska, see Guise, "Who Is Doctor Bauer?"

4   "On 17 October 1941, American military dependents of the naval government departed for Hawai'i on board the USS *Henderson*, leaving approximately 160 military personnel and local men of the Insular Force Guard to defend the island." The US invasion of Guam and eventual victory came to be celebrated annually as "Liberation Day." Notably, the United States placed Guam under martial law for two years beginning on July 21, 1944. Camacho, *Cultures of Commemoration*, 18, 41, 50, 64. On histories of colonialism and Catholicism in Guam, see Diaz, *Repositioning the Missionary*. On the history of US settler colonialism, militarism, and migration in Guam, see Kristin Oberiano's forthcoming book, *Territorial Discontent: Chamorros, Filipinos, and the Making of the United States Empire in Guam*.

5   See Hein and Selden, *Islands of Discontent*; Shigematsu and Camacho, *Militarized Currents*; and McCormack and Norimatsu, *Resistant Islands*.

6   Dower, *Embracing Defeat*.

7   Smith-Norris, *Domination and Resistance*, 6. Johnston, "Nuclear Landscapes," 182–84. See also Teaiwa, "bikinis and other s/pacific n/oceans"; Aguon, *What We Bury at Night*; and Dvorak, *Coral and Concrete*.

8   The Central Pacific circuit consisted of bases in the Gilbert Islands, the Marshall Islands, the Caroline Islands, the Mariana Islands, Palau, Luzon, and Taiwan. The Southwest Pacific circuit consisted of bases in Australia, New Caledonia, the New Guinea coast, the Bismark Archipelago, and Mindanao (Philippines). Blaker, *United States Overseas Basing*, 19.

9   On the "liminality" of Okinawa's condition at the threshold of US and Japanese colonial and military projects, see Lisa Yoneyama, "Liminal Justice: Okinawa," in *Cold War Ruins*, 43–80.

10 As stated in the introduction, today almost 75 percent of the US military installations in Japan are still located in Okinawa, yet the island does not even make up 1 percent of the total land area of Japan. Uenten, "Rising Up," 92. See also Ginoza, "R&R at the Intersection." For histories of militarized sexual violence across US military outposts in the Pacific Islands and Asia, see Gonzalez, *Securing Paradise*;

Gonzalez, *Empire's Mistress*; Moon, *Sex among Allies*; and Moon, "South Korean Movements."

11   Na'puti, "Disaster Militarism and Indigenous Responses," 2.

12   Through her analysis of the military base/camptown, POW camp, and unincorporated territory, Jodi Kim articulates the concept of "settler garrison" to analyze how US networks of military bases have depended upon the settler colonial theft of Indigenous land. Kim, *Settler Garrison*.

13   The constitution was adopted on October 5, 1945. Mari Matsuda, *Radical Wāhine of Honolulu, 1945*, printed by Apuni Space, on view February 4–March 8, 2023, at 729 Auaji Street, Honolulu, Hawai'i 96813. Many thanks to Christina Heatherton for sharing this resource with me.

14   Aikau and Camvel, "Cultural Traditions and Food," 545; Gupta, "Return to Freedom."

15   Chibana, "Resurgents Create a Moral Landscape," 135; Chibana, "Artful Way of Making."

16   On Kanaka Maoli protests against the TMT as critique of settler colonialism and capitalism, see Goodyear-Ka'ōpua, "Protectors of the Future"; Fujikane, *Mapping Abundance*; Maile, "On Being Late"; and Hobart, *Cooling the Tropics*.

17   Fujikane, *Mapping Abundance*, 5, 88.

18   Na'puti, "Disaster Militarism and Indigenous Responses," 2.

Bibliography

PRIMARY SOURCES

Center for Oral History, University of Hawai'i at Mānoa, Honolulu, Hawai'i

Hamilton Library, University of Hawai'i at Mānoa, Honolulu, Hawai'i

- Carey D. Miller Collection (CM)
- Government Documents Collection
- Hawaiian Collection (HC)
- Hawaii War Records Depository (HWRD)
- Japanese Internment and Relocation Files (JIR)
- University Archives

Hawaii Medical Library, Queen's Medical Center, Honolulu, Hawai'i

Japanese Cultural Center of Hawai'i, Honolulu, Hawai'i (JCCH)

- AR19: Japanese American Relocation and Internment—The Hawai'i Experience (AR19)
- Dan Toru Nishikawa Collection
- The Joichi Tahara Archival Collection

Northern Mariana Islands Museum of History and Culture, Saipan, NMI

National Archives and Records Administration II, College Park, Maryland (NA)

- RG 126: Records of the Office of Territories, Classified Files, 1907–1951 (RG 126)
- RG 494: Records of U.S. Army Forces in the Middle Pacific, 1942–1946, Military Government of the Territory of Hawaii (RG 494)

National Archives at San Francisco, San Bruno, California (NASF)

- RG 21: Records of District Courts of the United States, U.S. District Court, District of Hawaii, Honolulu, Civil Case Files, 1900–1984 (RG 21)
- RG 181: Records of Naval Districts and Shore Establishments, Naval Facilities Engineering Com. Western Division, Land Acquisitions, 1944–1961 (RG 181)

Adams, Romanzo Colfax. *Interracial Marriage in Hawaii: A Study of the Mutually Conditioned Processes of Acculturation and Amalgamation.* New York: Macmillan, 1937.

Aguon, Julian. *What We Bury at Night: Disposable Humanity.* Tokyo: Blue Ocean, 2008.

Aikau, Hōkūlani, and Ann Kemehaʻikū Camvel. "Cultural Traditions and Food: Kānaka Maoli and the Production of Poi in the Heʻeʻia Wetland." *Food, Culture, and Society* 19, no. 3 (2016): 539–61.

Allen, Gwenfread. *Hawaii's War Years: 1941–1945.* Honolulu: University of Hawaiʻi Press, 1950.

Aluli, N. E. "Prevalence of Obesity in a Native Hawaiian Population." *American Journal of Clinical Nutrition* 53, no. 6 (1991): 1556s–1560s.

Ammon, Francesca Russello. *Bulldozer: Demolition and Clearance of the Postwar Landscape.* New Haven, CT: Yale University Press, 2016.

Anderson, Karen. *Wartime Women: Sex Roles, Family Relations, and the Status of Women during World War II.* Westport, CT: Praeger, 1981.

Anderson, Warwick. *Colonial Pathologies: American Tropical Medicine, Race, and Hygiene in the Philippines.* Durham, NC: Duke University Press, 2006.

Anthony, Joseph Garner. *Hawaii under Army Rule.* Stanford, CA: Stanford University Press, 1955.

Arrighi, Giovanni. *The Long Twentieth Century: Money, Power, and the Origins of Our Times.* New York: Verso, 1994/2006.

Arvin, Maile. *Possessing Polynesians: The Science of Settler Colonial Whiteness in Hawaiʻi and Oceania.* Durham, NC: Duke University Press, 2019.

Arvin, Maile. "Still in the Blood: Gendered Histories of Race, Law, and Science in *Day v. Apoliona.*" *American Quarterly* 67, no. 3 (2015): 681–703.

Azuma, Eiichiro. *Between Two Empires: Race, History, and Transnationalism in Japanese America.* New York: Oxford University Press, 2005.

Azuma, Eiichiro. *In Search of Our Frontier: Japanese America and Settler Colonialism in the Construction of Japan's Borderless Empire.* Berkeley: University of California Press, 2019.

Bailey, Beth L., and David R. Farber. *The First Strange Place: Race and Sex in World War II Hawaii.* Baltimore: Johns Hopkins University Press, 1994.

Bazore, Katherine. *Hawaiian and Pacific Foods: A Cook Book of Culinary Customs and Recipes Adapted for the American Hostess.* New York: M. Barrows, 1940.

Beechert, Edward D. *Working in Hawaii: A Labor History.* Honolulu: University of Hawaiʻi Press, 1985.

Bender, Daniel E., and Jana K. Lipman, eds. *Making the Empire Work: Labor and United States Imperialism.* New York: NYU Press, 2015.

Bentley, Amy. *Eating for Victory: Food Rationing and the Politics of Domesticity.* Urbana: University of Illinois Press, 1998.

Bernstein, Robin. *Racial Innocence: Performing American Childhood from Slavery to Civil Rights.* New York: NYU Press, 2011.

Bhandar, Brenna. *Colonial Lives of Property*. Durham, NC: Duke University Press, 2019.

Bhattacharya, Tithi, ed. *Social Reproduction Theory: Remapping Class, Recentering Oppression*. London: Pluto, 2017.

Blaisdell, Richard Kekuni. "Historical and Cultural Aspects of Native Hawaiian Health." In *Social Process in Hawaii*, vol. 32., edited by Eldon Wenger, 1–21. Honolulu: Department of Sociology, University of Hawai'i at Mānoa, 1989.

Blaisdell, Richard Kekuni. "Historical and Philosophical Aspects of Lapa'an Traditional Kanaka Maoli Healing Practices." *In Motion*, April 28, 1996, www.inmotionmagazine.com/kekuni.html.

Blaker, James R. *United States Overseas Basing: An Anatomy of the Dilemma*. New York: Praeger, 1990.

Brown, Wendy. *Regulating Aversion: Tolerance in the Age of Identity and Empire*. Princeton, NJ: Princeton University Press, 2008.

Byrd, Jodi A. *The Transit of Empire: Indigenous Critiques of Colonialism*. Minneapolis: University of Minnesota Press, 2011.

Byrd, Jodi A., Alyosha Goldstein, Jodi Melamed, and Chandan Reddy. "Predatory Value: Economies of Dispossession and Disturbed Relationalities." *Social Text* 36, no. 2 (June 2018): 1–18.

Camacho, Keith L. *Cultures of Commemoration: The Politics of War, Memory, and History in the Mariana Islands*. Honolulu: University of Hawai'i Press, 2011.

Chauncey, George. *Gay New York: Gender, Urban Culture, and the Making of the Gay Male World, 1890–1940*. New York: Basic, 1995.

Chen, Kuan-Hsing. *Asia as Method: Toward Deimperialization*. Durham, NC: Duke University Press, 2010.

Chibana, Megumi. "An Artful Way of Making Indigenous Space." *Verge: Studies in Global Asias* 4, no. 2 (Fall 2018): 135–62.

Chibana, Megumi. "Resurgents Create a Moral Landscape: Indigenous Resurgence and Everyday Practices of Farming in Okinawa." *Humanities* 9, no. 4 (2020): 135.

Chinn, Sarah E. *Technology and the Logic of American Racism: A Cultural History of the Body as Evidence*. New York: Bloomsbury Academic, 2000.

Connolly, N. D. B. *A World More Concrete: Real Estate and the Remaking of Jim Crow South Florida*. Chicago: University of Chicago Press, 2014.

Coulthard, Glen. *Red Skin, White Masks: Rejecting the Colonial Politics of Recognition*. Minneapolis: University of Minnesota Press, 2014.

Davis, Angela. "Women and Capitalism: Dialectics of Oppression and Liberation." In *The Black Feminist Reader*, edited by Joy James and T. Denean Sharpley-Whiting, 146–82. Hoboken, NJ: Blackwell, 2000.

Davis, Sasha. *The Empires' Edge: Militarization, Resistance, and Transcending Hegemony in the Pacific*. Athens: University of Georgia Press, 2015.

Day, Iyko. *Alien Capital: Asian Racialization and the Logic of Settler Colonial Capitalism*. Durham, NC: Duke University Press, 2016.

Deloria, Philip J. *Playing Indian*. New Haven, CT: Yale University Press, 1999.

Diaz, Vicente M. *Repositioning the Missionary: Rewriting the Histories of Colonialism, Native Catholicism, and Indigeneity in Guam.* Honolulu: University of Hawai'i Press, 2010.

Diaz, Vicente M. "To 'P' or not to 'P': Marking the Territory between Pacific Islander and Asian American Studies." *Journal of Asian American Studies* 7, no. 3 (2004): 183–208.

Diaz, Vicente M., and J. Kēhaulani Kauanui, eds. "Native Pacific Cultural Studies on the Edge." Special issue, *Contemporary Pacific* 13, no. 2 (2001).

Dower, John W. *Embracing Defeat: Japan in the Wake of World War II.* New York: W.W. Norton, 1999.

Dower, John W. *War without Mercy: Race and Power in the Pacific War.* New York: Pantheon, 1986.

Drinnon, Richard. *Keeper of Concentration Camps: Dillon S. Myer and American Racism.* Berkeley: University of California Press, 1987.

Dudziak, Mary L. *Cold War Civil Rights: Race and the Image of American Democracy.* Princeton, NJ: Princeton University Press, 2000.

Dvorak, Greg. *Coral and Concrete: Remembering Kwajalein Atoll between Japan, America, and the Marshall Islands.* Honolulu: University of Hawai'i Press, 2020.

Edmond, Rod, and Vanessa Smith. *Islands in History and Representation.* New York: Routledge, 2003.

Else, 'Iwalani R. N. "The Breakdown of the Kapu System and Its Effect on Native Hawaiian Health and Diet." *Hūlili* 1, no. 1 (2004): 241–55.

Escobedo, Elizabeth R. *From Coveralls to Zoot Suits: The Lives of Mexican American Women on the World War II Home Front.* Chapel Hill: University of North Carolina Press, 2013.

Estes, Nick. *Our History Is the Future: Standing Rock versus the Dakota Access Pipeline, and the Long Tradition of Indigenous Resistance.* New York: Verso, 2019.

Faderman, Lillian. *Odd Girls and Twilight Lovers: A History of Lesbian Life in Twentieth-Century America.* New York: Columbia University Press, 2012.

Fanon, Frantz. *Black Skin, White Masks.* London: Pluto Press, 1986.

Federici, Silvia. *Caliban and the Witch: Women, the Body, and Primitive Accumulation.* Brooklyn: Autonomedia, 2004.

Federici, Silvia. "Silvia Federici." In *Revolutionary Feminisms*, edited by Brenna Bhandar and Rafeef Ziadah, 149–58. New York: Verso, 2020.

Foucault, Michel. *Discipline and Punish: The Birth of the Prison.* New York: Vintage, 1995.

Foucault, Michel. *The History of Sexuality: An Introduction.* Translated by Robert Hurley. New York: Vintage, 1990.

Foucault, Michel. *Security, Territory, Population: Lectures at the Collège de France, 1977–78.* Translated by Graham Burchell. New York: Picador, 2007.

Foucault, Michel. *"Society Must Be Defended": Lectures at the Collège de France, 1975–76.* Translated by David Macey. New York: Picador, 2003.

Friedman, Andrew. "US Empire, World War 2 and the Racialising of Labour." *Race & Class* 58, no. 4 (2017): 23–38.

Fujikane, Candace. *Mapping Abundance for a Planetary Future: Kanaka Maoli and Critical Settler Cartographies in Hawai'i.* Durham, NC: Duke University Press, 2021.

Fujikane, Candace, and Jonathan Y. Okamura, eds. *Asian Settler Colonialism: From Local Governance to the Habits of Everyday Life in Hawai'i*. Honolulu: University of Hawai'i Press, 2008.

Fujitani, T. *Race for Empire: Koreans as Japanese and Japanese as Americans during World War II*. Berkeley: University of California Press, 2011.

Fujitani, T. "Right to Kill, Right to Make Live: Koreans as Japanese and Japanese as Americans During WWII." *Representations* 99, no. 1 (Summer 2007): 13–39.

Fujitani, T., Geoffrey M. White, and Lisa Yoneyama, eds. *Perilous Memories: The Asia-Pacific War(s)*. Durham, NC: Duke University Press, 2001.

Gardiner, C. Harvey. *Pawns in a Triangle of Hate: The Peruvian Japanese and the United States*. Seattle: University of Washington Press, 1981.

Ginoza, Ayano. "R&R at the Intersection of US and Japanese Dual Empire: Okinawan Women and Decolonizing Militarized Heterosexuality." Special issue, *American Quarterly* 68, no. 3 (September 2016): 583–91.

Goldstein, Alyosha, ed. *Formations of United States Colonialism*. Durham, NC: Duke University Press, 2014.

Goldstein, Alyosha. "'In the Constant Flux of Its Incessant Renewal': The Social Reproduction of Racial Capitalism and Settler Colonial Entitlement." In *Colonial Racial Capitalism*, edited by Susan Kosher, Lisa Marie Cacho, Jodi A. Byrd, and Brian Jordan Jefferson, 61–87. Durham, NC: Duke University Press, 2022.

Goldstein, Alyosha. "Toward a Genealogy of the U.S. Colonial Present." In *Formations of United States Colonialism*, edited by Alyosha Goldstein, 1–30. Durham, NC: Duke University Press, 2014.

González, Roberto J., Hugh Gusterson, and Gustaaf Houtman, eds. *Militarization: A Reader*. Durham, NC: Duke University Press, 2019.

Gonzalez, Vernadette Vicuña. *Empire's Mistress, Starring Isabel Rosario Cooper*. Durham, NC: Duke University Press, 2021.

Gonzalez, Vernadette Vicuña. *Securing Paradise: Tourism and Militarism in Hawai'i and the Philippines*. Durham, NC: Duke University Press, 2013.

Gonzalez, Vernadette Vicuña. "Wars of Memory at Pu'uloa/Pearl Harbor." *Radical History Review* 129 (October 2017): 177–85.

Goodyear-Ka'ōpua, Noelani, "Introduction." In *A Nation Rising: Hawaiian Movements for Life, Land, and Sovereignty*, edited by Noelani Goodyear-Ka'ōpua, Ikaika Hussey, and Erin Kahunawaika'ala Wright, 1–33. Durham, NC: Duke University Press, 2014.

Goodyear-Ka'ōpua, Noelani. "Protectors of the Future, Not Protesters of the Past: Indigenous Pacific Activism and Mauna a Wākea." *South Atlantic Quarterly* 116, no. 1 (January 2017): 184–94.

Goodyear-Ka'ōpua, Noelani, Ikaika Hussey, and Erin Kahunawaika'ala Wright, eds. *A Nation Rising: Hawaiian Movements for Life, Land, and Sovereignty*. Durham, NC: Duke University Press, 2014.

Grenier, John. *The First Way of War: American War Making on the Frontier, 1607–1814*. Cambridge: Cambridge University Press, 2005.

Guglielmo, Thomas A. "'Red Cross, Double Cross': Race and America's World War II–Era Blood Donor Service." *Journal of American History* 97, no. 1 (June 1, 2010): 63–90. doi:10.2307/jahist/97.1.63.

Guise, Holly Miowak. "Who Is Doctor Bauer? Rematriating a Censored Story on Internment, Wardship, and Sexual Violence in Wartime Alaska, 1941–1944." *Western Historical Quarterly* 53, no. 2 (Summer 2022): 145–65.

Gupta, Clare. "Dairy's Decline and the Politics of 'Local' Milk in Hawai'i." *Food, Culture, and Society* 19, no. 3 (2016): 485–516.

Gupta, Clare. "Return to Freedom: Anti-GMO Aloha 'Āina Activism on Molokai as an Expression of Place-Based Food Sovereignty." *Globalizations* 12, no. 4 (2014): 529–44.

Hardt, Michael. "Affective Labor." *boundary 2* 26, no. 2 (1999): 89–100.

Harris, Cheryl. "Whiteness as Property." In *Critical Race Theory: The Key Writings That Formed the Movement*, edited by Kimberlé Crenshaw, Neil Gotanda, Gary Peller, and Kendall Thomas, 276–91. New York: New Press, 1996.

Harvey, David. *A New Imperialism*. Oxford: Oxford University Press, 2003.

Hau'ofa, Epeli. "Our Sea of Islands." *Contemporary Pacific* 6, no. 1 (1994): 147–62.

Hein, Laura Elizabeth, and Mark Selden, eds. *Islands of Discontent: Okinawan Responses to Japanese and American Power*. Lanham, MD: Rowman & Littlefield, 2003.

Hernández, Kelly. *City of Inmates: Conquest, Rebellion, and the Rise of Human Caging in Los Angeles, 1771–1965*. Chapel Hill: University of North Carolina Press, 2017.

Higashide, Seiichi. *Adios to Tears: The Memoirs of a Japanese-Peruvian Internee in U.S. Concentration Camps*. Seattle: University of Washington Press, 2000.

Hirsch, Arnold R. *Making the Second Ghetto: Race and Housing in Chicago 1940-1960*. Chicago: University of Chicago Press, 1998.

Hobart, Hi'ilei Julia Kawehipuaakahaopulani. *Cooling the Tropics: Ice, Indigeneity, and Hawaiian Refreshment*. Durham, NC: Duke University Press, 2023.

Hogue, Rebecca H. "Nuclear Normalizing and Kathy Jetñil-Kijiner's 'Dome Poem.'" *Amerasia Journal* 47, no. 2 (2021): 208–29.

Honey, Maureen. *Creating Rosie the Riveter: Class, Gender, and Propaganda during World War II*. Amherst: University of Massachusetts Press, 1984.

Hu Pegues, Juliana. *Space-Time Colonialism: Alaska's Indigenous and Asian Entanglements*. Chapel Hill: University of North Carolina Press, 2021.

Hughes, Judith R. "The Demise of the English Standard School System in Hawai'i." *Hawaiian Journal of History*, vol. 27 (1993): 65–89.

Inglis, Kerri A. *Ma'i Lepera: Disease and Displacement in Nineteenth-Century Hawai'i*. Honolulu: University of Hawai'i Press, 2013.

Jacobson, Matthew Frye. *Whiteness of a Different Color: European Immigrants and the Alchemy of Race*. Cambridge, MA: Harvard University Press, 1999.

Jenkins, Dustin and Justin Leroy, eds. *Histories of Racial Capitalism*. New York: Columbia University Press, 2020.

Johnson, Gaye Theresa, and Alex Lubin, eds. *Futures of Black Radicalism*. New York: Verso, 2017.

Johnston, Barbara Rose. "Nuclear Landscapes: The Marshall Islands and Its Radioactive Legacy." In *Militarization: A Reader*, edited by Roberto J. González, Hugh Gusterson, and Gustaaf Houtman, 181–86. Durham, NC: Duke University Press, 2019.

Jung, Moon-Kie. *Reworking Race: The Making of Hawaii's Interracial Labor Movement*. New York: Columbia University Press, 2010.

Kajihiro, Kyle. "The Militarizing of Hawai'i: Occupation, Accommodation, and Resistance." In *Asian Settler Colonialism: From Local Governance to the Habits of Everyday Life in Hawai'i*, edited by Candace Fujikane and Jonathan Okamura, 170–94. Honolulu: University of Hawai'i Press, 2008.

Kajihiro, Kyle. "Resisting Militarization in Hawai'i." In *The Bases of Empire: The Global Struggle against U.S. Military Posts*, edited by Catherine Lutz, 299–332. New York: New York University Press, 2009.

Kame'eleihiwa, Lilikalā. *Native Land and Foreign Desires: Pehea Lā E Pono Ai? How Shall We Live in Harmony?* Honolulu: Bishop Museum, 1992.

Kaplan, Amy. *The Anarchy of Empire in the Making of U.S. Culture*. Cambridge, MA: Harvard University Press, 2005.

Karuka, Manu. *Empire's Tracks: Indigenous Nations, Chinese Workers, and the Transcontinental Railroad*. Berkeley: University of California Press, 2019.

Kauanui, J. Kēhaulani. "Asian American Studies and the 'Pacific Question.'" In *Asian American Studies after Critical Mass*, edited by Kent A. Ono, 123–43. New York: Wiley-Blackwell, 2005.

Kauanui, J. Kēhaulani. "Colonialism in Equality: Hawaiian Sovereignty and the Question of U.S. Civil Rights." *South Atlantic Quarterly* 107, no. 4 (September 21, 2008): 635–50.

Kauanui, J. Kēhaulani. "False Dilemmas and Settler Colonial Studies: Response to Lorenzo Veracini: 'Is Settler Colonial Studies Even Useful?'" *Postcolonial Studies* 24, no. 2 (2021): 290–96.

Kauanui, J. Kēhaulani. *Hawaiian Blood: Colonialism and the Politics of Sovereignty and Indigeneity*. Durham, NC: Duke University Press, 2008.

Kauanui, J. Kēhaulani. "Hawaiian Nationhood, Self Determination, and International Law." In *Decolonizing Native Histories: Collaboration, Knowledge, and Language in the Americas*, edited by Florencia Mallon, 27–53. Durham, NC: Duke University Press, 2011.

Kauanui, J. Kēhaulani. *Paradoxes of Hawaiian Sovereignty: Land, Sex, and the Colonial Politics of State Nationalism*. Durham, NC: Duke University Press, 2018.

Kauanui, J. Kēhaulani. "A Sorry State: Apology Politics and Legal Fictions in the Court of the Conqueror." In *Formations of United States Colonialism*, edited by Alyosha Goldstein, 110–34. Durham, NC: Duke University Press, 2014.

Kauanui, J. Kēhaulani. "'A Structure, Not an Event': Settler Colonialism and Enduring Indigeneity," in "Forum: Emergent Critical Analytics for Alternate Humanities." *Lateral: Journal of the Cultural Studies Association* 5, no. 1 (Spring 2016): n.p.

Kelly, Marion, and Nancy Aleck. "Mākua Means Parents: A Brief Cultural History of Mākua Valley." American Friends Service Committee—Hawai'i Area Program, December 1997. www.dmzhawaii.org.

Kim, Jinah, and Nitasha Tamar Sharma. "Center-to-Center Relationalities: At the Nexus of Pacific Islands Studies and Trans-Pacific Studies." Special Issue, *Critical Ethnic Studies Journal* 7, no. 2 (2021).

Kim, Jodi. *Settler Garrison: Debt Imperialism, Militarism, and Transpacific Imaginaries.* Durham, NC: Duke University Press, 2022.

Kosher, Susan, Lisa Marie Cacho, Jodi A. Byrd, and Brian Jordan Jefferson, eds. *Colonial Racial Capitalism.* Durham, NC: Duke University Press, 2022.

Kosher, Susan, Lisa Marie Cacho, Jodi A. Byrd, and Brian Jordan Jefferson. "Introduction." In *Colonial Racial Capitalism*, edited by Susan Kosher, Lisa Marie Cacho, Jodi A. Byrd, and Brian Jordan Jefferson, 1–32. Durham, NC: Duke University Press, 2022.

Kramer, Arnold. "Japanese Prisoners of War in America." *Pacific Historical Review* 52, no. 1 (February 1983): 67–91.

Labriola, Monica. "Planting Islands: Marshall Islanders Shaping Land, Power, and History." *Journal of Pacific History* 54, no. 2 (2019): 182–98.

LaDuke, Winona. *The Militarization of Indian Country.* East Lansing: Michigan State University Press, 2013.

Lâm, Maivân Clech. "The Kuleana Act Revisited: The Survival of Traditional Hawaiian Commoner Rights in Land." *Washington Law Review* 64 (April, 1989): 233–88.

Laudan, Rachel. *The Food of Paradise: Exploring Hawaii's Culinary Heritage.* Honolulu: University of Hawai'i Press, 1996.

Lê Espiritu Gandhi, Evyn. *Archipelago of Resettlement: Vietnamese Refugee Settlers and Decolonization across Guam and Israel-Palestine.* Berkeley: University of California Press, 2022.

Lee, Erika. *At America's Gates: Chinese Immigration during the Exclusion Era, 1882–1943.* Chapel Hill: University of North Carolina Press, 2003.

Leong, Karen J., and Myla Vicenti Carpio. "Carceral States: Converging Indigenous and Asian Experiences in the Americas." In "Carceral States," special issue, *Amerasia Journal* 42, no. 1 (2016): vii–xviii.

Locke, John. *Two Treatises of Government.* Edited by Peter Laslett. Cambridge: Cambridge University Press, 1988.

Lowe, Lisa. "Afterword: Revolutionary Feminisms in a Time of Monsters." In *Revolutionary Feminisms*, edited by Brenna Bhandar and Rafeef Ziadah, 217–27. New York: Verso, 2020.

Maile, David Uahikeaikalei'ohu. "On Being Late: Cruising Mauna Kea and Unsettling Technoscientific Conquest in Hawai'i." *American Indian Culture and Research Journal* 45, no. 1 (2021): 95–121.

Man, Simeon. "Aloha, Vietnam: Race and Empire in Hawai'i's Vietnam War." *American Quarterly* 67, no. 4 (2015): 1085–108.

Man, Simeon. *Soldiering Through Empire: Race and the Making of the Decolonizing Pacific.* Berkeley: University of California Press, 2018.

Marlow, Mikaela L., and Howard Giles. "Who You Tink You, Talkin Propah? Hawaiian Pidgin Demarginalized." *Journal of Multicultural Discourses* 3, no. 1 (2008): 53–68.

Marx, Karl. *Capital: A New Abridgement.* Edited by David McLellan. Oxford: Oxford University Press, 2008.

Marx, Karl. *Karl Marx: Selected Writings*, 2nd ed. Edited by David McLellan. Oxford: Oxford University Press, 2000.

McCormack, Gavan, and Satoko Oka Norimatsu, eds. *Resistant Islands: Okinawa Confronts Japan and the United States*. Lanham, MD: Rowman & Littlefield, 2012.

McGregor, Davianna Pōmaikaʻi. *Nā Kuaʻāina: Living Hawaiian Culture*. Honolulu: University of Hawaiʻi Press, 2007.

Mei-Singh, Laurel. "Carceral Conservationalism: Contested Landscapes and Technologies of Dispossession at Kaʻena Point, Hawaiʻi." *American Quarterly* 68, no. 3 (2016): 695–721.

Melamed, Jodi. "Racial Capitalism." *Critical Ethnic Studies* 1, no. 1 (Spring 2015): 76–85.

Melamed, Jodi. *Represent and Destroy: Rationalizing Violence in the New Racial Capitalism*. Minneapolis: University of Minnesota Press, 2011.

Milkman, Ruth. *Gender at Work: The Dynamics of Job Segregation by Sex during World War II*. Urbana: University of Illinois Press, 1987.

Miller-Davenport, Sarah. *Gateway State: Hawaiʻi and the Cultural Transformation of American Empire*. Princeton, NJ: Princeton University Press, 2019.

Mohr, James C. *Plague and Fire: Battling Black Death and the 1900 Burning of Honolulu's Chinatown*. New York: Oxford University Press, 2006.

Moon, Katharine H. S. *Sex among Allies: Military Prostitution in U.S.-Korea Relations*. New York: Columbia University Press, 1997.

Moon, Katharine H. S. "South Korean Movements against Militarized Sexual Labor." In *Militarized Currents: Toward a Decolonized Future in Asia and the Pacific*, edited by Keith Camacho and Setsu Shigematsu, 125–45. Minneapolis: University of Minnesota Press, 2010.

Moran, Michelle T. *Colonizing Leprosy: Imperialism and the Politics of Public Health in the United States*. Chapel Hill: University of North Carolina Press, 2007.

Moreton-Robinson, Aileen. *The White Possessive: Property, Power, and Indigenous Sovereignty*. Minneapolis: University of Minnesota Press, 2015.

Morgan, Jennifer. *Reckoning with Slavery: Gender, Kinship, and Capitalism in the Early Black Atlantic*. Durham, NC: Duke University Press, 2021.

Morgensen, Scott Lauria. *Spaces between Us: Queer Settler Colonialism and Indigenous Decolonization*. Minneapolis: University of Minnesota Press, 2011.

Mōri, Tsuneyuki. *Rainbow over Hell: The Death Row Deliverance of a World War II Assassin*. Translated by Sharon Fujimoto-Johnson. Nampa, ID: Pacific, 2006.

Nakamura, Kelli Y. "'Into the Dark Cold I Go, the Rain Gently Falling': Hawaiʻi Island Incarceration." *Pacific Historical Review* 86, no. 3 (2017): 407–42.

Nakano Glenn, Evelyn. "From Servitude to Service Work: Historical Continuities in the Racial Division of Paid Reproductive Labor." *Signs: Journal of Women in Culture and Society* 18, no. 1 (1992): 1–43.

Nakano Glenn, Evelyn. *Issei, Nisei, War Bride: Three Generations of Japanese American Women in Domestic Service*. Philadelphia: Temple University Press, 1988.

Nakano Glenn, Evelyn. "Racial Ethnic Women's Labor: The Intersection of Race, Gender and Class Oppression." *Review of Radical Political Economics* 17, no. 3 (September 1, 1985): 86–108.

Na'puti, Tiara R. "Disaster Militarism and Indigenous Responses to Super Typhoon Yutu in the Mariana Islands." *Environmental Communication* (February 8, 2022): 612–29.

Nebolon, Juliet. "'Life Given Straight from the Heart': Settler Militarism, Biopolitics, and Public Health in Hawai'i during World War II." *American Quarterly* 69, no. 1 (2017): 23–45.

Nebolon, Juliet. "Settler-Military Camps: Internment and Prisoner of War Camps across the Pacific Islands during World War II." *Journal of Asian American Studies* 24, no. 2 (2021): 299–335.

Ngai, Mae M. *Impossible Subjects: Illegal Aliens and the Making of Modern America.* Princeton, NJ: Princeton University Press, 2004.

Nichols, Robert. *Theft Is Property! Dispossession and Critical Theory.* Durham, NC: Duke University Press, 2019.

O'Brien, Jean. *Firsting and Lasting: Writing Indians Out of Existence in New England.* Minneapolis: University of Minnesota Press, 2010.

Odo, Franklin. *Voices from the Canefields: Folksongs from Japanese Immigrant Workers in Hawai'i.* New York: Oxford University Press, 2016.

Okihiro, Gary Y. *Cane Fires: The Anti-Japanese Movement in Hawaii, 1865–1945.* Philadelphia: Temple University Press, 1991.

Okihiro, Gary Y. *Pineapple Culture: A History of the Tropical and Temperate Zones.* Berkeley: University of California Press, 2009.

Oliveira, Katrina-Ann R. Kapā'anaokalāokeola Nākoa. *Ancestral Places: Understanding Kanaka Geographies.* Corvallis: Oregon State University Press, 2014.

Oliveira, Katrina-Ann R. Kapā'anaokalāokeola Nākoa. "E Ola Mau ka 'Ōlelo Hawai'i: The Hawaiian Language Revitalization Movement." In *A Nation Rising: Hawaiian Movements for Life, Land, and Sovereignty,* edited by Noelani Goodyear-Ka'ōpua, Ikaika Hussey, and Erin Kahunawaika'ala Wright, 78–85. Durham, NC: Duke University Press, 2014.

Osorio, Jonathan Kamakawiwo'ole. *Dismembering Lāhui: A History of the Hawaiian Nation to 1887.* Honolulu: University of Hawai'i Press, 2002.

Osorio, Jonathan Kamakawiwo'ole. "Hawaiian Souls: The Movement to Stop the U.S. Military Bombing of Kaho'olawe." In *A Nation Rising: Hawaiian Movements for Life, Land, and Sovereignty,* edited by Noelani Goodyear-Ka'ōpua, Ikaika Hussey, and Erin Kahunawaika'ala Wright, 137–60. Durham, NC: Duke University Press, 2014.

Paik, A. Naomi. *Bans, Wall, Raids, Sanctuary: Understanding U.S. Immigration for the Twenty-First Century.* Berkeley: University of California Press, 2020.

Paik, A. Naomi. *Rightlessness: Testimony and Redress in U.S. Prison Camps since World War II.* Chapel Hill: University of North Carolina Press, 2016.

Park, K-Sue. "The History Wars and Property Law: Conquest and Slavery as Foundational to the Field." *Yale Law Journal* 131, no. 4 (2022): 1062–153.

Park, K-Sue. "Money, Mortgages, and the Conquest of America." *Law & Social Inquiry* 41, no. 4 (2016): 1006–35.

Parreñas, Rhacel Salazar. "Migrant Filipina Domestic Workers and the International Division of Reproductive Labor." *Gender and Society* 14, no. 4 (August 2000): 560–80.

Peattie, Mark R. *Nan'yō: The Rise and Fall of the Japanese in Micronesia, 1885–1945*. Honolulu: University of Hawai'i Press, 1988.

Polk, Khary Oronde. *Contagions of Empire: Scientific Racism, Sexuality, and Black Military Workers Abroad, 1898–1948*. Chapel Hill: University of North Carolina Press, 2020.

Polmar, Norman, and Thomas B. Allen. *World War II: The Encyclopedia of the War Years, 1941–1945*. New York: Dover, 2012.

Puhipau. "Puhipau: The Ice Man Looks Back at the Sand Island Evictions." In *A Nation Rising: Hawaiian Movements for Life, Land, and Sovereignty*, edited by Noelani Goodyear-Ka'ōpua, Ikaika Hussey, and Erin Kahunawaika'ala Wright, 131–35. Durham, NC: Duke University Press, 2014.

Reddy, Chandan. *Freedom with Violence: Race, Sexuality, and the U.S. State*. Durham, NC: Duke University Press, 2011.

Robinson, Cedric. *Black Marxism: The Making of the Black Radical Tradition*. Chapel Hill: University of North Carolina Press, 1983/2000.

Rohrer, Judy. *Haoles in Hawai'i*. Honolulu: University of Hawai'i Press, 2010.

Romaine, Suzanne. "Hawai'i Creole English as a Literary Language." *Language in Society* 23, no. 4 (1994): 527–54.

Romaine, Suzanne. "Hawaiian Creole English." In *Encyclopedia of Language & Linguistics*, 2nd ed., edited by Keith Brown, 227–28. Amsterdam: Elsevier Science, 2006.

Rosa, John P. *Local Story: The Massie-Kahahawai Case and the Culture of History*. Honolulu: University of Hawai'i Press, 2014.

Saranillio, Dean Itsuji. "Colliding Histories: Hawai'i Statehood at the Intersection of Asians 'Ineligible to Citizenship' and Hawaiians 'Unfit for Self-Government.'" *Journal of Asian American Studies* 13, no. 3 (2010): 283–309.

Saranillio, Dean Itsuji. *Unsustainable Empire: Alternative Histories of Hawai'i Statehood*. Durham, NC: Duke University Press, 2018.

Saranillio, Dean Itsuji. "Why Asian Settler Colonialism Matters: A Thought Piece on Critiques, Debates, and Indigenous Difference." *Settler Colonial Studies* 3, nos. 3–4 (2013): 280–94.

Scheiber, Harry N., and Jane L. Scheiber. *Bayonets in Paradise: Martial Law in Hawai'i during World War II*. Honolulu: University of Hawai'i Press, 2016.

Shah, Nayan. *Contagious Divides: Epidemics and Race in San Francisco's Chinatown*. Berkeley: University of California Press, 2001.

Shigematsu, Setsu, and Keith L. Camacho, eds. *Militarized Currents: Toward a Decolonized Future in Asia and the Pacific*. Minneapolis: University of Minnesota Press, 2010.

Silva, Noenoe K. *Aloha Betrayed: Native Hawaiian Resistance to American Colonialism*. Durham, NC: Duke University Press, 2004.

Singh, Nikhil Pal. *Black Is a Country: Race and the Unfinished Struggle for Democracy*. Cambridge, MA: Harvard University Press, 2005.

Singh, Nikhil Pal. "On Race, Violence, and 'So-Called Primitive Accumulation.'" In *Futures of Black Radicalism*, edited by Gaye Theresa Johnson and Alex Lubin, 39–58. New York: Verso, 2017.

Singh, Nikhil Pal. *Race and America's Long War*. Berkeley: University of California Press, 2017.

Smith-Norris, Martha. *Domination and Resistance: The United States and the Marshall Islands during the Cold War*. Honolulu: University of Hawai'i Press, 2016.

Stannard, David E. *Honor Killing: Race, Rape, and Clarence Darrow's Spectacular Last Case*. New York: Penguin, 2006.

Statham, Robert E. *Colonial Constitutionalism: The Tyranny of United States' Offshore Territorial Policy and Relations*. Lanham, MD: Lexington Books, 2003.

Sturken, Marita. *Tangled Memories: The Vietnam War, the AIDS Epidemic, and the Politics of Remembering*. Berkeley: University of California Press, 1997.

Swanson, Kara W. *Banking on the Body: The Market in Blood, Milk, and Sperm in Modern America*. Cambridge, MA: Harvard University Press, 2014.

Taira, Derek. "Embracing Education and Contesting Americanization: A Reexamination of Native Hawaiian Student Engagement in Territorial Hawai'i's Public Schools, 1920–1940." *History of Education Quarterly* 58, no. 3 (2018): 361–91.

Takaki, Ronald T. *A Different Mirror: A History of Multicultural America*. Boston: Back Bay, 2008.

Takaki, Ronald T. *Pau Hana: Plantation Life and Labor in Hawaii, 1835–1920*. Honolulu: University of Hawai'i Press, 1984.

TallBear, Kim. *Native American DNA: Tribal Belonging and the False Promise of Genetic Science*. Minneapolis: University of Minnesota Press, 2013.

Teaiwa, Teresia. "bikinis and other s/pacific n/oceans." *Contemporary Pacific* 6, no. 1 (Spring 1994): 87–109.

Tompkins, Kyla Wazana. *Racial Indigestion: Eating Bodies in the 19th Century*. New York: New York University Press, 2012.

Trask, Haunani-Kay. *From a Native Daughter: Colonialism and Sovereignty in Hawai'i*. Honolulu: University of Hawai'i Press, 1999.

Trask, Haunani-Kay. "Settlers of Color and 'Immigrant' Hegemony." In *Asian Settler Colonialism: From Local Governance to the Habits of Everyday Life in Hawai'i*, edited by Candace Fujikane and Jonathan Okamura, 45–65. Honolulu: University of Hawai'i Press, 2008.

Uenten, Wesley Iwao. "Rising Up from a Sea of Discontent: The 1970 Koza Uprising in U.S.-Occupied Okinawa." In *Militarized Currents: Toward a Decolonized Future in Asia and the Pacific*, edited by Setsu Shigematsu and Keith L. Camacho, 91–124. Minneapolis: University of Minnesota Press.

Vaughan, Mehana Blaich, and Adam L. Ayers. "Customary Access: Sustaining Local Control of Fishing and Food on Kaua'i's North Shore." *Food, Culture & Society* 19, no. 3 (2016): 517–38.

Vimalassery, Manu, Juliana Hu Pegues, and Alyosha Goldstein. "Colonial Unknowing and Relations of Study." *Theory & Event* 20, no. 4 (October 2017): 1042–54.

Vimalassery, Manu, Juliana Hu Pegues, and Alyosha Goldstein. "Introduction: On Colonial Unknowing." *Theory and Event* 19, no. 4 (2016). https://muse.jhu.edu/article/633283.

Vora, Kalindi. *Life Support: Biocapital and the New History of Outsourced Labor*. Minneapolis: University of Minnesota Press, 2015.

Vora, Kalindi. "Limits of 'Labor': Accounting for Affect and the Biological in Transnational Surrogacy and Service Work." *South Atlantic Quarterly* 111, no. 4 (October 2012): 681–700.

Wailoo, Keith. *Drawing Blood: Technology and Disease Identity in Twentieth-Century America*. Baltimore: Johns Hopkins University Press, 1999.

Waldby, Catherine. *The Visible Human Project: Informatic Bodies and Posthuman Medicine*. New York: Routledge, 2003.

Waldby, Catherine, and Robert Mitchell. *Tissue Economies: Blood, Organs, and Cell Lines in Late Capitalism*. Durham, NC: Duke University Press, 2006.

Walia, Harsha. *Border and Rule: Global Migration, Capitalism, and the Rise of Racist Nationalism*. New York: Haymarket, 2021.

"We Drank Our Tears": Memories of the Battles for Saipan and Tinian as Told by Our Elders. Saipan, NMI: Pacific STAR Center for Young Writers, 2004.

Weglyn, Michi. *Years of Infamy: The Untold Story of America's Concentration Camps*. Seattle: University of Washington Press, 1976.

Weinbaum, Alys Eve. *The Afterlife of Reproductive Slavery*. Durham, NC: Duke University Press, 2019.

Willens, Howard P., and Deanne C. Siemer. *An Honorable Accord: The Covenant Between the Northern Mariana Islands and the United States*. Honolulu: University of Hawai'i Press.

Winter, Kawika B., Kamanamaikalani Beamer, Mehana Blaich Vaughan, Alan M. Friedlander, Mike H. Kido, A. Nāmaka Whitehead, Malia K. H. Akutagawa, Natalie Kurashima, Matthew Paul Lucas, and Ben Nyberg. "The *Moku* System: Managing Biocultural Resources for Abundance within Social-Ecological Regions in Hawai'i." *Sustainability* 10, no. 10 (2018): 1–19.

Wolfe, Patrick. "Settler Colonialism and the Elimination of the Native." *Journal of Genocide Research* 8, no. 4 (2006): 387–409.

Woodward, Rachel. "Military Landscapes: Agendas and Approaches for Future Research." *Progress in Human Geography* 38, no. 1 (February 1, 2014): 40–61.

Yellin, Emily. *Our Mothers' War: American Women at Home and at the Front during World War II*. New York: Free Press, 2005.

Yoneyama, Lisa. *Cold War Ruins: Transpacific Critique of American Justice and Japanese War Crimes*. Durham, NC: Duke University Press, 2016.

Yoneyama, Lisa. *Hiroshima Traces: Time, Space, and the Dialectics of Memory*. Berkeley: University of California Press, 1999.

Yung, Judy. *Unbound Feet: A Social History of Chinese Women in San Francisco*. Berkeley: University of California Press, 1995.

Index

Note: page numbers followed by *f* refer to figures.

martial law (continued)
   land occupation and, 21, 44–45; Mākua Valley
      and, 40; MIS and, 126; primitive accumulation
      and, 31; public health programs and, 48, 50–52,
      54–58, 70–71, 73, 101; racial difference and,
      127; school occupations and, 106, 109; social
      reproduction of US settler militarism and, 79;
      violence of, 104; women and, 72–73
Marx, Karl, 14, 169–70nn54–56, 171n59
masculinity: heterosexual, 48; militarized, 16, 125;
      military, 63, 166n29; patriotic, 67
Maui, 26, 106, 126, 164n6; konohiki fisheries on,
      197n65; onions, 90
Mei-Singh, Laurel, 41, 184n108
Meiz, H. R., 1, 3f, 48
Melamed, Jodi, 11–12, 170n54, 171n58, 173n61,
      176n12, 193n4
men, 10, 54, 97, 214n4; biopower and, 10, 63, 71,
      189–90n69; Black, 21, 65; enlisted, 52, 140; Ha-
      waiian, 81; immigrant, 74, 96, 100; Indigenous,
      96, 100; in internment camps, 140; Japanese,
      125; military, 111; multiracial, 83
Meyer, Dillon, 147, 151
Micronesia, 18, 130, 133, 142, 146, 149–51, 206–7n6.
      See also Marshall Islands; Northern Mariana
      Islands (NMI)
Midway, 177n39; Battle of, 132
migration, 151–52; in Guam, 214n4; labor, 130–31;
      settler, 8, 130, 151, 164n5
militarization, 5–6, 8–9, 110, 131, 142, 158, 167n33,
      214n2; demilitarization, 161; eminent domain
      and, 29; of female-gendered patriotic duties,
      73; of land, 25–26, 71; language and, 115, 121;
      logics of, 22, 26, 46; resistance to, 41; in War on
      Terror, 160
military basing, 9, 46, 129, 146
Military Intelligence Service Language School
      (MIS), 17, 104; students, 124, 205n74; transla-
      tors, 125–26, 128
Miller, Carey D., 76–77, 80–85, 89–90, 96–100,
      102, 119, 199n103
missionaries, 24, 86
mobilization, 4; capitalist, 105; labor, 2, 11, 71, 109;
      military, 10; wartime, 2, 16–17, 27, 54, 71, 109,
      131–32, 155, 208n23
modernity, 14, 22, 28, 84, 91, 104, 121, 127
modernization, 30, 37, 45, 142–44, 157
Mōkapu peninsula, 28–30, 44. e also Heleloa tract;
      Kāne'ohe Bay
molasses, 33, 35
mo'olelo, 41, 183n100
morale, 105–6, 127, 134; high, 78; lack of, 16

Moreton-Robinson, Aileen, 12, 164n4, 169n48,
      176n11. See also white possession
mothering, 17, 72, 79, 99, 101; American, 156; as
      biopower, 174n67
mothers, 72, 75, 79, 101, 110, 156; military security
      and, 77, 88; nutrition and, 77, 89, 95; wartime
      mobilization and, 16
mountain apples, 86, 91
Muroda, Shigeo, 68, 136

Nakano Glenn, Evelyn, 100, 173n67, 193n3, 193n5,
      199n95
Nascimento, Isabel, 1, 4f
Native Hawaiians, 10, 64, 81, 93, 166n21; access
      to land and, 71; assimilation and, 13; eating
      practices of, 86–87; Hawaiian Homestead
      Lands and, 36–37; Hawaiian Organic Act and,
      168n40; Kaho'olawe and, 42; Mākua Valley
      and, 183n100; mandatory vaccination program
      and, 57; place-based counternarratives and, 41;
      racialization of, 166–67n29; wartime nutrition
      and, 80. See also Kanaka Maoli
natural resources, 19, 29, 58, 73, 77, 91–92, 102, 155,
      157; access to, 23, 57, 87; acquisition of, 130; ap-
      propriation of, 15; extraction of, 89; primitive
      accumulation of, 52; theft of, 34
Newlands Resolution, 7, 20, 24, 130
Nimitz, C. W., 141–42
Nisei, 5, 85, 125, 164n9, 207n21; Military Intel-
      ligence Service Language School and, 17, 104,
      124, 126, 128; soldiers, 8, 65, 67, 166n29
Nishikawa, Dan, 139, 209nn49–50
Northern Mariana Islands (NMI), 129–31, 142–45,
      206–7n14, 214n8; camps in, 12, 129–30, 132, 137,
      141, 143, 149–50, 153, 158–59, 206n4, 210n15;
      Carolinians in, 210n58; invasion of, 211n69; MIS
      students deployed to, 124; settler militarism
      and, 144; Tinian, 131, 145, 159; US military
      government land acquisition in, 145; US
      military occupation of, 131, 141, 159, 161. See also
      Chamorros; Saipan
nurses, 16, 47–48, 51–53, 71, 156, 180n64
nutrition, 17, 72, 75–83, 85–87, 100, 104, 119, 127;
      Americanized, 91; campaigns, 80, 84, 88,
      156–57; family and, 110; Kanaka Maoli access
      to, 24; sugar plantations and, 193n11; white
      settler women professionals and, 96. See also
      Territorial Nutrition Committee

O'ahu, 1, 10, 34, 42, 51, 126, 149; blood donation
      in, 59; domestic servants in, 100; internment
      camps in, 136; land in, 25–27, 33, 36, 182n88,

US annexation of Hawai'i, 7–8, 20, 24, 31, 41, 130

US Army, 2, 106, 125, 147, 190n82, 212n84; immunization and, 53; Kaho'olawe and, 41; land and, 44, 176n27; Mākua and, 40, 183n92; Quartermaster Department, 27; Territorial Board of Health and, 52

US Department of Agriculture, 78, 89

US Department of Defense (DOD), 26, 38–40, 42, 45, 161

US Marine Corps. *See* Marine Corps

US military, 2, 5–7, 9, 15–18, 102, 166n19, 190n82; bases, 130, 144, 158–59, 178n42; domestic science and, 99; education and, 104, 121; empire, 13, 18–19, 173n62; expansion, 7, 9, 91, 121, 126, 131, 146, 158, 161; food and, 91–92; Guam and, 159; internment and prisoner-of-war camps and, 129, 131, 134, 137, 141–44, 146, 149–52, 154, 158, 206n4; Japanese Americans volunteering for, 67; land and, 20, 22, 24–31, 36–40, 43–46, 57, 87, 131, 145, 154–56, 175n2; language and, 124, 126, 128; Marshallese and, 144–45; occupations, 11, 15, 41–42, 57, 158; Okinawa and, 214n10; public health and, 51, 53, 55–56, 60; school occupations and, 106, 127

US military government of Hawai'i, 2, 12–13, 16–17, 37, 70, 74, 106–9, 136–37; blood donation and, 62, 73, 127, 156; English language and, 121, 124; finger printing and, 54–55; immunization and, 53, 56, 73; internment and, 3, 138, 143, 146, 158; Japanese language and, 123–24, 126, 128; labor loan program, 15; land acquisition and, 131; in Marshall Islands, 144, 149; martial law and, 5, 99, 133–35, 179n64; in Northern Mariana Islands, 145; nutritional campaigns, 90–91; Pidgin and, 120; propaganda, 163n1; productivity and, 50, 56; public health policies of, 48, 54, 73, 75–77, 85; racial difference and, 11, 128; repatriation and, 211n83. *See also* Office of Civilian Defense (OCD)

US Navy, 1, 27, 106, 161, 177n38, 182n80; camps and, 141–43; health programs and, 51; Japanese, 149; land acquisition and, 26, 29–31, 34–37, 42–44, 176n27, 177n39, 178n53, 179nn59–60, 181n75; Secretary of, 146

US War Department/US Department of War, 5, 30, 132, 134, 139–40, 148

vaccination, 1–2, 50, 52–53, 55, 60, 106–7; mandatory, 1, 48, 55, 57; of Marshallese population, 143, 185n6

vegetables, 78, 80–84, 86–87, 89–92, 96, 102; gardens, 111, 138, 140

violence, 32, 58, 113–14, 160; of capitalism, 170n54; colonial, 12, 19, 63, 71, 86, 153, 171n58; environmental, 30; extractive, 38; liberal, 160n85; politics of, 99; racial, 54, 71, 86, 171n58; settler colonial, 116, 120, 157; settler militarism and, 17–18, 71, 94, 104, 152; sexual, 159, 166n25, 214n10; state, 4, 12, 138; wartime, 144

vitamin C, 81, 90

volunteers, 51, 53; in MIS, 126; multiracial, 63; women, 59

wages, 2, 15, 33, 37, 74, 109–10

wahi pana, 57, 183n100

War Relocation Authority (WRA), 132, 135, 147–48, 150–51, 206n4, 211n80

wartime mobilization, 2, 16–17, 27, 54, 131–32, 155, 208n23

well-being, 4, 17, 174n67; psychological, 75

white possession, 2, 12–13, 64, 164n4, 169n48, 176n11

white settler possession, 23, 45

white settlers, 8, 10, 50, 64, 95, 132, 166n29; as haole, 196n58; Hawaiian foods and, 80–81, 87, 91; Republic of Hawaii and, 166n21; Polynesia and, 169n48

white supremacy, 9–10

Wolfe, Patrick, 64, 165n13, 165n16

women, 10, 16, 54, 72, 79, 83, 103, 105, 107–8, 168n38, 171n59; affective labor of, 156; Black, 21; blood banks and, 59, 71; blood donation and, 63, 189–90n69; class-privileged, 173n67; of color, 92, 173–74n67, 193n3; cookbooks and, 93; defense laborers, 1; enlisted, 101; Hawai'i Youth for Democracy and, 160; homosexuality and, 98–99; immigrant, 74, 100–101; Indigenous, 74, 92, 100–101; in internment camps, 140; labor of, 74–75, 193n3; occupational statuses of, 5; white settler, 74, 77, 80, 92, 94–96

World War I, 116, 130

YMCA, 68, 123

Young, Sally, 1, 4f

YWCA, 81, 123